Kick'n' Back in TEXAS

D1231481

WEST
SIDE
PUBLISHING

Contributing Writers: Jeff Bahr, Fiona Broome, James Duplacey, Laura Hill, Jonathan Kelley, William Martin, Winter Prosapio, Lawrence Robinson, William Sasser, Paul Seaburn, Donald Vaughan, Nanette Lavoie-Vaughan, Michael Karl Witzel

Factual Verification: Christy Nadalin

Cover Illustration: Simon Fenton

Interior Illustrations: Art Explosion, Linda Howard Bittner, iStockphoto, Jupiter Images, RetroClipArt.com, Shutterstock

Contents

The Great State of Texas

The Lone Star State is a state of superlatives in every way. It's got the biggest ranch, the most wood harvested in the United States, more farmland than any other state, the most wool produced (yes, that also probably means it has the most sheep), and so on. Perhaps most important (or not?), there are more species of bats in Texas than in any other state.

The name *Texas* is said to have come from a word sometimes transcribed *Teyshas,* which may have meant "hello friend" in the language of the Hasinai people. It makes sense, then, that the motto of Texas is "Friendship"—and the people of Texas certainly live by that motto. Because of the state's size, Texas sometimes seems to embody all that's good, bad, and especially big about the United States.

There are enough strange, unusual, and special stories and people and places in Texas that it could fill 20 books. But the Armchair Reader™ staff has gone through the best of all that and pared it down to happily present this book to you.

Read about:

- The world's first rodeo, held during the 1800s in Pecos

- An iconic TV mansion just outside Dallas—not Southfork, but the Munsters' house

- Six thousand Chinese terra-cotta soldiers standing guard in a suburb of Houston

- A horned toad that spent 31 years inside a wall—and lived to croak about it

So now it's time to settle in to that big armchair, sit back and relax, and get to reading.

Enjoy!

P.S.—We are always trying to make our books the best that we can, so please, if you have any comments—whether good or bad—contact us at armchairreader.com.

Charro Days: A Tale of Two Cities

While the cities of New Orleans and Rio de Janeiro celebrate the pre-Lenten season with Mardi Gras and Carnaval, the Texas border town of Brownsville has its own kind of festival.

For a week in late February each year, Brownsville and its Mexican sister city Matamoros come together across the Rio Grande for a cross-border festival. Charro Days, which celebrates a cooperative climate between the two cities and their cultures, is marked by a spectacular country-to-country parade that begins in Brownsville, crosses the international bridge spanning the Rio Grande, and climaxes in the heart of Matamoros. The festival also features fireworks, musical performances, food fairs, art exhibits, mariachi competitions, a rodeo, and street dances.

Charro Days is named in honor of the distinctively dressed Mexican cowboys known as *charros*. Many participants wear the traditional costumes of the charro suit for men and the china poblana dress for women.

In the Beginning

The first official Charro Days celebration was held in February 1938, although the tradition is believed to date back to the mid-1800s. The earliest cross-border festivities took place when merchants in Matamoros heard of American settlers arriving on the other side of the river. The merchants dressed up in traditional costumes and traveled with their wares to trade with their new neighbors. Attendees at this initial bicultural celebration totaled no more than 100.

These friendly relations were interrupted in 1846 when war broke out between the United States and Mexico over the U.S.

annexation of Texas. After that, it was largely forgotten for nearly a century. But when the Brownsville members of the Pan American Round Table were looking for a way to boost the city's collective spirits during the Great Depression, they launched the current tradition.

That first "official" Charro Days festival in 1938 featured horse-drawn floats—all made by hand, of course. And while more events have been added to the fiesta over the years, much of the festivities remain the same as they were then. That event began with the traditional Mexican *grito,* a celebratory cry that dates back to Mexico's battle for independence. The mayors from the two cities next exchanged greetings and gifts over the Gateway International Bridge between the two countries. Flowers representing friendship and peace were then tossed into the river below.

The early years of Charro Days coincided with the birth of the Big Band musical era. From 1939 onwards, artists such as Desi Arnaz, the Ran Wilde Orchestra, Johnny Randolph's Band, and Pepe Sandoval entertained dancers at the festival's Grand Ball.

Up to Date

Today, Charro Days attracts an estimated 165,000 people and is regularly listed among the American Bus Association's prestigious Top 100 Events in North America. Since 1967, the festival has included the Mr. Amigo presentation honoring a Mexican celebrity or politician who serves as an ambassador of friendship between the United States and Mexico. In 1986, the Sombrero Fest was added. The huge street festival takes place in Brownsville's Washington Park for three days and features music and entertainment as well as a mouth-watering selection of traditional Mexican cuisine. A tortilla-eating contest in which entrants battle to see who can consume the most flour tortillas stuffed with beans in the shortest amount of time is also held.

Established as part of Charro Days in 1999, the Baile del Sol is now the first event of the weeklong festivities. This features children and college students dressed in native costumes performing traditional Mexican dances. The presidents of Charro Days, Sombrero Festival, the Mr. Amigo Association, and Fiestas Mexicanas (as the festival is called in Matamoros) then continue the tradition that began in 1938 by shouting out the *grito.*

A Meal as Big as Texas

Be warned: At the Big Texan Steak Ranch, the world-famous free 72-ounce steak dinner (if eaten in one hour) is only for the very hungry. Many have tried. Many have failed.

During the 1960s, signs sprouted up along Route 66 inviting travelers to dine on a free steak dinner. From across the Mother Road, they rolled into the Big Texan Steak Ranch to take up the challenge: Eat a 72-ounce top sirloin steak, a baked potato, a salad, one dinner roll, and a shrimp cocktail in one hour, and you didn't pay one red cent.

The steak ranch was the brainchild of midwesterner R. J. "Bob" Lee, whose family had previously been in the restaurant biz in Kansas City. After Lee and his family relocated to the Panhandle, he found a shortage of steak houses selling local beef. So, he decided to open his own.

Who Doesn't Like a Challenge?

The steak promo began shortly thereafter. One day, a cowboy working at a nearby ranch ambled in through the front door and bragged that he was so hungry he could "eat the whole darned cow!" Not one to shirk from a dare, Lee slapped down the first competition slab of meat on the grill. Game on!

When the cowboy finally yelled "calf-rope," he had single-handedly scarfed down four and a half pounds of Texas beef. Of course, his reward was dinner on the house. Customers enjoyed watching the culinary contest so much that Lee vowed that the "free" dinner gimmick would be a regular event.

In the early 1970s, Interstate 40 replaced Route 66 as the major conduit across the Panhandle, and a bigger and better Steak Ranch was built along the new route. But the people kept coming—and still do—eager to prove that they have the mettle to consume an unholy amount of food and fixins. They want to walk away with their stomach stretched but their wallet intact. The success stories number in the thousands. And the failures? No one can say.

The Mysterious Orb

If Texas were a dartboard, the city of Brownwood would be at the center of the bull's-eye. Maybe that's how aliens saw it, too.

Brownwood is a peaceful little city with about 20,000 residents and a popular train museum. A frontier town at one time, it became the trade center of Texas when the railroad arrived in 1885. Since then, the city has maintained a peaceful lifestyle. Even the massive tornado that struck Brownwood in 1976 left no fatalities. The place just has that "small town" kind of feeling.

An Invader from the Sky

In July 2002, however, the city's peace was broken. Brownwood made international headlines when a strange metal orb fell from space, landed in the Colorado River, and washed up just south of town. The orb looked like a battered metal soccer ball—it was about a foot across, and it weighed just under ten pounds. Experts described it as a titanium sphere. When it was x-rayed, it revealed a second, inner sphere with tubes and wires wrapped inside.

That's all that anybody knows (or claims to know). No one is sure what the object is, and no one has claimed responsibility for it. The leading theory is that it's a cryogenic tank from some kind of spacecraft from Earth, used to store a small amount of liquid hydrogen or helium for cooling purposes. Others have speculated that it's a bomb, a spying device, or even a weapon used to combat UFOs.

It's Not Alone

The Brownwood sphere isn't unique. A similar object landed in Kings-bury, Texas, in 1997, and was quickly confiscated by the Air Force for "tests and analysis." So far, no further announcements have been made.

Of course, the Air Force probably has a lot to keep it busy. About 200 UFOs are reported each month, and Texas is among the top three states where UFOs are seen. But until anything is known for sure, those in Texas at night should keep an eye on the skies.

Name the Mascot

The only things more sacred to Texans than high school and college football are the mascots and nicknames of their teams. Many Texas high school nicknames are funny, creative, odd, or just plain strange. Draw lines from the nickname to the high school:

Polar Bears	Winters High
Rockcrushers	Mason High
Red Ants	Rocksprings High
Kerberoes	Mesquite High
Skeeters	Knippa High
Parrots	Dallas Ursuline Academy
Yeguas	Somerville High
Cottonpickers	Tivy High
Sissies (the girls' team)	Frost High
Hippos	Van High
Blizzards	Cuero High
Gobblers	Fredericksburg High
Pied Pipers	Bridgeport High
Battlin' Billies	Robstown High
Vandals	Texas City High
Stingarees	Hamlin High
Paladins	Hutto High
Punchers	FW Polytechnic (Poly)
Antlers	Roscoe High
Angoras	Spring Providence Classical High
Honey Buns	Houston KIPP Academy
Plowboys	Progreso High

Answers: Bridgeport Sissies; Cuero Gobblers; Dallas Ursuline Academy Honey Buns; Fredericksburg Battlin' Billies; Frost Polar Bears; FW Polytechnic (Poly) Parrots; Hamlin Pied Pipers; Houston KIPP Academy Kerberoes; Hutto Hippos; Tivy Antlers; Knippa Rockcrushers; Mason Punchers; Mesquite Skeeters; Progreso Red Ants; Robstown Cottonpickers; Rocksprings Angoras; Roscoe Plowboys; Somerville Yeguas; Spring Providence Classical Paladins; Texas City Stingarees; Van Vandals; Winters Blizzards

---

12

Remember the Alamo!

Many myths abound regarding the Alamo and its legendary fighters. What's true, and what's not?

The story of the Alamo is known to every student of American history, and 2.5 million visitors tour the original structure in downtown San Antonio every year. With any epic conflict, the tales of bravery and the details of the battle become embellished over time, and the facts surrounding the Battle of the Alamo are no exception. In fact, much of what you think you know about that battle may be wrong.

Not What People Think

One of the most common myths about the battle, which was fought in 1836, is that there were no survivors. In truth, close to 20 women and children who were under siege during the conflict survived to return to their homes. William Travis's personal slave and about 14 pro-Texan Hispanics were also among the survivors.

There are two sides to every fight, and that is true of the Alamo. The event has often been simplified to paint the Texans as the good guys and the Mexicans as the bad guys, but each side had its own reasons for entering the battle. The Mexicans were fighting to defend their country, and the Texans were seeking changes to Mexican laws. Many of the Americans entering Texas were slaveholders, and there was much sentiment toward abolition in the Mexican government. In addition to seeking their independence, the Texans fighting at the Alamo wanted to make sure they kept the right to own slaves.

What Really Happened?

Myths also surround the most memorable figures in the battle: Davy Crockett and Jim Bowie. Many have heard the tale of how Davy Crockett heroically died clutching his favorite rifle, "Old Betsy," in his hands and leaving a swath of dead Mexicans in his wake. Although accounts vary, many historians agree that Crockett was captured along with the other surviving combatants and was most likely quickly executed.

Jim Bowie has come to symbolize the dedication of the Texans to their cause. According to legend, William Travis drew a line in the courtyard and challenged the soldiers who wished to stay and continue fighting to cross the line. Bowie, who was ill, is said to have asked for his cot to be carried across the line. Historians, however, have been unable to find records to support this account.

The story of the line in the sand led to another myth that the volunteers could have left at any time. Technically this is true, but these citizen soldiers had signed an oath of allegiance to the provisional government of Texas, and they chose to remain true to their oath.

William Travis, the leader of the freedom fighters, is often portrayed as pompous and disliked by the men who served with him. This myth has been supported by the fact that the volunteer fighters refused to take orders from him and instead elected Jim Bowie as their leader. But that decision wasn't based on personalities; Travis was respected by both the soldiers and the volunteers and was often described as gregarious and honorable. The only reason the volunteers elected Bowie was because they didn't want to take orders from an officer.

Another myth is that the flag of Texas proudly flew over the Alamo for the duration of the battle, but conflicting records suggest that the flag flown may actually have been that of the Louisiana Grays or even the Mexican flag. Most historians now conclude that it was the tricolor *Tejas y Coahuila* flag that hung over the embattled compound.

Did They Know Their Influence?

Perhaps the greatest patriotic myth is that the freedom fighters died without knowing that Texas had gained independence. The truth is that even though the garrison members were killed before hearing that the Declaration was signed, they fully expected it to happen and had sent delegates to the convention prior to the battle.

Even when these myths are dispelled, it is clear that the battle of the Alamo was a pivotal event in Texas history and that the players on both sides performed admirably under horrific conditions.

Fast Facts

- *Ever wonder why Spanish settlers tended toward the more arid part of Texas rather than congregate around the Gulf river-mouths? The answer may go back to Spain's climate. Spaniards had centuries of skill in wringing life from drought-prone land—in short, south and west Texas reminded them of home.*

- *In 1984, the management of the Texas Rangers decided to ban outside food from Arlington Stadium. This might not have made fans so angry had the security staff not been so obvious about chowing down the snacks they were confiscating.*

- *Oprah Winfrey almost started another civil war when she vowed in 1996 never again to eat hamburger (due to Mad Cow Disease). Some Texas ranchers sued her for defamation of food. Somehow they lost, though the case was tried in Amarillo, but the good news is that Oprah got to know Dr. Phil McGraw during the ordeal.*

- *Houston's "Silver Dollar" Jim West Jr. (1903–57) got his nickname giving those coins away at random—throwing them on the floor (or in swimming pools), just to watch people react. A police-ophile, Jim had about 40 blue Cadillacs with antennas sticking out listening to the police band. All the cars contained guns.*

- *Could an alcoholic goat out-govern a town's mayor? It's been tried. Lajitas (pop. 75) had a series of beer-guzzling goats named Clay Henry as mayors. Given that the town has done it several times, perhaps goats make good mayors.*

- *Grand Saline is well named, for it sits on a salt dome three miles thick by a mile and a half across. Clearly, it was necessary to build a Salt Palace from the material. However, salt doesn't weather well—the city has gone through three of them.*

- *On December 23, 1927, a bank robber in a Santa suit stuck up the First National Bank of Cisco. "Santa" turned out to be a local ne'er-do-well, and his friends and neighbors weren't in a jolly mood. They stormed the jail and lynched the faux Santa on a pole.*

The State Symbols of Texas

How many people know the official state insect of Texas?
How about the official state flying mammal? Never fear!
Following is a complete list of the Lone Star State's official
symbols and emblems, and the years they were adopted.

- **Flower:** Bluebonnet (all types) (1901, again in 1971)
- **Tree:** Pecan (*Carya illinoensis*) (1919)
- **Bird:** Mockingbird (*Mimus polyglottos*) (1927)
- **Song:** "Texas, Our Texas," words by William J. Marsh and Gladys Yoakum Wright, music by William J. Marsh (1929)
- **Flower Song:** "Bluebonnets," written by Julia D. Booth and Lora C. Crockett (1933)
- **Gemstone:** Texas blue topaz (1969)
- **Stone:** Petrified palmwood (1969)
- **Grass:** Sideoats grama (1971)
- **Dish:** Chili (1977)
- **Gemstone cut:** Lonestar cut (1977)
- **Shell:** Lightning whelk (1987)
- **Air force:** Commemorative Air Force (1989) (Formerly known as the Confederate Air Force)
- **Fish:** Guadalupe bass (*Micropterus treculi*) (1989)
- **Bluebonnet trail:** Ennis Bluebonnet Trail (1991)
- **Folk dance:** Square dance (1991)
- **Fruit:** Texas red grapefruit (1993)
- **Reptile:** Horned lizard (1993)
- **Flying mammal:** Mexican free-tailed bat (*Tadarida brasiliensis*) (1995)
- **Insect:** Monarch butterfly (*Danaus plexippus*) (1995)

- **Large mammal:** Longhorn (1995)
- **Pepper:** Jalapeño (1995)
- **Plant:** Prickly pear cactus (1995)
- **Ship:** USS *Texas* (1995)
- **Small mammal:** Nine-Banded armadillo (*Dasypus novemcinctus*) (1995)
- **Bluebonnet city:** Ennis (1997)
- **Bluebonnet festival:** The Chappell Hill Bluebonnet Festival (1997)
- **Dinosaur:** Brachiosaur sauropod, Pleurocoelus (1997)
- **Fiber/Fabric:** Cotton (1997)
- **Musical instrument:** Guitar (1997)
- **Native pepper:** Chiltepin (1997)
- **Shrub:** Crape myrtle (1997)
- **Sport:** Rodeo (1997)
- **Vegetable:** Sweet onion (1997)
- **Railroad:** Texas State Railroad (2003)
- **Snack:** Tortilla chips and salsa (2003)

- **Bread:** Pan de campo (cowboy bread) (2005)
- **Cooking implement:** Cast-iron Dutch oven (2005)
- **Dog breed:** Blue lacy (2005)
- **Native shrub:** Texas purple sage (2005)
- **Tall ship:** *Elissa* (2005)
- **Vehicle:** Chuck wagon (2005)
- **Footwear:** Cowboy boot (2007)
- **Precious metal:** Silver (2007)
- **Tejano music hall of fame:** Tejano Music Hall of Fame Museum, Alice (2001)
- **Tie:** Bolo tie (2007)

Texas's Musical Holy Trinity

Texas has always been a fertile and fruitful fountain of diverse and distinct music. Three individuals—Guy Clark, Townes Van Zandt, and Jimmy Dale Gilmore—were instrumental in introducing a blend of folk-fried country blues and deft finger-picking guitar work with poetic, precise parables that made the song, not the singer, the star of the show.

The musical trends of Texas have ranged from the fun, rollicking rock 'n' roll of Buddy Holly and flamboyant Tex-Mex styling of Flaco Jiménez to the outlaw oeuvre of Willie Nelson and big-band gospel-tinged spirituality of Lyle Lovett. But these three songwriters truly set themselves apart.

Guy Clark—Country Chronicler

The genius of Guy Clark rests in his emotional versatility, simplistic storytelling, and compelling compositions. Like the other members of this trio, Clark uses his voice as an instrument to deliver the message without overwhelming the structure of the piece. A native of Monahans, a small community tucked away in the southwestern corner of the state, Clark grew up listening to and reciting poetry, which may account for his intricate phrasing and love of language.

After learning the fine art of guitar making in Los Angeles, Clark relocated to Nashville, where he honed his songwriting skills while immersing himself in the community's rich history and creative culture. It was in Music City that Clark joined a singer-songwriter fraternity that included Townes Van Zandt, Rodney Crowell, Steve Earle, John Hiatt, and David Allan Coe.

Many of his songs relate to the everyday events and ordinary people that have influenced his life: from the appearance of the first streamlined train in his hometown ("Texas, 1947") or his move to California to seek fame and fortune ("L.A. Freeway") to the struggle to find peace in his father's death ("Randall Knife") and meaning in his grandfather's life ("Desperados Waiting for a Train"). Born in 1941, Clark has recorded more than a dozen studio albums and

Guy Clark

Townes Van Zandt

Jimmy Dale Gilmore

released numerous live and anthology collections. He continues to tour and craft songs that "strike at the heart of the matter."

Townes Van Zandt— The Troubled Troubadour

Unconventional in style and unrepentant in life, Townes Van Zandt wrote piercing, often turbulent tunes about loss, love, yearning, and returning, and he sang them in a voice punctured by pain and creased by calamity. Born in Fort Worth in 1944 to a prominent family with a pedigree that can be traced back to the roots of the republic, Van Zandt always marched to a different drummer. He preferred the solitude of the road, the company of a good book, and a full bottle to the higher aspirations expressed by his family. Damaged by depression and addled by addictions, Van Zandt found solace in his ability to construct perfectly appointed parables, songs that combined his expressive blues-filtered guitar work with precise lyrics and flowing melodies.

Although he was revered as a singer-songwriter—both Merle Haggard and Willie Nelson had hits with his material—he wasn't able to translate that success into mainstream acceptance. Each of his more than two dozen recordings were released on small, independent labels. "Pancho and Lefty," "If I Needed You," and "No Place to Fall" are the best examples of his handsomely honed, image-immersed compositions.

Unfortunately, Van Zandt's erratic behavior, dependence on alcohol, and inability to exorcise the demons that were smothering him plagued and undermined the creative output of his final years. Ironically, when he died on New Years Day, 1997, he was just about to begin recording an album for Geffen Records, which would have been his first release on a major record label.

Jimmy Dale Gilmore—Honky Tonk Cowboy

A native of Lubbock—the home of Buddy Holly and the birthplace of the "Lubbock Sound," a carousing compilation of country honk and rock 'n' roll—Jimmy Dale Gilmore has fashioned a creative career that blends folk, blues, country, and rock into a compelling combination. Though not as prolific a songwriter as Clark or Van Zandt—even if some of his compositions have been featured in movies such as *Terminal Velocity*—Gilmore's contribution to the musical legacy of Texas is no less impressive.

In 1971, Gilmore and two local lads, Butch Hancock and Joe Ely, formed a band called The Flatlanders, a seminal unit that is often credited with introducing a synthesis of sounds that would later be dubbed progressive, alternative country. Featuring minimal, lo-fi instrumentation and subtle arrangements, The Flatlanders became local legends, but their fame remained confined to a cult following.

Although each of these musicians went on to have successful and creative solo careers, Gilmore has garnished the greatest critical praise of the three. This is largely due to his intuitive selection of first-rate material by fellow songwriters and the unique focus of his own songs that approaches common themes such as loving and leaving and filters them through a spiritual, mystical light. And, of course, there is his voice, a remarkable instrument that has been variously described as "oddly resonant" and "like a hinge that needs a shot of WD-40."

Gilmore has released eight solo albums, including the critically acclaimed *One Endless Night* and *Spinning Around the Sun*. The Flatlanders, who still reunite occasionally for live performances and recording sessions, have five albums on their resume, including *More a Legend than a Band*, originally recorded in 1972 but not released until 1990. Gilmore widened his appeal by appearing in *The Big Lebowski*, the Joel and Ethan Coen cult movie about bowling, nihilism, and survival of the slacker.

Calling All Munster Fans

The house at 1313 Mockingbird Lane is now open for business.

Sandra and Charles McKee are the ultimate fans of the 1960s TV show *The Munsters*. Thus, setting out to build their dream home involved watching all 70 episodes of the horror show/sitcom and poring over pictures from the popular program. The result: an exact replica of the Munster home, right down to the doorknobs.

Construction of the 5,825-square-foot house was enough to cause a stir in the small town of Waxahachie. But once onlookers realized what was taking shape, the curiosity seekers started to arrive.

A Dream Home—or a Nightmare?

Sandra admits to being a bigger Munsters fan than her husband, but don't call her odd; she prefers to think of herself as a Munsters enthusiast. Her love of the TV series was the perfect inspiration for her and Charles's dream home.

The McKees tried to be as faithful as possible to the Munsters' monstrous home as it appeared on television, but they have left room for some personal space and bathrooms, which viewers never actually saw. After all, the house is their home—because it's their personal residence and not a museum, visitors are reminded to respect the couple's privacy. However, pictures are allowed through the front gate, the final detail that lends authenticity to the Victorian abode.

For fellow Munsters fans and the curious, the McKees open their house to visitors once a year for a Halloween event. The two-day festivities include house tours, costume contests, Munsters trivia, and celebrity guests, with proceeds donated to charity. People have even had a chance to spot their favorite Munster family member on the tour, as Butch Patrick (Eddie), Al Lewis (Grandpa), and Pat Priest (Marilyn) have all attended the Halloween party in the past.

The McKees continue to work on the exterior of the house and have been experimenting with different techniques to create a realistic dilapidated look. This final renovation will make their home a true Munster Mansion.

Taste of Texas

Texas foods are sometimes called a foreign cuisine within the United States, but Texans are abundantly proud of them. Here are a few of the many dishes that have been invented or popularized in the Lone Star State.

- Chili, the official state dish of Texas, is said to have been invented in San Antonio's Military Plaza in the 1880s. Enterprising local women set up stands on the plaza selling the spicy meat stew, adding to the festive energy of the city's nightlife. Pretty young women enlisted to serve it up became known as Chili Queens. The health department, however, closed the stands in the early 1940s.

- Chili powder, the key ingredient of the Tex-Mex food revolution, was invented by German immigrant William Gebhardt in 1896 in New Braunfels. A café owner, Gebhardt pulverized dried chiles using a meat grinder. Gebhardt's Eagle Chili Powder is still found on grocery store shelves today. Sparing home cooks the task of drying and pulverizing chiles, his spicy dust caught on like wildfire in Texas and spread to the rest of the nation.

- As the state is home to millions of head of cattle, it's not surprising that a Texan claims to have invented hamburgers. The story goes that café owner Fletcher Davis first put ground beef inside a bun in the East Texas town of Athens sometime in the late 1880s. In 1904 he took his invention to the World's Fair in St. Louis, where the quintessential American fast food entrée went national. Billions of burgers later, a historic marker in downtown Athens now marks where Fletcher's café once stood.

- Born on the cattle trail, chicken fried steak went on to become a mainstay of roadside diners from coast to coast. Historians say cowboy cooks invented the dish to make tough Longhorn beef more appetizing. After beating the meat tender, they dipped it in milk and dredged it in flour before frying it up in a Dutch oven. Gravy was made from the pan drippings. Diners today only need to add salt and pepper to taste.

Houston Is Where It Happens

Anyone who's ever watched a space launch on television is probably familiar with the Kennedy Space Center at Cape Canaveral, Florida, but any Texan knows that Houston is where the hardest work is being done.

The Lyndon B. Johnson Space Center (JSC) is the home of NASA's Mission Control Center, which coordinates and monitors all space flights. The center was the hub for all of the Gemini and Apollo missions, and that building is now designated a National Historic Landmark. Today, the space shuttle missions and all activities aboard the International Space Station are monitored from the Johnson Space Center.

The center consists of 100 buildings scattered across 1,620 acres in southeast Houston. Originally known as the Manned Spacecraft Center, the facilities opened in 1963, and in 1973, the center was renamed for the late president.

Setting It Up

In 1962, President John F. Kennedy made it a goal to put an American on the moon by the end of the decade. The administrator of NASA, James E. Webb, headed a selection team to find a site where test facilities and research laboratories could be built to mount the space program. Requirements included the availability of water transport and an all-weather airport, proximity to a major telecommunications network, availability of established industrial workers and contractor support, an available supply of water, a mild climate permitting year-round outdoor work, and a culturally attractive community. Another factor Houston had over the competition—and one of the reasons it was initially considered—was its proximity to the U.S. Army San Jacinto Ordnance Depot, the Houston Shipping Channel, and regional universities.

Today, roughly 3,000 civilians and 110 astronauts are employed at JSC. The bulk of the workforce is the 15,000 contract workers representing about 50 contracting firms.

What It Takes to Be an Astronaut

In addition to being the Mission Control Center, the JSC is the home of the astronaut corps and is responsible for training astronauts from both the United States and its international partners. Astronauts receive training on the shuttle system and in basic sciences, which include mathematics, guidance and navigation, oceanography, astronomy, and physics. Candidates are put through military water survival training, SCUBA certification, and flying instruction, and they learn to handle emergencies associated with atmospheric pressure and space flight.

Astronauts begin their formal training by reading manuals and taking computer-based training programs. From there, they move on to the orbiter systems trainer, where they practice orbiter landings and prepare for malfunctions and corrective actions. The next step is the shuttle mission simulators, which provide training on shuttle operations and specific tasks they may have to perform.

The neutral buoyancy laboratory, a large pool containing 6.2 million gallons of water, allows astronauts to practice tasks in an environment that simulates zero gravity conditions. It also prepares them for space walks.

Research and Development

But the center is much more than an astronaut training facility—the Johnson Space Center leads NASA's flight-related scientific and medical research programs. The technologies that support space flight are now in use in civilian medicine, the energy industry, transportation, agriculture, communications, and electronics. Current research studies include the prebreathe reduction program, which is intended to help walks in space from the International Space Station become safer and more efficient.

A Tourist Site

The visitor center and grounds contain historical and archival information that chronicles the history of the astronaut program and its contributions to NASA. One can see the lunar receiving laboratory where the first astronauts were quarantined after returning from space. The center's landing and recovery division was responsible for retrieving astronauts after splashdown during the Gemini and Apollo missions and is housed at JSC. The majority of moon rocks and lunar samples are also stored at the complex.

One of the artifacts displayed at JSC is a Saturn V rocket made of actual surplus flight-ready materials. An incomplete Apollo Capsule Service Module (CSM), intended to fly on the cancelled Apollo 19 mission, is also displayed on the grounds. An educational center provides student internships, day camps, and materials for educators, and it trains volunteers, as well.

Security Is Vital

The Johnson Space Center has its own security headquarters and maintains a high level of monitoring due to the sensitive nature of its business and the equipment housed at its facilities. Only one reported security incident has occurred in its several decades of history when, in 2007, a hostage situation occurred in the communication and tracking development laboratory. A gunman killed one employee and injured another before taking his own life.

The center is also vulnerable to the effects of nature. In 2008, Hurricane Ike hit as a Category 3, destroying several airplane hangars and damaging a number of buildings.

The Johnson Space Center will continue to provide services to NASA and the International Space Station as the space program moves forward. Those missions may take humans back to the moon, to Mars, or into the deep reaches of space. One thing is certain: The crew at JSC Houston will be there to make sure everything runs smoothly.

• *Amazon.com founder Jeff Bezos, through his company Blue Origin, has built a spaceport on land near Van Horn in West Texas. Activities there have been quite secretive so far, although in 2006, a spokesperson for the Federal Aviation Administration said, "We have received permit applications from Blue Origin and are evaluating them for safety and other considerations."*

Talkin' About Texas

"We are marching through a beautiful country—its face presents a scene of grandeur and magnificence rarely, if ever witnessed. It is the most beautiful and sublime scene. Rome itself with all its famous hills could not surpass the natural scenery of Waterloo [Austin's original name]."

—James Jones, early colonist, letter to Republic of Texas President
Mirabeau B. Lamar, 1839

"The notion of the cowboy has always been one of America's most precious gifts to the children of the world.... When Anne Frank's secret annex was revisited after World War II, pictures of American cowboy stars were still fluttering from the walls where she had left them."

—Kinky Friedman, author and musician

"I love to come to Houston because there are more writers here than anywhere outside New York City."

—Susan Sontag, author, *In America*

"What others have called braggadocio we Texans call pride... after all, 'It ain't braggin' if it's true.' We're crazy about our home state and we want the world to know it."

—Texas Department of Transportation

"Texas has always been an enigma having an affair with a contradiction."

—Jonathan Eisen and Harold Straughn, authors, *Unknown Texas*

"And now, in my nineties I still see Texas as a land of opportunity for all people. And through all these years, the one thing I've always noticed about Texans is a genuine friendliness, not just for each other because Texans have never been clannish, but there is a real eagerness about Texans. Texans are proud of this land and I think Texans want everybody to experience the spirit of Texas."

—As told to author Mary Elizabeth Goldman by her father

"There has never been anything quite like Texas."

—David Nevin, author, *The Texans*

Molly Ivins Can't Say That, Can She?

Say the word Texas *to almost any journalist in the nation, and Molly Ivins's name is likely to come back in response, generally spoken with reverence. Well-known and loved around the country, she wrote columns that are still quoted. Molly Ivins stories abound and have not been slowed by her 2007 death at age 62 from breast cancer. But in Texas, where she was raised, this one-of-a-kind pundit is a legend.*

Writer Molly Ivins could—and did—say practically anything, especially if it involved skewering the powerful, the poseurs, and the just plain politically dumb. And what she said over the course of nearly 40 years as an unabashedly liberal newspaper columnist and reporter was nearly always witty and often deliciously on target.

Ivins in Action

Take the title of this piece, which was also the title of her first book. When Ivins, writing for the *Dallas Times Herald,* said of Texas Republican congressman Jim Collins, "If his I.Q. slips any lower, we'll have to water him twice a day," she created an uproar. Advertisers cancelled. Readers (and the congressman) protested. And the newspaper rented billboards in her support, declaring, "Molly Ivins can't say that, can she?"

Or this, from the *Charleston Gazette* in 1994 about gun control. "I am not anti-gun, I'm pro-knife. Consider the merits of the knife. In the first place, you have to catch up with someone in order to stab him. A general substitution of knives for guns would promote physical fitness. We'd turn into a whole nation of great runners. Plus, knives don't ricochet. And people are seldom killed while cleaning their knives."

Ivins referred to the second President Bush as "Shrub" for years, and she once famously derided a speech by conservative Pat Buchanan: "It probably sounded better in the original German."

Starting Out

Ivins was born in California but moved as a young child to Houston with her family, who were staunch Republicans. After graduating from Smith College in 1966, she attended Columbia Graduate School of Journal-ism. Her first newspaper job was in the complaint department of the *Houston Chronicle,* followed by a stint at the *Minneapolis Tribune,* where she was the first woman to cover the police beat.

In 1970, Ivins came home to Texas to become coeditor of the feisty independent *Texas Observer,* where she began her long career covering the antics of the Texas legislature—a goldmine of columns for the rest of her life. But she wasn't content to remain there.

A Legend Grows

It was no surprise when one of the country's great journalists joined the staff of one of its greatest papers. But Ivins wrote of *The New York Times,* where she worked from 1976 to 1982, that it was "a great newspaper: it is also No Fun." She was the *Times*'s Rocky Mountain bureau chief and covered major news stories for the paper, among them the Son of Sam and the death of Elvis Presley (she later joked that she was the only reporter on the scene whose stories referred to the late singer as "Mr. Presley"). But her idea of hell, she said, was "being edited by the *Times* copy desk for all eternity."

Back home in Texas in 1982, Ivins wrote for the *Dallas Times Herald,* despite the fact that she said Dallas "would have rooted for Goliath to beat David." After that paper folded, she moved on to the *Fort Worth Star-Telegram* before becoming a nationally syndicated independent columnist in 2001.

Ivins authored seven books, made innumerable television appearances, and was a tireless fund-raiser for causes she championed, particularly the *Texas Observer* and groups that supported the First Amendment, such as the American Civil Liberties Union.

A liberal voice heard around the world, she said of her home, "I dearly love the state of Texas, but I consider that a harmless perversion on my part, and discuss it only with consenting adults."

The Sutton-Taylor Feud

When disputes fester, they can turn deadly. Such was the case with Texas's version of the Hatfields and McCoys. When the smoke cleared, and this long-standing feud died out, dozens lay dead in its wake.

Texas's fight between the Suttons and the Taylors claimed an estimated 30 to 50 people. In one of the state's longest and deadliest disputes, William E. Sutton and Creed Taylor did their hateful best to mow each other down. Eventually, family and friends joined each combatant in their unquenchable quest for revenge. For such loyalty, many paid the ultimate price.

So, What Do We Know?

Hatred between the families may have begun as early as the 1840s, when Sutton and Taylor lived in Georgia. By the 1860s, both families had relocated to Texas's DeWitt County, bringing their loathing with them. In March 1868, a pivotal event occurred when accused horse thieves Charles Taylor and James Sharp were shot to death. This was followed by the Christmas Eve murders of Buck Taylor and Dick Chisholm. William Sutton was believed to be involved in both episodes.

With the gauntlet thrown down, there was no turning back. The Taylors staged deadly ambushes, claiming a number of Sutton's soldiers. In 1872, Pitkin Taylor was shot and wounded, and he died six months later. His family swore revenge and enlisted kinsman and notorious outlaw John Wesley Hardin. Soon, Hardin and Jim Taylor disposed of Jack Helm, an agent of Sutton.

Settled?

This deadly tit-for-tat continued until the late 1870s, when Texas Rangers arrested eight men from the Sutton camp for killing Dr. Phillip Brassel and his son. By this time, the feud was so widespread and fragmented that no one was sure who fought for what or for whom. With witnesses understandably scared to testify against either side, the legal case fell apart. But the feud appeared to be over. With a whimper instead of a bang, the Sutton-Taylor feud had finally come to an end.

Ludicrous Laws

Everything is big in Texas, and that includes seemingly pointless laws. Here are some of the stranger statutes currently on the books.

- When two trains meet each other at a railroad crossing, each shall come to a full stop, and neither shall proceed until the other has gone.

- A citizen cannot work for the state government if his supervisor has "reasonable grounds to believe that the person is a communist."

- It is illegal to sell a secondhand watch without an invoice that clearly states the watch is used "in letters larger than any other letters on the invoice."

- It is illegal to carry wire cutters in your pocket in the city of Austin.

- It is illegal to sell armadillos.

- In Galveston, it is against the law for camels to wander unattended.

- Criminals must give their intended victims 24 hours notice, either orally or in writing, to explain the nature of the crime about to be committed against them.

- Littering is never a good idea, but throwing garbage out of a plane might land one in jail in Galveston.

- No feather dusters in Clarendon! It's against the law to use them to dust public buildings.

- People wanting to enjoy a nice, cold beer had better be sitting down. They can take as many as three sips while standing up, but if they draw that fourth one, they're crossing the line into criminality.

- Speaking of beer, the authorities really don't want anyone making it without proper authorization. In fact, the *Encyclopedia Britannica* has been banned in Texas because it contains instructions for how to brew your own. Yep, not just *B,* but every single volume of it.

- Riding a horse at night can be dangerous. That's why Texarkana requires horses to be equipped with tail lights after dark.

The Great Camel Experiment

One of the most interesting military experiments prior to the Civil War involved 77 camels and a native of Syria called Hi Jolly. Who came up with the idea of camel caravans in Texas?

In 1836, Major George Crosman recommended to Congress that the U.S. Army consider using camels, which require less water and forage than mules and horses. He also passed that suggestion to Major Henry Wayne, who, in the late 1840s, began to investigate the feasibility of using camels as pack animals.

Wayne proposed that camels would move faster than mules, carry more supplies, and naturally adapt to the Southwest, which mimicked the geographic areas he called "Camel Land." He submitted a formal proposal to the War Department recommending the importation of camels to test the feasibility of a camel cavalry. The cause was also supported by Army Lieutenant Edward Beale, who had surveyed Death Valley and agreed that camels were hardy animals that could assist the Army in developing the Texas territory and surrounding Southwest.

A Growing Consensus

Jefferson Davis, U.S. Secretary of War in the 1850s, had listened closely to Wayne and Beale and set out to do his own research. Being an avid historian, he knew that the French had used camels during the Napoleonic campaign in Egypt. Davis had previously served in the Mexican War and was keenly aware of the challenges of a desert climate. With Davis's backing, Congress appropriated $30,000 to purchase camels and hire camel drivers.

So with visions of camel caravans winding their way across Texas, Major Wayne and Lieutenant David Porter were sent to the eastern Mediterranean on a Navy supply ship to purchase camels. Wayne, an experienced horse trader, haggled with the natives and chose a team of 33 camels. The savvy businessman paid $250 per beast and gained two more through the birth of two colts during the voyage.

The Triumphal Arrival

On the excursion's return to Texas, locals watched as the camels were unloaded at Powder Point, near Indianola. Displaying typical camel stubbornness and aggravated by the long period of confinement onboard ship, the animals snorted, reared, broke halters, and kicked handlers. Many onlookers thought a circus had come to town. And indeed the circuslike atmosphere continued as the beasts were herded towards Houston with their drivers wearing colorful red coats and blue pants and the jingle of bells on the camels' harnesses echoing through the countryside.

In February 1857, a second cargo of 41 camels landed on the Texas coast. Eventually, a permanent camel camp was established near San Antonio. Camp Verde became the proving ground for the Texas Camel Experiment.

Hadji Ali, a Syrian camel wrangler, was hired to teach the soldiers how to handle the camels and pack and load supplies on a camel's back. The Texans had trouble pronouncing his foreign name, so they gave him the nickname Hi Jolly.

Into the Desert

The first caravan, led by Beale and Jolly, left Texas in June 1857 and made its way to California. The camels carried 600 to 800 pounds each and traveled an average of 25 to 30 miles a day. The caravan made it to California and back successfully.

However, the grand plans for the camel experiment were cast aside as the Civil War loomed. Although the next secretary of war petitioned Congress for 1,000 additional camels, the affiliation of the project with Jefferson Davis, who would become president of the Confederacy, soured the enthusiasm.

The camels that were already available were eventually seized by the Confederates, who quickly lost interest in them. Many wandered away from the forts, and some were taken by Mexicans across the border. For many years after, there were camel sightings across Texas and the Southwest, with the last official sighting in 1901. Unsubstantiated sightings, however, lasted into the 1940s.

Fast Facts

- *Lyndon Baines Johnson, a colorful and well-known soul, was also an extremely frugal man. He'd go around the White House shutting off lights in empty rooms and would gladly wash and reuse Styrofoam cups. The man just did not believe in needless waste.*

- *Oil mogul Tom Slick Jr. had the curious hobby of abominable snowman hunting. He went to the Himalayas looking for a yeti (similar to Bigfoot) and spent a lot of time in the United States looking for one, as well. Slick never spotted any, but he probably had fun anyway.*

- *One lasting Spanish legal principle in Texas is estate law. In Texas, an executor doesn't need a court order to do things not specified in the will. About a dozen states now handle estates this way, which means, in short, that people need an executor they trust.*

- *Ninety percent of the world's known exploitable helium is under Amarillo. (Residents there have been listening to jokes about gas for a long time, so please, no more.) The helium is mixed in with the natural gas reserves underground and gets separated during refining.*

- *Rocker Meat Loaf, formerly known as Marvin Lee Aday (Dallas), got his nickname in his teens when someone dared him to let a Volkswagen run over his head. Marvin followed through on the dare, whereupon a perceptive onlooker accused him of having meatloaf between his ears.*

- *Most of the* Hindenburg, *of course, was incinerated in 1937 at Lakehurst, New Jersey. Somehow, however, the radio operator's chair wasn't roasted—and it made its way to Dallas. See it, and a few other* Hindenburg *artifacts, at the Frontiers of Flight Museum.*

- *Dallas Cowboys kicker Rafael Septien (1978–86) became famous for his creative excuses for missing kicks. Funniest ever: the time he blamed a field goal miss on the deep grass at Texas Stadium. What's wrong with that? The stadium had artificial turf.*

Decadent Christmas with Neiman Marcus

Do dreams come true? They do for those who can afford them.

The name Neiman Marcus is synonymous with upscale retail in the United States. In 1907, the first Neiman Marcus store opened in Dallas and featured exclusive women's clothing never seen before in Texas. The savvy owners, Carrie Marcus Neiman; her husband, Al Neiman; and her brother, Herbert Marcus, lavishly decorated the store and selected clothing they knew would appeal to the wives of oil-rich Texans eager to flaunt their wealth and sophistication. The idea worked—the store's entire inventory sold out in just a few weeks.

Big Sales from Big Money

During the early years, sales were bolstered by the influx of money into the Texas economy from cattle, cotton, and oil. A men's clothing line was added in 1928, and word spread about the high-end merchandise. Soon the rich and glamorous from Hollywood, New York, and Europe made their way to Dallas to shop at Neiman Marcus.

In the years that followed, Neiman Marcus expanded its brand with the addition of more stores in Texas; a direct-mail catalog; and the Fortnight, a presentation of fashions and culture from a particular country, which went on display each autumn.

Is This Where Santa Shops?

But the ultimate in decadence was the Neiman Marcus Christmas catalog. This world-famous book started in 1915 as a Christmas card inviting customers to shop for the holidays at the store in Dallas. The first actual Christmas catalog premiered in 1926 and was a modest 16 pages of beautiful and unusual items at a variety of prices.

The ante was raised in 1959 when Herbert's sons, Stanley and Edward, brainstormed about an unusual and extraordinary Christmas item they could add to the catalog for that year. They decided on a Black Angus steer delivered on the hoof or in steaks complete with a silver-plated cooker. The response was overwhelming.

Buoyed by the publicity, the brothers decided to push even further the next year and introduced a "His and Her" gift. They were going for over-the-top, and they achieved it with a pair of matching Beechcraft airplanes for the couple who thought it already had everything. Once again, the response was tremendous, and a yearly tradition was launched. Prior to the release of the catalog each year, famed journalist Edward R. Murrow and his then-assistant, Walter Cronkite, called the Marcuses to find out about the latest outrageous "His and Her" gift to be featured.

Defining Extravagance

Over the years, the catalog has offered "His and Her" Egyptian mummy cases, personalized action figures, hot air balloons, submarines, Chinese junks, camels, robots, and windmills. This ultimate wish book has also featured fantasy items such as a dirigible, an Empress chinchilla coat, polo ponies, a chocolate Monopoly game, and a 14-karat gold train set with a diamond engine whose train cars held rubies, emeralds, and sapphires. The most expensive item ever offered was an unfinished Boeing business jet for more than $35 million.

Presentation Is Everything

What makes the Neiman Marcus Christmas catalog unique is not only the items offered but also the way they are presented. Each item is displayed with a photograph and a detailed description that leaps off the page with its snappy lines and a plethora of adjectives. The catalog was an infomercial before infomercials ever aired on television. Here are a few samples from the 2008 catalog:

- **Titanium Fighter Motorcycle, $110,000:** "There's the startling, dare-we-say sexy, design that fuses raw power with crisp simplicity. It's an evolution of the machine, at once taken back down to the core elements while being reinvented and re-engineered for optimal performance. It's our street legal sci-fi dream come to life, in the form of the limited edition Fighter Motorcycle."

- **Thirty-Five–Year Collection of 45 RPM Records, $275,000:** "In this age of soulless digital downloads and MP3 mumbo-jumbo, we gleefully turn to that treasured icon of our American pop culture childhood: the 45 RPM vinyl single.... We present our exclusive, definitive collection. To be clear, it contains each and every 45 RPM vinyl record that was listed on the Billboard Top 100® Rock and Pop charts from Jan. 1, 1955, through Dec. 31, 1990. Absolutely every disc for 35 years, every No. 100 up to every No. 1. There are some 18,400 records total."

- **His & Hers Life-Size Lego Sculptures, $60,000 each:** "Acclaimed artist Nathan Sawaya... fills his New York studio with more than 1.5 million of the interlocking toy building blocks, and he can sculpt anything out of them.... Given the skill and depth of his devotion to his art, it makes perfect sense to immortalize your own magnificent self with our 2008 His & Hers gifts. Send in detailed photos and measurements, then Nathan gets to snapping and BOOM! One-of-a-kind life-size sculptures of yourselves in Lego bricks."

- **Jack Nicklaus Custom Backyard Golf Course, Beginning at $1,000,000 (Construction and site preparation costs not included):** "Yes, THE Jack Nicklaus. Jack will study topography, aerial photos, and landscape maps for the site, then send his team to survey the property. He'll create a formal design plan and color renderings for up to three holes and a practice area. Your construction crew builds from it, with supervision from Jack's world-class design team. When your course is finished, the Golden Bear himself will stop by to play the first round with you, personally. He'll sign his club and ball for your collection and throw in a custom set of Nicklaus clubs, including a personalized bag."

A Work of Art

Since its inception, Neiman Marcus has commissioned leading artists to design the cover of the catalog. Cover artists have included Al Hirshfield, Ben Shahn, Robert Indiana, and Saul Steinberg.

And the catalog wouldn't be complete without celebrity fashion models. Those whose careers were boosted by their appearance in the catalog include Cybill Shepherd, Andie MacDowell, Morgan Fairchild, Heidi Klum, and Cindy Crawford. Today, the Neiman Marcus Christmas catalog is distributed to more than one million homes worldwide.

Texas Tawk

Not everyone can understand what a Texan is saying, but they can certainly feign a deep understanding by nodding their head and repeating the words yup *or* yessir *at strategic intervals. If possible, they should stuff a chaw of* snuff (tobacco) *into their cheek and, every so often, spit out the excess juices to the side, always maintaining eye contact with the raconteur at hand.*

Mark Twain once wrote that "the difference between the almost right word and the right word is really a large matter—it's the difference between the lightning bug and the lightning." Well, it must be rainin' a frog strangler down in Texas, with big bolts hurled down by the legendary Pecos Bill himself, considering the colorful way that Texans choose their words.

For newcomers just moving in and tourists just passing through, mastering interpersonal communication in the Lone Star State *can* be challenging. Y'all, from the first unfamiliar word heard, frustration sets in quickly. Intimidated by Texas-speak, neophytes feel like a one-legged man at a butt-kickin' contest when they try to converse with the natives. Certainly, there are transplants who speak perfect English, but there are an equal number of old-timers who will leave listeners scratchin' their heads in dazed wonderment.

The challenges for the untrained ear—be it Yankee, Midwestern, or West Coast—are numerous. First thing out of the chute, Texans have a penchant for stretching out words and sentences with a distinct drawl, trying the patience of those accustomed to a quicker cadence. Hyperbolic colloquialisms in the form of sayings, adages, boasts, brags, insults, and put-downs also ooze forth from the Texan tongue with great frequency.

Fortunately, at its core, this language is still English. Once newcomers grow accustomed to the idiosyncrasies of Texas-speak, there's hope they'll catch on rather quickly. And dad gum it, once an ear is tuned in to the sarcastic slant of Texafied sayings, it's on its way to wisdom.

Lone Star Lexicon

- **howdy:** The standard Texas greeting used universally in place of *hello, hi, good day, pleased to meet you, glad to make your acquaintance,* and *how do you do?* "*Howdy* folks! Y'all come in from that frog strangler and dry off for a spell."

- **agger-vated:** With the emphasis on "vated," used to describe the entire gamut of human irritations, from everyday minor annoyances to the type of rage resulting in homicide.

- **fess up:** To admit or confess. For example, "Dad gum it, you'd better *fess up* now about what you did, young man. There's no way that tree chopped itself down."

- **over yonder:** A phrase used to give directions or to "clarify" which way to go. Describes an unquantified distance or direction of travel, usually accompanied by a vague pointing of a finger.

- **galoot:** Nothing to do with a woman robbing a bank, but rather an old cowboy reference meaning "old rascal." Generally, it's an endearing term meant in an affable, kind-hearted way.

- **taken to:** The act of adapting to or liking something. "For an iced-tea lover, Mary Lou has *taken to* drinking tequila rather quickly."

- **whole nuther thing:** Another obfuscated Texas term that's used to describe something else entirely, wherein the word *nuther* equates to the word *other,* the rest of the phrase being self-explanatory.

- **shoot:** A common, garden-variety expletive that is used in place of the other more common, similar-sounding swear or "cuss" word that refers to . . . well, you know.

- **conniptions:** Similar to a seizure or other uncontrollable movement of the body in reaction to some negatively perceived circumstance, a *conniption* fit can raise quite a ruckus.

- **blue norther:** A fast-moving storm front (accompanied by wind and rain) that arrives as a gargantuan, blue-black cloud of frigid air, rolling quickly over warm gulf air, often with freezing temperatures.

One Person's Junk...

This ever-growing edifice invites audience participation.

The Cathedral of Junk in Austin occupies the backyard of an inconspicuous house on the city's south side. It has been created over the past couple of decades by homeowner Vince Hannemann, who estimates that his sculpture contains more than 60 tons of junk—much of it brought by strangers who come to admire his creation.

In part covered by twisting strands of native flora, the magical construction is packed with all manner of mass-produced castoffs, with stairways leading to higher levels of strange juxtapositions—lawnmower wheels, fast-food kids'-meal toys, car parts, kitchen utensils, bottles, computer boards, bicycle castoffs, neon beer signs, electrical components, snow skis, trophies, street signs, and many objects that are unidentifiable. The cathedral is constantly growing and changing, with old things moving around and new pieces of junk popping up. It currently stands 30 feet high and contains an estimated 1,500 square feet—bigger than Hannemann's house.

An Unassuming Birth

Hannemann's ongoing found-art opus began in 1989 with just a few hub caps he hung on a backyard fence of the house he was renting. Luckily, his landlord didn't seem to mind the massive structure that was soon taking shape. Hannemann says he built it for his own amusement and to create a private space where he could sit and think. When his landlord passed away a few years ago, Hannemann bought the home from his widow.

While it started as a hobby, the cathedral has become more like a public art attraction and community service organization. Hannemann's backyard has hosted weddings, concerts, birthday parties, fundraisers, and school field trips, and it has served as a set for TV commercials and movies.

Hannemann has visitors coming from all over the world, at all hours. He doesn't mind the visitors, though, and if in the mood, he'll offer a tour.

Texas Timeline

November 1527
The first hurricane on record to strike the Texas coastline makes landfall near present-day Galveston, claiming a fleet of merchant ships and some 200 lives.

November 6, 1528
Spanish explorer Álvar Nuñez Cabeza de Vaca is shipwrecked near what is now Galveston. He and his shipmates become the first Europeans to explore the interior of Texas.

1540
Spanish conquistador Francisco Vázquez de Coronado launches a massive expedition in search of the fabled golden city of Cibola. The expedition travels throughout much of the Southwest, including northern Texas, over the next two years.

March 20, 1687
Searching for the mouth of the Mississippi River, French explorer René-Robert Cavelier, Sieur de La Salle, finds Texas instead.

May 25, 1690
The Mission San Francisco de los Tejas, Texas's first mission, is established in the Piney Woods, near present-day Nacogdoches.

May 1, 1718
The Mission San Antonio de Valero is founded near present-day San Antonio. It comes to be known more commonly as the Alamo.

March 20, 1721
Spanish dominion over Texas is established as governor Aguayo of Coahuila crosses into Texas to drive out the French.

May 29, 1813
The first edition of Texas's first newspaper, *Gaceta de Tejas,* is printed.

February 22, 1819
The United States and Spain sign the Adams-Onis Treaty, relinquishing Texas to Spain in exchange for Spain releasing all claims on Florida.

June 23, 1819
Unhappy with the signing of the Adams-Onis Treaty, 300 Americans in a filibustering expedition led by Mississippi doctor James Long occupy Nacogdoches and declare Texas an independent republic.

January 17, 1821
The Mexican government grants Moses Austin permission to colonize an area of its Texas territory with some 300 American families. Austin dies soon after, but his son Stephen carries on with the colonization plan.

January 24, 1822
Alabama planter Jared Ellison Groce arrives in the Austin colony, bringing with him what is thought to be the seed of Texas's first cotton crop.

September 15, 1829
Slavery is abolished in Mexico, including Texas, by order of President Vicente Guerrero.

September 25, 1829
The *Texas Gazette,* Texas's first newspaper that enjoys any success and longevity, is launched in San Felipe de Austin.

(Continued on p. 87)

Texas TV!

The Lone Star State is all over the boob tube.

Anyone who watches a lot of television has seen a lot of Texas. Over the decades, the Lone Star State has been the setting for an array of dramas, situation comedies, and animated series. Here are a few:

- *Anchorwoman.* Don't remember this 2007 Fox series? Not many people do—it was canceled after just two episodes aired back to back. A bizarre hybrid of comedy and reality, the show followed Lauren Jones—a former model, beauty pageant winner, and World Wrestling Entertainment (WWE) Diva—as she strove to become an anchorwoman at KYTX, a CBS affiliate in Tyler.

- *Dallas.* Remember when J. R. was shot? It's a question only fans of this groundbreaking prime-time CBS soap opera can answer. Between 1978 and 1991, *Dallas* was one of the most popular series on network television, launching one spin-off (*Knots Landing*) and inspiring numerous imitators. The series revolved around the oil-wealthy Ewing clan and scheming son J. R., played with evil gusto by Larry Hagman.

- *Davy Crockett.* Not exactly a series, *Davy Crockett* aired in five segments on the ABC show *Disneyland* in the mid-1950s—call it one of television's first miniseries. It starred Fess Parker as frontiersman Davy Crockett and Buddy Ebsen as his pal George Russel. In the series, Davy's adventures took him throughout the American West and included the battle of the Alamo.

- *Flo.* A spin-off of the popular CBS comedy *Alice, Flo* starred Polly Holliday as wise-cracking Florence Castleberry, a waitress who impulsively buys a run-down roadhouse in her hometown of Cowtown, Texas. You may not remember the series, but you probably remember Flo's hilarious catchphrase: "Kiss my grits!"

- *Friday Night Lights.* Based on the book and movie of the same name, this critically acclaimed NBC drama, still airing in 2009, revolves around the citizens of fictional Dillon, Texas, where high school football is king.

- *Judd, for the Defense.* This ABC legal drama, which ran for two seasons in the late 1960s, starred Carl Betz as Houston-based attorney Clinton Judd, who traveled the country tackling one tough case after another. The series is significant for addressing a number of then-taboo topics, including homosexuality and draft-dodging.

- *King of the Hill.* The brainchild of writer Mike Judge, who gave the world *Beavis and Butthead,* this long-running animated Fox series was cocreated with Greg Daniels and featured propane salesman Hank Hill, his loving wife Peggy and young son Bobby, and his beer-swilling, oddball friends, all of whom lived in the fictional town of Arlen, Texas.

- *Laredo.* Neville Brand, Peter Brown, and William Smith played Texas Rangers in this NBC western, set in the post–Civil War West. The series was novel for incorporating a healthy dose of humor around the action and gunplay.

- *Reba.* Country songbird Reba McEntire starred in this popular sitcom, which first aired on the WB Television Network. McEntire played a divorced single mom living in the suburbs of Houston, who was forced to deal with a variety of family issues, including her teenage daughter's high school pregnancy and subsequent marriage.

- *The Rebel.* Another western set after the Civil War, *The Rebel* starred Nick Adams as Johnny Yuma, a former Confederate soldier who roamed the Texas frontier looking for adventure. It ran on ABC between 1959 and 1961. Johnny Cash sang the show's popular theme song, "The Ballad of Johnny Yuma."

- *The Texan.* Rory Calhoun played Big Bill Longley in this CBS western series set in—that's right—Texas after the Civil War. Though not a lawman, Longley often found himself fighting for justice on the side of the innocent.

- *Walker, Texas Ranger.* Martial arts expert Chuck Norris dispensed his own form of butt-kicking justice as Cordell "Cord" Walker, a modern Texas Ranger, in this extremely popular CBS western. It's doubtful that real Texas Rangers routinely beat the stuffing out of criminals, but Norris's legion of fans couldn't get enough of his weekly fists of fury.

The First Texan

Sam Houston, whose name is almost synonymous with Texas, lived a life full of action, controversy, and risk.

A statue of Sam Houston towers over the East Texas city of Huntsville, easily visible to motorists traveling along Interstate 45. At 67 feet tall, it is the world's largest freestanding statue of an American figure. Samuel Houston was such an important character in the history of Texas, though, that many Texans argue that the statue isn't nearly large enough.

Born in Virginia in 1793, Houston successfully led the Texas rebels in their battle for independence from Mexico, famously defeating Santa Anna's army in the decisive battle of San Jacinto in 1836. He was then elected as the new Lone Star Republic's first president and had the city of Houston founded in his name. When Texas joined the Union in 1846, Houston became one of the new state's U.S. senators and later served two terms as governor.

Houston's renowned fondness of alcohol, women, and brawling, however, meant that his life was never far from controversy. He spent years living among the Cherokee, who referred to him by his Indian name "the Raven," or more simply as "Big Drunk." Houston took a Native American as the second of his three wives, and he was once arrested and convicted for beating a U.S. congressman.

Houston came close to being nominated to run for U.S. president in 1860, but his ardent opposition to secession and his refusal to take the oath of loyalty to the newly formed Confederate States of America saw him removed from the governor's mansion in 1861.

The Land of Promise

Sam Houston's public life didn't start with his arrival in Texas in 1832. By that point, he had already served under Andrew Jackson in the War of 1812, suffering three near-fatal wounds at the Battle of

Horseshoe Bend; had served two terms in Congress; and had been elected governor of Tennessee. He resigned as governor in 1829 at the age of 36, after his 11-week marriage to 19-year-old Eliza Allen ended amid mysterious circumstances. Since both Houston and his young bride maintained a lifelong silence about their brief marriage, the circumstances of its demise remain vague to this day.

Houston left Tennessee and went to live among the Cherokee in modern-day Oklahoma, with whom he had spent two years as a teenager. He was granted Cherokee citizenship and became a tribal emissary, a role in which he took great pride. When William Stanbery, a U.S. representative from Ohio, delivered a speech on the House floor in 1832 that Houston believed insulted him over an Indian rations contract, the Raven confronted him on Pennsylvania Avenue in Washington, D.C., and thrashed Stanbery with a hickory cane. In the subsequent criminal trial, Houston was found guilty but instead of paying the fine, he simply left the country. His second wife remained among the Cherokee while Houston moved to the Mexican state of Texas, a place he described as a "land of promise."

The Texas War of Independence

Houston quickly gained prominence within the rebellion movement that was building against the Mexican government. He was a member of the convention that met at Washington-on-the-Brazos in 1836 to declare independence from Mexico, and after the fall of the Alamo and the Goliad Massacre, he took charge of the ragtag Texan army.

Despite being outnumbered, Houston led his forces in the Battle of San Jacinto on April 21, 1836, and defeated the Mexican army led by that country's president, Santa Anna. The actual battle lasted less than 20 minutes, but along with the capture of Santa Anna the following day, it proved decisive and paved the way for the Republic of Texas to become an independent country.

Sam Houston was officially a Texas hero and became the first regularly elected president of the republic, serving until 1838. As the constitution of the fledgling nation barred a president from succeeding himself, Houston became a Texas congressman until 1841, when he was again eligible to be elected for another term as president. After Texas joined the United States in 1845, Houston served as first a senator and then governor.

The Problem of Slavery

Although Houston was a slaveowner and opposed abolition, he consistently voted against the expansion of slavery into other states beyond the South. As the issue became more and more heated, he also used his position as governor to vehemently oppose the growing support for Texas to secede from the Union. This proved a hugely unpopular move to his constituents, as did his refusal to pledge allegiance to the newly formed Confederacy in 1861. President Abraham Lincoln repeatedly offered Houston the use of federal troops to keep him in office, but Houston flatly declined, wishing to avoid bloodshed and civil unrest in his beloved Texas. Instead, he peacefully left the governor's mansion in March 1861, with only a prophetic warning for his opponents. An American Civil War, Houston predicted, would result in a Northern victory and the destruction of the South. The following month, hostilities broke out between the North and South when Confederate forces attacked a U.S. military base in South Carolina.

Houston retired to Huntsville with his third wife, Margaret Lea, who had provided him with eight children. A year later, Houston died from pneumonia at age 70. Fittingly, his final recorded words were: "Texas, Texas, Margaret!"

In addition to the city of Houston and the statue in Huntsville, numerous other places in Texas have been named in Sam Houston's honor, including a state university, a national forest, a regional library and research center, and a U.S. Army installation.

- *Spanish Texas Governor Manuel de Salcedo (1808–1813) respected his Anglo citizens quite a bit. His words: "The Anglo-Americans are naturally industrious. If this were not true, they would not love to live in deserts, where their sustenance depends on their industry."*

- *What was the currency of the Republic of Texas? The Texas dollar banknotes' reddish reverses led to the colloquial name Texas redbacks. Unfortunately, most of the time the redback wasn't worth much. In some times and places, TX$1.00 was worth about US$0.02.*

The Texas Pig Stand
Introduces Front-Seat Dining

*The drive-in restaurant wasn't born in California, nor did
the McDonald brothers invent the fast food genre. Carhops,
curb service, and the Pig Sandwich are what started it all.*

In 1921, Texas mercantile wholesaler Jesse Granville Kirby made the
proclamation, "People in their cars are so lazy that they don't want to
get out of them to eat!" At the time, he was trying to hook Reuben
Jackson, a Dallas physician, to invest $10,000 in a new idea for a
roadside stand, one that paired the Lone Star State's love for the car
with another pastime: eating barbecue.

For the era, Kirby's idea was revolutionary: Texans were to drive up
to the food stand and make their requests for food directly from behind
the wheel of their cars (or trucks, of course, this being Texas). A young
lad would take the customers' orders directly through the window of
the car and then deliver the food and beverages right back out to the
curb. The novelty of this new format was that hurried diners could
consume their meals while they were sitting in the front seat.

Convenience over All

When Kirby and Jackson's Texas Pig Stand opened along the busy
Dallas–Fort Worth Highway in the fall of 1921, legions of Texas
motorists tipped their ten-gallon hats to what was advertised as
"America's Motor Lunch." Prepared with tender slices of roast pork
loin, pickle relish, and barbecue sauce, Kirby and Jackson's Pig
Sandwich quickly gained a loyal following among cabbies, truckers,
limousine drivers, police officers, and other mobile workers.

But curbside cuisine wasn't the only attraction at America's first
drive-in restaurant. The daredevil car servers who worked the curb—
or *carhops,* as someone coined the phrase—were a sight. "Carhops
were very competitive," recalled Richard Hailey, successor to the Pig
Stand throne and former president of Pig Stands, Inc. "As soon as they
saw a Model T start to slow down, they'd race out to see who could
jump up on the running board first, while the car was still moving."

An Explosion of Pork Barbecue

With its good food and derring-do curb service, the legend of the Texas carhop grew as the reputation of the Pig Stands and its signature sandwich spread. Propelled beyond the borders of Texas by franchising, the number of pork stands multiplied. Between 1921 and 1934, more than 100 Pig Stands were serving up "A Good Meal at Any Time" across America. Drive-in curb service had gone nationwide, and scores of operators duplicated the successful format.

In 1930, Royce Hailey, future patriarch of the Pig Stands clan and father to Richard, started as a Dallas carhop at age 13. Moving up through the ranks to take the president's job, he became sole owner in 1975. A self-made Texan with a knack for food, he's credited with inventing the chicken-fried steak sandwich and the super-sized slice of grilled bread called "Texas Toast." Food historians also cite onion rings as one of his more famous works of culinary art.

Modern Hard Times

Unfortunately, the novelty of the drive-in restaurant and the nostalgic comfort food it served wasn't enough to carry the operation into the new millennium. In recent years, all of the Texas locations have ceased car and dining room service for one financial reason or another. A single exception exists in San Antonio. Although it was closed with the others, what is now known as Mary Ann's Pig Stand was saved from the scrap heap of history when longtime employee Mary Ann Hill came up with the money to reopen it. Starting as a carhop at age 18 in 1967, Hill had never worked anywhere else. With its original Georges Claude neon pig-shaped sign, vintage Coke machine, shelves of pig memorabilia, and canopied lot, the restaurant operates under trustee status.

Fortunately, then, longtime fans and curious newcomers can still get a milkshake, a Pig Sandwich, and many of the classic fast food entrees that Hailey pioneered—including his signature Texas Toast and giant onion rings. For fans of "The World's First Drive-in Restaurant," there's still nothing that compares with chowing down in America's favorite dining room: the front seat of the car.

- According to Dwight D. Eisenhower, 700 Texas Aggies died in World War II, including 46 soldiers who perished helping defend Bataan. The second-in-command of the Doolittle Raid over Tokyo was Major John Hilger (Class of '32). Seven Aggies have earned the Medal of Honor.

- When will teams learn? Never give door prizes that make good projectiles. April 26, 1986, was Ball Night for the Texas Rangers in Arlington, with a free baseball given to each fan. By the seventh inning of a pounding by the Milwaukee Brewers, Rangers fans lost patience and began raining the balls onto the field.

- Suppose someone could gather former governor Ann Richards, linebacker Mike Singletary, coach Hayden Fry, Hewlett-Packard CEO Mark Hurd, author Thomas Harris, Watergate prosecutor Leon Jaworski, and sit-com actress Angela Kinsey together. What would they have in common? The Baylor Line. All went to college in Waco.

- Herb Kelleher, who relocated to Texas after law school, built Southwest Airlines, which seems to have done all right for him. In 1992, both Southwest and Stevens Aviation were using the slogan "Plane Smart." Kelleher offered to arm-wrestle the Stevens CEO for the phrase—even though Kelleher lost, Stevens's chief let Southwest keep it.

- Texas has an international reputation for actually carrying out the death sentences its courts hand down, never mind what anyone else thinks. It's fitting, then, that the prison museum in Huntsville keeps the old electric chair on display. "Old Sparky" was retired in 1982 when Texas changed its execution method to the lethal injection.

- Anson outlawed dancing from 1933 into the 1990s, except at the Cowboy Christmas Ball held the weekend preceding the holiday. In 1941, a muralist painted some dancing cowboys on the Anson post office, an act that got her into big trouble.

The City Beneath the City

The San Antonio River Walk provides a unique perspective on a vibrant community.

It's not obvious today, but the more than two miles of walkways below the street level of San Antonio, lined with restaurants and shops, got their start as drainage and irrigation ditches built before the Alamo. The River Walk, Paseo del Rio, is the evolution of bypass channels from the San Antonio River, which flows through the city to join the Guadalupe River and then continues on to the Gulf of Mexico. Early settlers depended on the San Antonio River for drinking water and crop irrigation, but they soon realized that it also had a destructive side; annual flooding destroyed buildings and settlements along its banks. To avoid these factors, bypass channels were built.

Everything Starts Somewhere

To understand how this popular tourist attraction of modern-day San Antonio came about, one must become acquainted with the history of the river and the settling of the surrounding city. Álvar Nuñez Cabeza de Vaca, a shipwrecked captive of the Native Americans in the area, was exploring central Texas. He first described the river in 1536. In 1691, the first governor of the Spanish province of Texas, Domingo Teran de los Rios, named it the San Antonio River in commemoration of Saint Antony's Day while camping on its shores.

Early in the 1700s, settlement began with a fortified presidio, villa, and mission being built at the location of today's city. The settlers called it San Antonio de los Llanos. As the settlement grew, so did its need for water. Throughout the remaining 1700s and most of the 1800s, ditches were dug and aqueducts were built to funnel water from the San Antonio River. In 1900, the San Juan Ditch Corporation was founded, and engineers cautioned the citizens that heavy flooding was possible. A series of dams and locks was built to control flooding.

In the 1920s, as the city continued to grow, the San Antonio Conservation Society organized and began discussing the construction of shops along the bypass channel. The Depression put a halt to these plans, which were revisited in 1939. Throughout the early 1940s, walkways, stairways to street level, footbridges, and rock walls were built. In 1946, the first restaurant, Casa Rio, opened.

During the 1950s, the area was turned over to the Department of Parks and Recreation, which placed park rangers along the walkways for visitor safety and established a small botanical garden. At the close of the decade, a Tourist Attraction Committee was formed to explore expansion and attract economic development. Committee members listened to ideas from the Disney Corporation and took junkets to New Orleans to garner ideas.

In 1963, a full-scale development plan was unveiled that included a convention center, major hotels, a mall, and more restaurants, in addition to parks and gardens. Construction and renovation continued through the 1980s.

A Burgeoning River Culture

Today major hotels, a three-story shopping mall, the Henry B. Gonzales Convention Center, and a wide variety of restaurants and shops flank the River Walk. Visitors can traverse the 2.5-mile stretch on foot or by water taxi, or they can take a guided tour on a boat.

Restaurants are plentiful and suit every taste and pocketbook. History buffs can dine in one of several restaurants that have been in San Antonio or on the River Walk since its early days, such as Schilos (1917) and Casa Rio (1946). For the gourmet, there is Boudro's, rated one of the top 50 restaurants in the United States.

Shopping for souvenirs, handicrafts, or clothing is easy at any one of the many specialty stores and street vendors scattered along the waterway. Special festivals and events throughout the year bring in vendors specializing in unique items.

Dining and shopping are not the only options on the River Walk; there are many botanical gardens, nature parks, and alcoves for photos, leisure activities, or just sitting and enjoying the scenery. One such popular spot is Marriage Island, located across from the CPS Energy building. For a nominal fee, couples can arrange a brief wedding ceremony on the island, which can hold as many as 30 people.

The River Walk is also a scenic way to connect to other landmarks and attractions in San Antonio. Stairways to street level bring visitors close to the Alamo, museums, the Tower of the Americas, and downtown.

Keeping It All Together

Maintaining the River Walk is an annual affair. Every January, the water is drained from the canals during the Mud Festival, named for the muddy residue that remains at the bottom of the waterways. While Department of Operations employees remove debris, repair the brick walls, and perform minor renovations, citizens and tourists can enjoy an arts and crafts fair, musical performances, and mud-related activities, and they can join in the crowning of the Mud King and Queen.

Debris cleanup has yielded some interesting finds. The most common items found include sunglasses, cameras, cell phones, strollers, deck chairs, and silverware from the restaurants that line the waterway. Historical items occasionally surface from the mud and have included glass inkwells, medicine bottles, and even a casket handle. The more unique items are on display at the Department of Operations office. The largest item ever recovered was a small foreign car that had been submerged in the deeper North canal.

San Antonio's River Walk continues to expand, with current plans to upgrade the electrical lighting and landscaping along the entire 2.5 miles and refurbish and attract new business to the North canal region. The city continues to attract thousands of convention-goers and other visitors each year because of the River Walk. This unique "city beneath the city" will remain a popular vacation spot for years to come.

* * *

- *Canary Islanders founded the villa of San Fernando de Béxar in 1731. It became the first city in Spanish Texas and has grown into modern-day San Antonio. Most accounts don't flatter the Islanders, who are variously described as lazy, arrogant, and quarrelsome.*

Flags a' Flyin'

Ask true Texans about "Six Flags over Texas," and they won't talk about any amusement parks. Instead, they'll share some history.

The six national flags that have flown over Texas belong to Spain, France, Mexico, the Republic of Texas, the Confederate States of America, and the United States. Each of these has waved over a specific era and provides a glimpse into the history of the state.

Texas Under Spain, 1519–1821

The red, white, and gold Spanish flag depicts the lions of León and the castles of Castile. Spain was the first European nation with a presence in what is now Texas, beginning in 1519 when Hernán Cortés established a Spanish foothold in Mexico. Alonso Álvarez de Piñeda mapped the Texas coastline, and soon after came explorers Francisco Vasquez de Coronado and Juan De Oñate. Despite this early presence, it was nearly 160 years before Spain established its first settlement, Ysleta Mission, near present-day El Paso. Gradually expanding north out of Mexico, other Spanish missions, forts, and settlements were established for nearly a century, until Mexico threw off the European rule and became an independent country in 1821.

Texas Under France, 1685–90

The French flag features a host of golden fleur-de-lis emblazoned on a field of white. Planning to expand its base from French Louisiana, France took a bold move in 1685, planting its flag in eastern Texas near the Gulf Coast. Although the territory had already been claimed by Spain, the Spanish had very little presence in the area, and the nearest Spanish settlements were hundreds of miles away. French explorer René-Robert Cavelier, Sieur de LaSalle established Fort St. Louis on Matagorda Bay, between modern-day Houston and Corpus Christi, but the tiny town of 150 was doomed from the start.

Many settlers suffered from shipwreck disease and famine, while the remaining were plagued by hostile Native American attacks and internal fighting. By 1690, France's bold claim to Texas had evaporated.

Texas Under Mexico, 1821-36

The Mexican flag pictures an eagle, a snake, and a cactus on bars of brilliant red, green, and white. Texas was a frontier for Hispanics from the south and Anglos from the north and east who settled the land and became Mexican citizens. Unfortunately, the divergent cultures had conflicting social and political beliefs, and skirmishes broke out between the settlers. The final blow was dealt by General Santa Anna, who discarded the Mexican constitution and declared himself dictator of Texas. Texans revolted and won their independence from Mexico on April 21, 1836.

Republic of Texas, 1836-45

After gaining independence from Mexico, the new republic elected Sam Houston as president and established a capital in the small town of Waterloo. During the ten years Texas existed as an independent republic, Texans endured epidemics, financial crises, and volatile clashes with Mexico. But this decade also saw the birth of the American cowboy, the use of the Colt six-shooter, and the rise of Sam Houston as a paragon of rugged individualism. In 1845, Texans voted to join the United States, and statehood was declared on December 29 of that year. The state flag featuring the lone star on a red, blue, and white background seen today is the same flag that flew over the proud republic.

Texas in the Confederacy, 1861-65

The original flag of the Confederate States of America featured a circle of stars on a blue background with two red stripes and one white stripe. The cross-barred banner most people associate today with the Confederacy was actually a battle flag. Sixteen years after Texas declared statehood, the Civil War erupted. Texans joined their Confederate brothers in the epic battle and suffered the devastation and economic collapse shared by all the Southern states. The last battle of the Civil War was fought at Palmito Ranch near Brownsville a month after the formal surrender of General Lee. Texas was re-admitted to the Union as a state on March 30, 1870.

Texas in the United States, 1845–1861, 1865–present

Struggling through Reconstruction after the Civil War, Texans marshaled their strength and self-reliance to rebuild their economy and guide the future of this proud state. The Texas Longhorn provided beef for the nation; the vast farmlands yielded crops; and the discovery of oil pushed Texas into the spotlight.

But That's Not All

In addition to the formally recognized national flags, Texas has rallied around a variety of other standards. In the mid-1830s when the idea of gaining independence from Mexico was gaining support, Captain William Scott had a flag made to rally the cause. It featured a lone star and the word *independence* in capital letters.

Another revolutionary flag was an alteration of the Mexican flag, which replaced the center emblem with the number 1824 in reference to the Mexican constitution of that year. Although no one knows for certain, many believe that this flag flew over the Alamo during the infamous battle. It is sometimes called the Alamo Battle Flag.

The Texas Troutman Flag was created by Joanna Troutman, an 18-year-old girl in Macon, Georgia, in 1835. A group of Georgians were going to Texas to support the cause of independence, and she wanted them to have their own battle flag. The flag features a lone star and the words *Liberty or Death.*

The First Flag of the Republic, created after the first Constitutional Convention declared Texas an independent republic, featured a lone star surrounded by the word *Texas.* However, the most defiant flag created during this period was perhaps the Republic of Texas Gonzales Flag, which featured a lone star and a cannon with the words *Come and Take It* emblazoned beneath.

In November 1835, the Republic of Texas Navy was commissioned. The flag of the Navy was created by Charles Hawkins, the first commodore, and featured a lone star on a blue background and thirteen stripes, alternating red and white.

No matter which flag has flown over Texas, its people have vigorously defended their heritage, culture, and independence. Texans can be proud of their history and the six flags that have officially flown over the Lone Star State.

The Texas Snake Man

Breaking into Guinness World Records can be hard work. And faced with competitors, records must constantly be broken and reclaimed.

In March 2009, 58-year-old Jackie Bibby shared a bathtub with 195 venomous rattlesnakes (his previous November 2007 Guinness World Record of 87 snakes in a tub for a skin-crawling 45 minutes had been surpassed). And as of this writing, Bibby also held the official record for holding the most rattlesnakes in his mouth (12) and unsanctioned records for climbing into a sleeping bag headfirst with 30 rattlesnakes and feet-first with 112. Maybe this is why Jackie Bibby is better known as "The Texas Snake Man."

Dublin is about 120 miles southwest of Dallas and is home to the self-proclaimed "World's Largest Rattlesnake Roundup," not surprisingly a favorite event of the Texas Snake Man. A rattlesnake roundup is the reptile equivalent of a rodeo. Snake handlers perform tricks, attempt records, and compete in events such as sacking, in which competitors try to put ten rattlers into a burlap sack faster than their opponents. Bibby is the Tiger Woods of this world.

Home on the Rattlesnake Range

Hailing from Rising Star, Texas, Bibby attended his first rattlesnake roundup at the age of 17 and started attempting records soon after. He constructed a special see-through tub to break the bathtub record, enabling the audience to have a clearer view. None of the 195 snakes had been defanged, and once in the tub they were free to slither under Bibby's arms, around his legs, and just about everywhere else while Bibby sat coolly with his head resting on a pillow. None of the rattlesnakes bit him, which is an accomplishment he attributes to remaining as still as possible. "Rapid movement scares a rattlesnake. If you move real slow and gentle, that doesn't seem to bother them," he said afterward.

In all his years as the Texas Snake Man, Bibby claims he has only been bitten eight times. He does, however, limit his count only to bites that require a trip to the emergency room.

You Can Thank Texas

Believe it or not, there once was a time when automobiles didn't come with radios—or any music whatsoever. But luckily for generations of crooners, that changed in 1920 when Dallas inventor Henry "Dad" Garrett installed the first car radio and set the automotive industry on its ear.

Combining cars and music was just one of Garrett's many inspired ideas. In 1923, in an attempt to reduce the number of traffic accidents, he installed Dallas's first automated traffic light system, which proved so successful that it was picked up by municipalities across  the country. (Ironically, Garrett's wife, Lillian, was injured in a traffic accident seven years later, dying after two and a half months.) Garrett was also instrumental in installing two-way radios in the city's police cars and fire trucks.

An Inventive Life

Garrett, whom historian A. C. Greene called "Dallas's Inventive Genius," was a fascinating man. Born in Canada in 1861 to Episcopal Archbishop Alexander Garrett and his wife, Letitia, he traveled with his family to California and Nebraska before the clan put down roots in Dallas. Eschewing his father's religious calling, Garrett earned a degree in electrical engineering and entered into a number of occupations, including positions with Southwestern Bell and the Dallas Street Railway Company.

In the early 1900s, Garrett developed a fondness for automobiles and soon established himself as Dallas's first car dealer. Later, he became superintendent of the Dallas Police and Fire Signal System, and in 1920, he installed a 50-watt radio transmitter at the central fire station. When the transmitter was not being used to send alarms to other fire stations (and the portable receiver in Garrett's car), Garrett enjoyed entertaining local listeners by broadcasting the news and playing selections of classical music from his sizable record collection.

Henry Garrett, who died in 1952, was a true renaissance man. So drivers and passengers should think of him the next time they're rocking out to their favorite songs while cruising down the highway.

The Top Ten Places to See Bluebonnets

Texas has five state flowers, and all five are varieties of bluebonnets.

1. The Bluebonnet Trails start at Ennis, the Official Bluebonnet City of Texas, where more than 40 miles of flower-covered trails extend on both sides of Interstate 45.

2. The Willow City Loop in Texas's Hill Country is off Route 16, northeast of Fredericksburg.

3. Brenham in Washington County, off Route 290, between Houston and Austin, is reliable for its annual, lavish displays of bluebonnets. Many photographers start here.

4. Locals recommend the historic town of Chappell Hill, a once-flourishing stagecoach stop.

5. Not far from Chappell Hill, the quaint and photogenic town of Independence attracts international tourists and photojournalists.

6. Montgomery, Anderson, and other towns in Grimes County—around Sam Houston National Forest—feature glorious bluebonnet displays when other areas are sparse.

7. East of Dallas along Route 20, Van Zandt County is famous for its wildflowers, especially bluebonnets, along country roadsides.

8. Abilene is the hometown of celebrities such as Jessica Simpson and the Gatlin Brothers. It's at the heart of Texas "Big Country," with a celebrated display of bluebonnets along Highway 84.

9. Heading west in remote and historic Coke County, bluebonnets flourish just south of the dam at Lake Spence. Visitors may also see bison grazing along the roadside.

10. Last but not least, anyone looking for "Barbara Bush" bluebonnets can see their unique shades of lavender throughout Texas, including around El Paso.

The Great Debates

Abraham Lincoln and Stephen Douglas may have defined the art, but the debating team at Wiley College opened eyes that had previously been glued shut.

There is perhaps nothing more satisfying than a true come-from-behind story. Most people can identify in some way with the plight of the down-trodden, the ignored, the oppressed—the true underdogs of our world. When members of that camp are somehow able to rise above, to take on the omnipotent powers that be and to win, it triggers a feeling deep down inside us that anything is indeed possible. During the Great Depression, such a Cinderella story was set into motion at Marshall, Texas. After it had played itself out, racial stereotypes about intellect would be forever turned upside down, and a group of previously unknown college students would come to national prominence.

Seeds Take Root

Noted African American poet and educator Melvin B. Tolson (1898–1966) believed strongly that all people should stand up for their rights. Given the era and Tolson's skin color, such a mindset was forward thinking and controversial. But this was simply the way that Tolson, an English professor at all-black Wiley College from 1924 to 1947, operated. Nothing, it seemed, could stand in his way for long.

In addition to his teaching duties, Tolson wrote poetry and novels, directed plays, and even coached football. By living his life with such a can-do attitude, Tolson deconstructed racial stereotypes and gained considerable fame throughout the Southwest. Poet/playwright Langston Hughes wrote of him, "Melvin Tolson is the most famous Negro professor in the Southwest. Students all over that part of the world speak of him, revere him, remember him, and love him."

Many also strived to emulate him. When Tolson formed a debating team to help his students build up their confidence, the teacher wasn't lacking for applicants. Using radical techniques of his own design, Tolson taught his debaters how to become formidable opponents. He drilled them repeatedly on the finer points of physical gesturing and appropriate pauses, effectively showing them the importance of skillful acting during debate. He also taught them to pre-guess their opponent's strategy, and he wrote specific rebuttals for them to study before each event. Such preparedness promised that his students would always have a counterpunch at the ready.

Thumping the Competition

In most contests, a certain amount of time is required before a rookie participant can get up to speed. Perhaps owing to the intense training rendered by Tolson, this was *never* the case for the Wiley Debating Team. Beginning with its very first debate, the group continually mowed opponents down, one by one; it then set its sights on its next "victim." Slowly but steadily, the debaters' notoriety grew. From 1929 until 1939, the Wiley team proved to be wily indeed. Debating 75 total times, the team lost only one competition. Lying in its wake were such noted African American schools as Tuskegee, Howard, and Fisk universities. But, by far Wiley's greatest moment came in 1935 when the-little-team-that-could vanquished the vaunted University of Southern California, the reigning national debating champ. This upset victory proved far and away that capability rests where you find it and is not the domain of any single ethnicity. It was a mighty heady statement for 1935.

Hollywood Takes Notice

This celebrated debate proved so powerful that Hollywood later immortalized it in *The Great Debaters* (2007). With Denzel Washington cast as Professor Tolson (in addition to directing the film), the movie substituted Harvard University for USC, but otherwise the plot was the same. Much like David versus Goliath, the young debaters cut their champion opponents down to size and scored a major strike against racial prejudice for their efforts. Not too many tales, real or imagined, work out better than that.

Jack the Ripper's Eerie Austin Connection

Could America's first serial killer be one of Austin's best-kept and most grisly secrets?

Before Jack the Ripper made his bloody trail through London, Austin experienced a similar murder spree. The Ripper-like murders began on New Year's Eve, 1884. Someone killed Mollie Smith, a servant girl, and put a large hole in her head. Two more women were butchered in similar attacks a few months later.

A Trail of Blood

The killings weren't limited to servants, however. As the Austin murder spree continued, victims became more upscale. Each death was a little more gory. The final murders recorded occurred on Christmas Eve, 1885, almost a full year after they had begun. The victims included Mrs. Eula Phillips, a wealthy woman who—for amusement—worked as a prostitute.

To stop the binge of killing, Austin police began questioning men on the streets after dark. The city erected "moonlight towers" to illuminate the streets. Seventeen of those towers still light downtown Austin and are listed in the National Register of Historic Places. The city's efforts were apparently successful, as the slaughter ended.

The Whitechapel Murders

Jack the Ripper began killing women in London as early as the day after Christmas in 1887. The Ripper's physical description, style of killing, and victims seemed eerily similar to the Austin murders. Possible killers included a man called "the Malay Cook," who left Austin late in January 1886 and was interviewed in London in 1888. According to that interview, he said he'd been robbed by a woman "of bad character." Unless he recovered his money, he planned to murder and mutilate women in London's Whitechapel area.

No one knows if Austin was the training ground for Jack the Ripper, of course, but the possibility is chilling.

Blue Hole: Wimberley's Quintessential Texas Swimming Hole

Blue Hole is a much-adored destination for Hill Country residents and visitors alike. Its pristine, spring-fed waters, old growth cypress trees, and wildlife make it an idyllic spot to relax, swim, picnic, and temporarily escape the heat of summer.

Long before the "cement pond" came into vogue and many back-yards boasted their own swimming pools, Texans enjoyed more natural means to cool off during the dog days of summer. Once upon a time, the proverbial swimming hole reigned supreme, and spots such as Wimberley's Blue Hole were where people preferred to splash and swim.

These days, Blue Hole still attracts a loyal following to the village of Wimberley, a quaint hill-country town located about an hour southwest of Austin. Hidden near the town center, the swimming hole is an idyllic retreat fed by an artesian spring known as Jacob's Well. The underwater cave (which has been identified as being the longest in the state) is the primary water source to the Cypress Creek and Blue Hole.

Back When a Swimming Hole Meant Something

In its heyday, Blue Hole was part of 500 acres owned by the John R. Dobie family. During the 1920s, the family decided to share its natural treasure and opened Blue Hole to the public. For locals and visitors alike, the cerulean waters of the natural pool became an antidote to the summer heat. People thought the fun would never end—that is, until the swimming hole was sold to a private partnership group in Austin. Swimming and camping were still allowed, but plans were being made for residential development.

Fortunately, Wimberley's municipal government stepped up to save the local landmark from being turned into tract homes. To the town's good fortune, it entered into an agreement to buy a tract of 126 acres along the Cypress Creek so it could set it aside for public use. With grants and donations from Texas Parks and Wildlife, Hays County, the Lower Colorado River Authority, the Trust for Public Land, and a number of individuals, the town completed the land acquisition portion of the Blue Hole project in 2005. Currently underway is a master plan to restore, develop, and transform the one-of-a-kind creekside preserve into a regional park that will feature primitive camping, tennis courts, soccer fields, and restroom facilities.

Swimming as It's Meant to Be

Lined by majestic old-growth cypress trees, rocky outcroppings, native grasses, and wildflowers, Blue Hole takes visitors back to simpler days when an afternoon spent at the water park was far less complicated. Seventy or so years ago, the only aquatic "rides" in Texas were the kind that could be seen at the typical Texas swimming hole: long, braided ropes with big knots tied at the bottom, dangling from overhanging tree limbs. To get a thrill, swimmers grabbed onto the rope with both hands, jumped up so their feet straddled the knot, and swung out over the water as far as they could manage. When the time was just right, they simply let go and plunged in!

The Simple Joys of Water

Those were the days when being able to skip a rock across the glassy surface on multiple hops was an envied skill. People didn't worry about the SPF rating of their sunscreen, if their iPod was charged, or whether there was a fast-food restaurant nearby. A day at the swimming hole was pure fun, with a homemade picnic lunch if mom and pop happened to join in.

Like a time machine, the serene waters of Blue Hole transport swimmers back to those summers that seemed to last forever—to a carefree time of youth when riding a bicycle, eating ice cream cones, and catching fireflies were the most important things in life. Back in the good old days—and still today, at least at Blue Hole—nothing was more exciting than swinging from the bank and dropping like a cannonball into the cool, clear water with a big splash.

Texans Who Would Make John Heisman Proud

The Heisman Trophy is awarded annually to the most outstanding college football player in the National Collegiate Athletic Association. Presented by the Heisman Trophy Trust, the award is named for college football coach John Heisman, the first athletic director of the late, great Downtown Athletic Club in New York City. These Heisman Trophy winners played their college football in Texas, were born in Texas, or have a strong Texas connection. John Heisman himself had a tie to the state, coaching at Rice Institute (now Rice University) in Houston from 1924 to 1927.

- 1938: Davey O'Brien, Texas Christian University, quarterback
  Davey O'Brien was born in Dallas.

- 1948: Doak Walker, Southern Methodist University, running back
  Doak Walker was born in Dallas.

- 1957: John David Crow, Texas A&M University, running back

- 1963: Roger Staubach, Navy, quarterback
  Roger Staubach had a Hall of Fame career with the Dallas Cowboys from 1969 until 1979. After retiring from football, he continues to live in the Dallas area, where he has a successful career as a businessman and speaker.

- 1977: Earl Campbell, University of Texas, running back
  Earl Campbell was born in Tyler.

- 1987: Tim Brown, Notre Dame University, wide receiver
  Tim Brown was born in Dallas.

- 1989: Andre Ware, University of Houston, quarterback
  Andre Ware was born in Dickinson.

- 1990: Ty Detmer, Brigham Young University, quarterback
  Ty Detmer was born in San Marcos and moved with his family to San Antonio.

- 1998: Ricky Williams, University of Texas, running back

The Great Texas Airship Mystery

Roswell, New Mexico, may be the most famous potential UFO crash site, but did Texas experience a similar event in the 19th century?

One sunny April morning in 1897, a UFO crashed in Aurora, Texas.

Six years before the Wright Brothers' first flight and 50 years before Roswell, a huge, cigar-shape UFO was seen in the skies. It was first noted on November 17, 1896, about a thousand feet above rooftops in Sacramento, California. From there, the spaceship traveled to San Francisco, where it was seen by hundreds of people.

A National Tour

Next, the craft crossed the United States, where it was observed by thousands. Near Omaha, Nebraska, a farmer reported the ship on the ground, making repairs. When it returned to the skies, it headed toward Chicago, where it was photographed on April 11, 1897, the first UFO photo on record. On April 15, near Kalamazoo, Michigan, residents reported loud noises "like that of heavy ordnance" coming from the spaceship.

Two days later, the UFO attempted a landing in Aurora, Texas, which should have been a good place. The town was almost deserted, and its broad, empty fields could have been an ideal landing strip.

No Smooth Sailing

However, at about 6 A.M. on April 17, the huge, cigar-shape airship "sailed over the public square and, when it reached the north part of town, collided with the tower of Judge Proctor's windmill and went to pieces with a terrific explosion, scattering debris over several acres of ground, wrecking the windmill and water tank and destroying the judge's flower garden."

That's how Aurora resident and cotton buyer S. E. Haydon described the events for the *Dallas Morning News*. The remains of the ship seemed to be strips and shards of a silver-colored metal. Just one body was recovered. The newspaper reported, "while his remains are badly disfigured, enough of the original has been picked up to show that he was not an inhabitant of this world."

On April 18, reportedly, that body was given a good, Christian burial in the Aurora cemetery, where it may remain to this day. A 1973 effort to exhume the body and examine it was successfully blocked by the Aurora Cemetery Association.

A First-hand Account

Although many people have claimed the Aurora incident was a hoax, an elderly woman was interviewed in 1973 and clearly recalled the crash from her childhood. She said that her parents wouldn't let her near the debris from the spacecraft, in case it contained something dangerous. However, she described the alien as "a small man."

Aurora continues to attract people interested in UFOs. They wonder why modern Aurora appears to be laid out like a military base. Nearby, Fort Worth seems to be home to the U.S. government's experts in alien technology. Immediately after the Roswell UFO crash in 1947, debris from that spaceship was sent to Fort Worth for analysis.

Is There Any Trace Left?

The Aurora Encounter, a 1986 movie, documents the events that began when people saw the spacecraft attempt a landing at Judge Proctor's farm. Today, the Oates gas station marks the area where the UFO crashed. Metal debris was collected from the site in the 1970s and studied by North Texas State University. That study called one fragment "most intriguing": It appeared to be iron but wasn't magnetic; it was shiny and malleable rather than brittle, as iron should be.

As recently as 2008, UFOs have appeared in the north central Texas skies. In Stephenville, a freight company owner and pilot described a low-flying object in the sky, "a mile long and half a mile wide." Others who saw the ship several times during January 2008 said that its lights changed configuration, so it wasn't an airplane. The government declined to comment.

Today, a plaque at the Aurora cemetery mentions the spaceship, but the alien's tombstone—which, if it actually existed, is said to have featured a carved image of a spaceship—was stolen many years ago.

Fast Facts

- Law graduates of SMU have served on the supreme courts of Texas and Missouri, as well as the supreme courts of several nations, such as Japan, Indonesia, the Philippines, Egypt, Brazil, and Colombia.

- Marfa's Blaze Foley, the "Duct Tape Messiah," came by the nickname honestly; he performed with the tape all over him. It started when he decided to parody the movie Urban Cowboy by putting duct tape on his boots, and the joke gathered momentum from there.

- After a revolt led by Philip Nolan in the Hill Country in 1801, Spanish authorities made nine of the captured rebels roll two dice; the low roller would be hanged. That was unfortunate for Ephraim Blackburn: He rolled a four and earned an exclusive invitation to the necktie party.

- Every Labor Day, Bertram holds its annual Oatmeal Festival, conceived in parody of the numerous chili cookoffs all over Texas. Bertram wrote to oatmeal makers for support, and only National Oats chose to join the fun. A silo in town advertises 3-Minute Oatmeal and the festival in red and yellow.

- Texas rodeo hero Bill Pickett (1870–1932) came from Taylor. Part African American and part Native American, he was a master of the delicate art of bulldogging, which is biting a steer's upper lip to help wrestle the beast. Rodeo riders can't do that today, of course, but Pickett was 100 percent old-school Texas cowboy.

- John McCall of Spicewood, the "Shampoo King from Dripping Springs," used to call his Austin-area mansion the "Taj McCall." He's said to consider himself a Baptist Buddhist. It's no surprise that he donated more than $1 million to Kinky Friedman's 2006 gubernatorial campaign.

- University of Texas Longhorn mascot Bevo III (1945–48) once got loose on campus and went on a two-day tear before finally being corralled. Who would want a dull, docile Bevo anyway? Evidently someone did. Bevo III retired to the San Antonio Zoo.

Hot Under the Collar

Texas oil-well firefighter Red Adair truly led a blazing life.

If ever there were a character as big as Texas, Paul Neal "Red" Adair would be that man. Born in 1915 in Houston during the oil-boom era of the early 20th century, Adair left school early to support his family and eventually landed in the Army. Serving in a bomb disposal unit during World War II exposed Adair to a high degree of danger and quite possibly whetted his appetite for a life lived on the edge. After the war, Adair returned to Texas and signed on with the M. M. Kinley Company, a pioneer in the field of oil-well firefighting. His new job upped the danger quotient tenfold and provided a grand outlet for his talent, skill, and daring.

Hot Texas Geysers

There aren't many fires more difficult to extinguish than those at oil wells. Fed by what seems a nearly endless supply of fuel, these conflagrations can rocket hundreds of feet into the air, looking much like Dante's Inferno burning completely out of control. Such fires are also quite costly: A single oil-well fire can burn millions of barrels of crude each day. Because halting the oil flow is nearly impossible, firefighters try to cut off the fire's oxygen source, which is usually accomplished by setting explosives near the base of the flames (using special heat-shielded vehicles). If that attempt is successful, the battle is only halfway won. Oil continues to gush from the well and must then be capped. This part of the operation is considered the most dangerous of all, since any spark or remnant of flame can trigger a massive explosion.

Under the early tutelage of Myron Kinley, Adair furthered the art of firefighting by developing a set of "Wild Well Control Techniques." Using special tools and explosives, the gutsy firefighter began to routinely extinguish fires previously thought to be unstoppable. Adair's unique mix of nerve, ingenuity, and skill later came in handy on a mega-fire that solidified his fame.

The Big One

It was called "The Devil's Cigarette Lighter." At 800 feet tall, this Algerian natural gas fire, which started in November 1961 but wasn't capped until May '62, burned almost as high as New York's famed RCA building. It was so intense that it melted sand into glass as far as half a mile away, and it was bright enough to be seen by astronaut John Glenn in space. When a firefighting company needed to kill the beast, the newly formed Red Adair Company was tapped for the job. With trusty lieutenants Asger "Boots" Hansen and Ed "Coots" Matthews at his side, Adair precariously introduced 750 pounds of highly unstable nitroglycerine into the base of the fire. With a resounding boom that rocked the desert floor, the deed was done. In an instant, an impossibly huge fire had been tamed by perhaps the only man in the world skilled enough to do the job. Texan Red Adair had become a star.

Gone Hollywood

When John Wayne was cast for the 1968 movie *Hellfighters,* the role seemed tailor-made for him. He played oil-well firefighter Chance Buckman, swaggering his way past burning wells, vanquishing his blazing foe as he went. Red Adair, of course, inspired the character, and he and Wayne formed a friendship on the movie set. As occasional drinking buddies, these two "hard chargers" exchanged war stories that most people could only dream of.

But Adair wasn't ready to call it a day yet. Still based out of Houston, he tackled major oil platform disasters from the North Sea to the Gulf of Mexico. He topped off his career with what may have been his finest moment, capping 117 oil well fires in Kuwait after the first Gulf War in 1991. Finally, at age 79, he hung up his asbestos suit and retired. Red Adair's personal flame was extinguished on August 7, 2004. During his life he had conquered more than 2,000 fires. Even in death, his legend continues to burn brightly.

People Nicknamed *Tex* or *Texas*

You don't have to be from Texas to be nicknamed Tex, *although it does make the explanation a lot easier. It's a popular nickname for cowboy actors, musicians, and baseball players, but you could probably find a Tex in almost any line of work.*

- **Woodard Maurice "Tex" Ritter**—singing cowboy in western movies and father of actor John Ritter.

- **Gordon "Tex" Beneke**—singer and saxophonist in the Glenn Miller Orchestra, and a bandleader in his own right.

- **Sollie Paul "Tex" Williams**—Texas swing bandleader of Tex Williams and His Western Caravan Band.

- **Herbert Jon "Tex" Antoine**—longtime New York City TV weather forecaster.

- **Charles "Tex" Watson**—member of the Charles Manson family and convicted murderer.

- **Texas Earnest "Tex" Schramm Jr.**—first president and general manager of the Dallas Cowboys; inducted into the NFL Hall of Fame in 1991.

- **John Wilson "Texas Jack" Vermillion**—Old West gunfighter, also known as "Shoot-Your-Eye-Out" Vermillion.

- **Frederick Bean "Tex" Avery**—cartoon director for Walter Lantz Studios, Warner Brothers, and MGM who worked on the *Merrie Melodies* and *Looney Tunes* cartoon series; created Daffy Duck, Droopy, Screwy Squirrel, and Chilly Willy; and invented Bugs Bunny's famous "What's up, Doc?"

- **Randall "Tex" Cobb**—kickboxer, heavyweight boxer (who went 15 rounds with then-champion Larry Holmes), actor.

- **"Tex" Fletcher (real name: Geremino Bisceglia)**—singing cowboy, movie actor.

Ludicrous Laws

- An Odessa city ordinance prohibits anyone riding in a parade vehicle or on a parade float or animal from throwing, dropping, or handing out candy, food, toys, souvenirs, or similar items to persons along the parade route.

- In Houston no one may drive cattle, horses, mules, hogs, sheep, or goats over public streets without written permission from the chief of police.

- Houston also does not allow its citizens to light candles in or on the grounds of certain public and government buildings, including the Sam Houston Coliseum, the Jesse H. Jones Center for the Performing Arts, the Albert Thomas Convention Center and its underground parking garages, City Hall, the Police Administration Building, the Municipal Court, the Public Library, and the Emergency Operating Center.

- In Galveston don't even think about landing an airplane on the beach or what is commonly known as Seawall Boulevard.

- The city of Galveston does, however, allow partiers to get drunk in its parks. Any alcoholic beverages may be consumed in a city park or even on a city playground, as long as written permission is obtained from the director of parks and recreation.

- A parent or person who has the duty of control and reasonable discipline of a child is liable for any property damage caused by the child. Hotels and inns may seek up to $25,000 in damages for the malicious conduct of a child between the ages of 10 and 18.

- Gun Barrel City protects its citizens against cotton fires by prohibiting the storage of cotton within 50 feet of a house or building where fire is kept or used.

- It is illegal to sell, purchase, or possess an alligator in the great state of Texas. But that's not all—monitor lizards, anacondas, cobras, crocodiles, cougars, lions, tigers, chimpanzees, gorillas, elephants, bears, weasels, dingos, and jackals are not considered pets in the Lone Star State.

Satisfaction Guaranteed

After a rough round of ropin', ridin', and ranchin', red-blooded rowdies in need of a little romancin' often headed for the Chicken Ranch in La Grange, Texas, where the beer was cold, the food was hot, and the women were legal.

At one time, the Chicken Ranch was possibly the oldest continually operating brothel in the United States. It fulfilled the appetites of Texas students, politicians, soldiers, cowboys, and farmers for almost 130 years. Located on the outskirts of La Grange, a small community in Fayette County, Texas, near the Colorado River, the operation was originally founded in 1844 by a widow known only as Mrs. Swine. She imported three young ladies of questionable repute but unquestionable beauty from New Orleans and set them up in the world's oldest profession. Business was brisk and the profits were lucrative, at least until she was accused of holding "Yankee sympathies" during the Civil War. The operation quickly took on a lower profile.

The business was eventually taken over by a woman named Jessie Williams, who relocated the establishment near the highway just outside of town. Jessie and her girls stayed on the proper side of the law, indulging politicians and other community officials and discouraging drunken and rowdy behavior.

Widespread Attention

The ranch continued to service its customers until 1973, when a consumer-affairs reporter named Marvin Zindler from Houston's KTRK-TV decided to do a week-long exposé on the real "food" being sold at the Chicken Ranch and its possible connections to organized crime. Zindler's disclosure was front-page news around the country, causing panic rather than profit. Within days, the best-known secret in Texas was shut down, obliged to live on in song, memory, and movies. The Broadway musical and subsequent motion picture *The Best Little Whorehouse in Texas* was based on the infamous Chicken Ranch, as was the boisterous blues bender "La Grange" by ZZ Top, the biggest little band in Texas.

Texas Tea

The modern American oil industry was born in southeastern Texas on January 10, 1901. That's when the Lucas #1 well on a hill known as Spindletop blew a gusher more than 100 feet in the air. Until then, the nation's leading oil-producing state had been Pennsylvania.

Native Americans had known about the oil under the Texas soil for centuries and had used what seeped to the surface as a home remedy for a variety of ailments. Spanish explorers later discovered black tar along the beaches of eastern Texas and used it to waterproof their boots.

In the late 1800s, small amounts of oil were produced in the area around Nacogdoches, a region that eventually became known as Oil Springs. This attracted several oil companies eager to tap the area's natural oil reservoirs. The first major oil-producing field was Corsicana, which, like many other fields, was discovered by accident when locals drilling for water hit oil instead. Many ignored the oil and drilled around it to reach the deeper water wells—after all, you can't drink oil. These early oil wells produced roughly 25 barrels a day, just a fraction of what was being produced in the larger Pennsylvania fields.

A Visionary Pioneer

It would take Patillo Higgins, an amateur geologist who had lost an arm in a teenage encounter with the police, to turn the focus to Spindletop and change everything. Higgins was a forward thinker who believed the coal industry would ultimately be replaced by oil. He was also convinced that large amounts of oil could be found under salt domes—salt domes such as Spindletop.

In 1882, Higgins formed the Gladys City Oil, Gas and Manu-facturing Company. Many years of frustration—not to mention deri-sion from local geologists and petroleum industry officials—followed as attempt after attempt to drill proved unsuccessful. The situation finally turned around with the help of John Galey and James Guffey, who had previously left Texas after the Corsicana field failed to pro-duce significant amounts of oil. The men surveyed the area around Beaumont and picked the spot at Spindletop to drill. Exploration began on October 27, 1900. The drill site that produced the famous gusher was the work of Anthony Lucas, a Louisiana mining engineer and oil prospector.

That Spindletop well produced more than 75,000 barrels a day, with peak annual production of 17.5 million barrels in 1902. The boom was on, and an influx of wildcatters descended on the area. With them came related services, supply and manufacturing firms, and refineries. Unfortunately, so did speculators, scam artists, pros-titutes, gamblers, and liquor dealers. Such a volatile combination led to gunfights, murders, and mayhem, all of which added to the color-ful tales that Texans love to tell about their history.

The Ever-Expanding Industry

Within several years, additional fields were tapped in Sour Lake, Baston, and Humble within the 150-mile radius around Spindletop. Companies were established to develop the burgeoning oil fields, and these evolved into the giants of today's oil industry. Among them were Gulf Oil, Sun Oil, Magnolia Petroleum, the Texas Company, and Humble Oil, which later affiliated itself with Standard Oil of New Jersey to become Esso and then Exxon. The refineries, pipelines, and export facilities that grew along the coastline near Beaumont and Port Arthur became a major industrial region that made millionaires out of the company owners.

Between 1902 and 1910, however, oil fever spread to North Texas. Water-well drillers found oil in Wichita County, and the Electra oil field was created. Subsequent oil fields were found in Burkburnett, Ranger, Mexia, and eventually in the Panhandle and all across the state. The largest of the discoveries occurred in Rusk County in East Texas when the Daisy Bradford #3 well blew. A free-for-all atmosphere ensued, and derricks started popping up like weeds across the surrounding area. At the time, no regulations for spacing or limits on production existed. Local sheriffs had to institute martial law to control the wildcatters. Bitter rivalries and concern over the exploding industry led to two years of legal battles to institute the regulations that are still used today.

People Swarmed In

The burgeoning industry led to a sudden growth in population in the areas surrounding all these oil fields. This became known as the boomtown phenomenon as hastily erected shacks, tents, and vehicles served as living quarters for the oil-field workers. Businesses in the surrounding rural communities were overrun by workers, and lines were long at eating and banking establishments. Many historians have compared it to the famous California Gold Rush in which whole towns appeared overnight.

By the time the East Texas field was fully developed, the economy had shifted from an agricultural base to the petroleum industry as king. Gradually, the oil industry began to affect ordinary Texans in a trickle-down effect that saw the mechanization of farm work, the replacement of farmland by manufacturing plants, the displacement of the population to the oil fields and manufacturing centers, and the growth of urban areas.

By the Numbers

In the first quarter of 1929, Texas oil operators produced 69,541,834 barrels of so-called black gold. At the end of 1935, there were more than 1,000 operators in the field producing 158,599,275 barrels. With the start of World War II, however, exports to Europe fell by a quarter, and the industry was producing just 60 percent of its potential.

The end of the war brought another boom in the oil industry as postwar markets for oil and gas expanded. For the first time in eight years, the Texas Railroad Commission ordered no shutdown days to keep the oil barrels moving. However, the boom didn't last, and in the 1950s a decrease in domestic demand and the increase of imports once again caused the oil industry to cut back its production. The most notable developments over the next two decades were the improved management of oil production, the expansion of the petro-chemical industry, and the discovery of natural gas.

Undercut by Imported Oil

Toward the end of the 1970s, it became evident that the U.S. oil industry was being controlled by decisions made in Washington, D.C., that were related to oil imports from the Middle East and the pivotal changes resulting from the fall of the Shah of Iran's government. Over the next decade, the increased cost of production and exploration, the political environment, and a decline in the price of domestic oil led to failures of oil production, finance, and real estate in Texas.

By the 1990s, the Texas industry started a period of downsizing, and although it continues to produce domestic oil, the percentage of state government revenue contributed by oil money has dropped into the single digits.

Texas education benefited from the oil industry over the years as lands endowed for the building of state universities and public schools yielded oil-producing wells. The income produced from land grants and drilling, as well as mineral rights, produced millions of dollars in revenue for the school system.

In addition, most of the individuals who made their millions in the oil and petroleum industry gave generously to charities and organizations throughout the state of Texas. Health research, hospitals, education, fine arts, engineering, and technology have all benefited from the generosity of petroleum millionaires.

Today, oil is no longer the driving force behind Texas's economy. However, in the century since Spindletop blew that geyser of Texas Tea into the air, oil has touched the lives of many Texans. The oil industry continues to provide benefits to the citizens of Texas and is still considered a major player in the international oil market.

* *Ever heard of Notrees, Texas, 79759? It may have the most literal name of any town in the state. When the community, which is 20 miles north of Odessa, got a post office during the first oil boom, it needed to come up with a name quickly. And since there are no trees . . .*

* *Texas is home to 27 petroleum refineries, which together can process more than 4.7 million barrels of crude oil daily.*

🎗 Bragging Rights

- **The inauguration of Pappy Lee O'Daniel:** In 1941, the governor of Texas invited every Texan to an inaugural dinner at his mansion to celebrate the beginning of his second term. More than 20,000 people took him up on the invitation. The mansion grounds and nearby streets served as the dining room. Guests devoured 19,000 pounds of barbecue, 1,000 pounds of potato salad, and 1,100 pounds of pickles and onions. As many as 32,000 cups of coffee were served to wash it all down.

- **Wildseed Farms:** This farm in Fredricksburg is the largest working wildflower farm in the United States. More than 200 acres of fields in the Hill Country and an 800-acre packing-and-distribution center produce 88 varieties of wildflower seeds. Wildseed Farms attracts the public through retail sales, catalog sales, and consumer education. More than 300,000 people drop by the Market Center yearly, especially in April, when the wildflowers bloom.

- **Lakewood Church:** Pastor Joel Osteen, author of *Your Best Life Now: 7 Steps to Living Your Full Potential,* is the leader of a Christian mega-church in Houston, the largest in the country. Mega-churches are known for their large congregations and grandiose sanctuaries, but Lakewood Church has outdone all the others by moving into the former Compaq Center, the arena that was home to the Houston Rockets. The arena was renovated to accommodate a worship center, home offices, and classrooms for the some 40,000 parishioners who, the church reports, worship weekly with Osteen.

- **Gigantic spiderweb takes over Texas park:** Entomologists had a field day in 2007 when a spiderweb was found covering a 200-yard stretch of a trail in a Wills Point park. This seldom-seen occurrence was not the lair of Spider-Man but a phenomenon known as "ballooning," created by multiple spiders spinning at the same time. Texas A&M University staff identified 11 types of spiders in the collected sample, including the Guatemalan long-jawed spider. The wet conditions during the summer of 2007 created the perfect environment for the spiders to build the giant web to capture midges and mosquitoes.

Death from on High

When a troubled man exacted revenge from a lofty perch, a stunned nation watched in horror and disbelief. What could cause a man to kill indiscriminately? Why hadn't anyone seen it coming? Could such a thing happen again? Decades later the mystery continues.

In an America strained by an escalating war in Vietnam, the 1966 headline still managed to shock the senses. The "Texas Tower Sniper" had killed his mother and wife before snuffing out the lives of 13 innocents on the University of Texas (UT) campus at Austin. At least the Vietnam conflict offered up motives. Like most wars, battle lines had been drawn, and a steady buildup of threats and tensions had preceded the violence. But here, no such declarations were issued. Bullets came blazing out of the sky for no apparent reason. After the victims breathed their last and the nightmare drew to a close, a stunned populace was left with one burning question: Why?

Undercurrents

Charles Whitman appeared to have enjoyed many of life's advantages. Hailing from a prominent family in Lake Worth, Florida, the future was Whitman's to make or break. But friction with his abusive father found Whitman seeking escape. After a brutal incident in which he returned home from a party drunk only to be beaten—and nearly drowned in a swimming pool—by his father, the 18-year-old Whitman enlisted in the U.S. Marines. He served for five years, distinguishing himself with a Sharpshooters Badge. After that he attended college at UT. During that period, he also married his girlfriend, Kathy Leissner.

Whitman's life plan appeared to be straightforward. After obtaining a scholarship, he would seek an engineering degree, hoping to follow it up with acceptance at officer's candidate school. But things didn't go as planned.

Opportunity Lost

After leaving the military, Whitman worked toward a variety of goals in and out of school. Unfortunately, the ex-Marine was fraught with failure, and his frustrations multiplied. In the spring of 1966, Whitman sought the help of UT psychiatrist Dr. Maurice Dean Heatly. In a moment of ominous foretelling, Whitman remarked that he fantasized "going up on the [campus] tower with a deer rifle and shooting people." The doctor, having heard similar threats in the past, was mostly unimpressed. Since Whitman hadn't previously exhibited violent behavior, Heatly took his statement as nothing more than an idle threat.

Surprise Assault

During the wee hours of August 1, 1966, Whitman's demons finally won out, and his killing spree began. For reasons still uncertain, the murderer kicked off his blood quest by first stabbing his mother in her apartment and his wife while she slept. Both died from the injuries.

Whitman then made his way to the UT campus and ascended the soon-to-be infamous tower. At his side he had enough provisions, weapons, and ammo to hole up indefinitely. Just before noon, he lifted a high-powered rifle and began shooting. He picked off victims one by one from the observation deck of the 307-foot-tall tower. Whitman's sharpshooting prowess (he once scored 215 points out of a possible 250 in target practice) added to the danger. When people finally realized what was happening, quite a few had already been cut down.

Lives Cut Short

As the attacks progressed, Austin police hatched a plan. Officers Ramiro Martinez and Houston McCoy snuck into the tower, surprising Whitman. Both sides exchanged fire. The 96-minute attack ended with two fatal shots to Whitman's head, compliments of McCoy's 12-gauge shotgun. The horror was over. In its ultimate wake lay 16 dead and 31 wounded. An autopsy performed on Whitman revealed a brain tumor that may have caused him to snap.

The authorities later found a note at his home. Its matter-of-fact tone is chilling to this day: "I imagine it appears that I brutaly [*sic*] kill [*sic*] both of my loved ones. I was only trying to do a quick thorough job. If my life insurance policy is valid...please pay off all my debts....Donate the rest anonymously to a mental health foundation. Maybe research can prevent further tragedies of this type."

Talkin' About Texas

"Just to think about old Texas
    Makes a fellow proud, gee whiz!

How could anybody blame us
    When you know how big she is?"

—Jennie Lee Blanton

"Each year El Paso gets more sunny days—over 300—than any other U.S. city."

—Jerome Pohlen, author, *Oddball Texas*

"Texas could get along without the United States, but the United States cannot, except with great hazard, exist without Texas."

—Sam Houston

"Fraudulent debtors in the United States skipped away from their creditors during the night, and chalked on their shutters the three cabalistic letters 'G.T.T.'—'Gone to Texas.'"

—Nevin O. Winter, describing some of the early American pioneers to Texas

"Texas is the number-one bird-watching destination in the United States, and the Rio Grande Valley is the number-one bird-watching area in Texas. Some 465 species of birds, including 34 species found nowhere else in the country, have been spotted in Texas. Most can be found in the Rio Grande Valley."

—June Naylor, author, *Off the Beaten Path—Texas*

"These Texians are the most independent people under the whole canopy of heaven."

—J. Frank Dobie, writer and folklorist

"Most people who are real Texans by birth or at least by attitude know that a 'Mexican breakfast' consists of a cup of black coffee and a cigarette."

—Clay Reynolds, novelist

"On the eighth day God created Texas."

—Anonymous

Strange Lights in Marfa

According to a 2007 poll, approximately 14 percent of Americans believe they've seen a UFO. How many of them have been in Marfa?

If anyone is near Marfa at night, they should watch for odd, vivid lights over nearby Mitchell Flat. Many people believe that the lights from UFOs or even alien entities can be seen. The famous Marfa Lights are about the size of basketballs and are usually white, orange, red, or yellow. These unexplained lights only appear at night and usually hover above the ground at about shoulder height. Some of the lights—alone or in pairs—drift and fly around the landscape.

From cowboys to truck drivers, people traveling in Texas near the intersection of U.S. Route 90 and U.S. Route 67 in southwest Texas have reported the Marfa Lights. And these baffling lights don't just appear on the ground. Pilots and airline passengers claim to have seen the Marfa Lights from the skies. So far, no one has proved a natural explanation for the floating orbs.

Eyewitness Information

Two 1988 reports were especially graphic. Pilot R. Weidig was about 8,000 feet above Marfa when he saw the lights and estimated them rising several hundred feet above the ground. Passenger E. Halsell described the lights as larger than the plane and noted that they were pulsating. In 2002, pilot B. Eubanks provided a similar report.

In addition to what can be seen, the Marfa Lights may also trigger low-frequency electromagnetic (radio) waves—which can be heard on special receivers—similar to the "whistlers" caused by lightning. However, unlike such waves from power lines and electrical storms, the Marfa whistlers are extremely loud. They can be heard as the orbs appear, and then they fade when the lights do.

A Little Bit About Marfa

Marfa is about 60 miles north of the Mexican border and about 190 miles southeast of El Paso. This small, friendly Texas town is 4,800 feet above sea level and covers 1.6 square miles.

In 1883, Marfa was a railroad water stop. It received its name from the wife of the president of the Texas and New Orleans Railroad, who chose the name from a Russian novel that she was reading. A strong argument can be made that this was Dostoyevsky's *The Brothers Karamazov*. The town grew slowly, reaching its peak during World War II when the U.S. government located a prisoner of war camp, the Marfa Army Airfield, and a chemical warfare brigade nearby. (Some skeptics suggest that discarded chemicals may be causing the Marfa Lights, but searchers have found no evidence of such.)

Today, Marfa is home to about 2,500 people. The small town is an emerging arts center with more than a dozen artists' studios and art galleries. However, Marfa remains most famous for its light display. The annual Marfa Lights Festival is one of the town's biggest events, but the mysterious lights attract visitors year-round.

The Marfa Lights are seen almost every clear night, but they never manifest during the daytime. The lights appear between Marfa and nearby Paisano Pass, with the Chinati Mountains as a backdrop.

Widespread Sightings

The first documented sighting was by 16-year-old cowhand Robert Reed Ellison during an 1883 cattle drive. Seeing an odd light in the area, Ellison thought he'd seen an Apache campfire. When he told his story in town, however, settlers told him that they'd seen lights in the area, too, and they'd never found evidence of campfires.

Two years later, 38-year-old Joe Humphreys and his wife, Sally, also reported unexplained lights at Marfa. In 1919, cowboys on a cattle drive paused to search the area for the origin of the lights. Like the others, they found no explanation for what they had seen.

In 1943, the Marfa Lights came to national attention when Fritz Kahl, an airman at the Marfa Army Base, reported that airmen were seeing lights that they couldn't explain. Four years later, he attempted to fly after them in a plane but came up empty again.

Explanations?

Some skeptics claim that the lights are headlights from U.S. 67, dismissing the many reports from before cars—or U.S. 67—were in the Marfa area. Others insist that the lights are swamp gas, ball lightning, reflections off mica deposits, or a nightly mirage.

At the other extreme, a contingent of people believe that the floating orbs are friendly observers of life on Earth. For example, Mrs. W. T. Giddings described her father's early 20th-century encounter with the Marfa Lights. He'd become lost during a blizzard, and according to his daughter, the lights "spoke" to him and led him to a cave where he found shelter.

Most studies of the phenomenon, however, conclude that the lights are indeed real but cannot be explained. The 1989 TV show *Unsolved Mysteries* set up equipment to find an explanation. Scientists on the scene could only comment that the lights were not made by people.

Share the Wealth

Marfa is the most famous location for "ghost lights" and "mystery lights," but it's not the only place to see them. Here are just a few of the legendary unexplained lights that attract visitors to dark roads in Texas on murky nights.

- In southeast Texas, a single orb appears regularly near Saratoga on Bragg Road.
- The Anson Light appears near Mt. Hope Cemetery in Anson, by U.S. Highway 180.
- Since 1850, "Brit Bailey's Light" glows five miles west of Angleton near Highway 35 in Brazoria County.
- In January 2008, Stephenville attracted international attention when unexplained lights—and perhaps a metallic spaceship—flew fast and low over the town.

The Marfa Lights appear over Mitchell Flat, which is entirely private property. However, the curious can view the lights from a Texas Highway Department roadside parking area about nine miles east of Marfa on U.S. Highway 90. Seekers should arrive before dusk for the best location, especially during bluebonnet season (mid-April through late May), because this is a popular tourist stop.

The Marfa Lights Festival takes place during Labor Day weekend each year. This annual celebration of Marfa's mystery includes a parade, arts and crafts booths, great food, and a street dance.

Texas Tawk:
Pronunciation Guide

*Want to tawk real Texan? Well sir, first of all ya got to slow
down and stretch out your vowels, son, turn 'em into a
single note sound, or what Yankees call a* monophthong.

Visitors can step into Texas and parrot back a few folksy aphorisms
all they want, but none of it will do them any good unless they know
how to pronounce words like a Texan.

At the core of the Texas twang is the *monophthong.* This is a
single note "pure" vowel sound, or flattened vowel sound; it accounts
for why many words sound similar when spoken by a Texan, such as
the merging of *fire* and *far,* or why *night* sounds like *naht.*

Don't Rush It

The stereotypical Texas accent has a slow, lazy cadence, as well.
Natives meander around consonants and linger over vowels. Visitors
who do the same will be able to utter one-syllable words correctly.
Take the word *bad* for instance. In Texas, it's pulled like a piece of
taffy into *bay-uhd.* Similarly, *kid* is transformed into *kee-uhd.*

At the same time, listeners have to pay attention to the peculiar
ways that words are altered. One of the prime examples is a word
ending in *ing.* Texans regard the *g* as silent. Saying that someone
is "fixing to go to the store" is a dead giveaway that the speaker is a
Yankee. To use the proper pronunciation, say "fixin' to go."

Put 'Em Together

Similarly, visitors should listen for word combining. The word *of* is
often slurred with others and used as a bridge. A "chest of drawers"
becomes "chester drawers." Three or more words can be combined
into a single phrase, too: "How are you?" is recast as "hairyew?"

So, ya'll take notice of pronunciation. Soon as tourists get the
knack of droppin' a *g*, roundin' an *o*, and flattenin' vowels, they'll
shore nuff be shootin' the breeze with the best of 'em!

Fast Facts

- Rice's Marching Owl Band (MOB) went over the line in 1973 with their parody of the Texas Aggies. When the band's halftime routine insulted A&M's canine mascot, it was too much. A number of A&M cadets besieged the MOB after the game, and police had to smuggle the band members out in groups by truck.

- Did Sor María de Jesús de Ágreda, "The Blue Nun," visit Texas in the late 1620s? At about that time, a group of the Jumano people presented themselves to a Spanish mission to learn more about Christianity, citing a "Lady in Blue." Yet Sor María had never left Spain!

- Ben Hogan, the famous Texan golfer, wasn't the sociable kind. Late in his career, he had a ten-room mansion built in Fort Worth. Only one of those rooms was a bedroom. Apparently Hogan didn't plan on guests spending the night.

- Remember the Ala ... Mao? On March 20, 1980, some Revolutionary Communist Party comrades snuck into the Alamo. They struck the Texas flag for a Communist Red Flag, which, not surprisingly, was down in 30 minutes.

- When Beaumont was late paying its electric bill in the first half of the 20th century, wealthy madam Grace Woodyard lent the town tens of thousands of dollars to bail it out of the crisis.

- Austin psychedelic rocker Roky Erickson has had a few colorful moments. The low point might be in 1969 when he was arrested for having one marijuana cigarette, pled insanity, and did three years in a hospital for the criminally insane—where he was subjected to shock therapy.

- Poor sanitation, vile cockroaches, voracious mosquitoes, punishing heat, 100-percent humidity, disgusting food, and frequent infections: a World War II POW camp in the Philippines? Nope, worse: Houston Oilers training camps from 1960 to '63. That torment also produced a 37–18–1 record, three division titles, and two AFL titles.

Getting Back to the Basics in Luckenbach, Texas

Take two beers, listen to a country fiddle, smile and laugh, strum a guitar, kick your boots up, and don't call until morning. "Luckenbach," said the doctor, "is a habit-forming antidote for modern life."

The small community of Luckenbach is tucked away among the rolling hills and prickly pear cacti of the Texas Hill Country, 75 miles west of Austin. Oil wasn't discovered here; neither was gold, silver, or diamonds. Nobody especially famous was born and raised  here, either. It's off the beaten path, difficult to find, and far from the modern conveniences of the 20th century.

But that's the whole point. The late Hondo Crouch, celebrated Texas folklorist, writer, humorist, and self-styled "Clown Prince" of Luckenbach, orchestrated it to be that way. With a couple of buddies, in 1970 he purchased the ten-acre town for $30,000. At the time, only three residents remained, which meant that it was teetering on the brink of becoming a ghost town.

Starting from Scratch

"Downtown" Luckenbach consisted of nothing more than a combination general store and tavern, an old-time dance hall, and a blacksmith shop. Nothing much had changed here since the German pioneers first arrived during the mid-1800s. In fact, the last time something newsworthy had happened was in 1849 when Minna Engel, the daughter of an itinerant preacher, opened the general store. She also named the town after her fiancé, Carl Albert Luckenbach.

After Crouch bought the town, he maintained the status quo by keeping growth to a minimum. He wasn't thinking of putting in a master-planned community, a strip mall, or even a theme park. He merely kicked back, began whittling, and invited some friends over to play some music. His most extravagant ambition was to greet visitors with a hearty welcome and to make them smile.

Building a Reputation

Single-handedly, Hondo Crouch invented Luckenbach and styled it as if it were the living room of his imagination. In fact, he referred to the town as a "free state...of mind."

As the town "mayor," he had a duty to act as both irreverent thinker and ringmaster. He liked to poke fun at politicians and often lampooned the "Texas White House," President Lyndon Johnson's ranch on the nearby Pedernales River. He also staged crazy festivals such as a women-only chili cook-off and the Luckenbach Great World's Fair. "Hug-ins" were a regular event, as was Mud Daubers' Day. "Everybody's Somebody in Luckenbach," decreed Crouch... and people took his word for it.

Then, one summer night in 1973, musician Jerry Jeff Walker and the Lost Gonzo Band recorded a live album there called *Viva Terlingua.* The antithesis of the Nashville scene, the record became a classic of the country-rock "outlaw" genre. More notoriety came in 1977 after Waylon Jennings and Willie Nelson released their hit "Luckenbach, Texas (Back to the Basics of Love)." Suddenly, the town's reputation as a venue to relax and strum a guitar transformed it into a cult destination.

Modern Times

Today, Luckenbach is still all about the music. On any night of the week, you can find musicians dressed in boots and faded jeans, wearing cowboy hats, sitting around pickin', grinnin', and singin'. Eager to be inspired by Luckenbach's muse, hopeful artists travel from across America just to play their new song at the dance hall. Somehow, they hope that a small amount of Luckenbach's legend will rub off on their tune and bless it with fortune.

Around these parts, they like to say that "you can't find a place more laid-back without being unconscious," and they're right. In an age when people are obsessed with money, social status, and the so-called trappings of success, Luckenbach exists as a virtual tranquilizer—an antidote to life that has to be experienced rather than swallowed.

Texas Timeline

(Continued from p. 40)

February 20, 1830
In an effort to obtain a Texas land grant offered only to Mexican citizens, James Bowie takes an oath of allegiance to Mexico.

April 6, 1830
Mexico establishes a law prohibiting further American settlement in Texas, thus sowing discontent.

December 10, 1832
Former Tennessee governor Sam Houston arrives in Texas on orders from President Andrew Jackson.

January 27, 1834
Stephen F. Austin is arrested by Mexican authorities for inciting insurrection in Texas. He is held for nearly a year.

September 1835
Sarah Bradley Dodson creates a red, white, and blue banner with a single star for her husband to carry into battle. It becomes Texas's first flag.

October 2, 1835
The Texas Revolution begins with the Battle of Gonzales, in which Texans force the retreat of some 160 Mexican soldiers.

October 17, 1835
The Texas Rangers are formed to guard Texas's borders against invaders and incursions by Native Americans.

November 28, 1835
Sam Houston calls for the immediate organization of a Texas Army in San Felipe.

February 8, 1836
Davy Crockett arrives at the Alamo with a contingent of Tennessee volunteers.

February 17, 1836
Mexican troops annihilate Texas forces in San Patricio as they march north toward San Antonio and the Alamo.

March 2, 1836
Texas's Declaration of Independence from Mexico is adopted in Washington-on-the-Brazos, declaring the territory to be an independent and sovereign republic.

March 6, 1836
Mexican General Santa Anna, backed by 4,000 troops, captures the Alamo from some 150 brave Texans who defend the garrison to the end.

May 14, 1836
Revolutionary President David Burnet meets Mexican General Santa Anna to sign the Treaties at Velasco, ending hostilities and granting Texas its independence.

January 19, 1837
The city of Houston is established on Galveston Bay.

December 10, 1838
Sam Houston's two-year term as president of Texas, during which the republic earned recognition by the United States, ends.

January 19, 1840
Austin, known as Waterloo before being renamed to honor Stephen F. Austin, becomes Texas's capital.

(Continued on p. 133)

The House that Doak Built

There was a time when athletic achievement was measured by integrity, intelligence, and on-field accomplishments rather than bank balances, contract clauses, and off-field romances. The undisputed star of this era was a humble, honest, and hard-hauling running back from Southern Methodist University named Doak Walker, a perpetual All-American who became so popular that the Cotton Bowl Stadium was resized to seat all the spectators who scrambled to see him soar and score.

It's been written that Doak Walker was so shifty that he could evade tacklers in a phone booth, so humble that he wrote thank-you notes to the scribes who regularly chose him as an All-American, and so popular that he appeared on the cover of 47 major magazines during his illustrious years playing for the SMU Mustangs and NFL's Detroit Lions. Not content to limit his athletic talents to the gridiron, Walker also lent his skills to the SMU basketball and baseball teams. However, it was on the football field that the Dallas native excelled and evolved.

An Unquestionable Sensation

Walker attended Highland Park High School in Dallas, where he shared the sporting spotlight with future NFL Hall of Fame quarterback Bobby Layne. After graduating in 1944, Walker stayed close to home and attended SMU, where he tore up the turf for the Mustangs as a star halfback, defensive back, punter, and kick returner.

Walker's athletic prowess, combined with SMU's on-field success and a soaring spectator interest, forced the Mustangs to relocate their home games. The team moved from Ownby Stadium, located at the south end of the SMU campus in the University Park neighborhood in Dallas, to the larger Cotton Bowl Stadium at the Texas State Fair. The stadium, which sat more than 40,000 fans, was also the home of the annual Cotton Bowl Classic, a postseason match that initially pitted a Texas team against a top-rated independent school.

Classing Up the Cotton Bowl

Founded in 1937, the Cotton Bowl game was a financial liability in its early years, rarely attracting sellout crowds despite the presence of a hometown host, and often losing money. In 1941, the powers that be decided that the champion of the Southwest Conference (SWC) would host the annual Cotton Bowl game, but the advent of World War II and a drop in the quality of competition continued to undercut the showcase.

However, once Doak Walker and the Mustangs became the park's regular tenants during the season, attendance soared and interest intensified. Walker, who solidified his standing among the all-time gridiron giants by winning the 1948 Heisman Trophy, led the SMU team to a pair of Cotton Bowl game appearances, including a title-winning victory over Oregon in 1949. He was named MVP in both his Cotton Bowl games.

Almost 30,000 seats were added to the stadium to meet the demand for tickets, raising its capacity from 46,200 to 75,504. This could only help to promote the prestige and popularity of the game, which became a nationally followed favorite. Walker's role in the ascension of the game and the stadium that hosts it up to full-fledged classic status was solidified when scribes began referring to the Cotton Bowl as "The House that Doak Built," placing Walker's name alongside Babe Ruth's as athletes whose acclaim transcended the playing field.

The SMU Mustangs continued to use the Cotton Bowl stadium as their home turf until 1979, when the school moved its home games to Texas Stadium, home of the NFL's Dallas Cowboys. The House that Doak Built saw its most enduring tenant, the Cotton Bowl Classic, host its final game in the stadium in 2009, as plans were made for the bowl game to relocate to the new Cowboys Stadium in Arlington beginning in 2010.

• *In the 1954 Cotton Bowl, Rice Owl running back Dickie Moegle got loose along the Alabama Crimson Tide sideline. 'Bama's Tommy Lewis jumped off the bench to stop him. Moegle was awarded a TD.*

🍺 Taste of Texas

When it comes to Texas, there's always more food. Here are another handful of dishes that come out of Texas kitchens.

- Not all Texas cuisine was invented by cowboys. In the 1950s, New Yorker Helen Corbitt moved to Dallas to become the doyenne of the Neiman Marcus kitchens. Among the Texas favorites Corbitt brought to the national scene is monkey bread—a pull-apart sweet loaf made from frozen dough and pudding mix. Over the decades, the once simple dessert has become a delicacy featuring a coating of caramel and nuts.

- Corbitt also invented "Texas caviar," which doesn't involve fish eggs at all but rather the down-home black-eyed pea. Corbitt took the cowpea upscale, pickling it in a vinaigrette marinade. First served at a New Year's soiree at a Houston country club, the dish moved on to Austin's Driskill Hotel, where it won the caviar moniker.

- Another Texan made black-eyed peas the national dish of New Year's. In 1947, the Henderson County Chamber of Commerce hired agricultural consultant Elmore Torn Sr. to boost the fortunes of some local pea canneries. He invented a fable that serving black-eyed peas for New Year's was a long-cherished antebellum tradition, suppressed by the Yankees during Reconstruction. Newspaper editors across the South ran his story for years to come—an Oscar-worthy performance that won the legume national stardom. Incidentally, Torn's son Elmore Jr., better know as "Rip," became a veteran Hollywood character actor who's been nominated for an Oscar and won an Emmy Award.

- Whether first mixed in Texas or just across the border, the margarita made its world debut in the Lone Star State. Some say the sweet and frozen Tequila cocktail was first poured just across the Rio Grande in Juarez, others that it happened at the Kentucky Club in Galveston. As a matter of fact, however, it was perfected by Mariano Martinez at Mariano's Mexican restaurant in Dallas in the 1970s, when he put his family's secret margarita recipe into an Icee machine.

White Man Sees Red

*When Apache kidnapped Adolph Korn from his Texas farm, his
life seemed all but over. But then something strange happened:
Rather than curse his captors, he decided to join them. The
unlikely alliance stands as one of Texas's more improbable tales.*

While tending sheep on New Year's Day, 1870, 10-year-old Adolph
Korn's life took a sudden twist when he was attacked by three
Apache. Knocked unconscious, he was taken captive and forcibly
thrust into Apache life. At first Korn resisted his captors, but over
time such impulses subsided as he adjusted to his new setting. Korn
eventually found peace among his new family, and with it a sense of
dutiful purpose. Against all odds, he became one with his captors.

Rebirth

Korn wasn't the first white boy to be abducted by Native Americans.
The practice had been used to increase the ranks of native cultures,
giving them a fighting chance against a flood of hostile Europeans.
And with Korn, they hit pay dirt. Not only was the youth willing to
stand beside his new "brothers" in solidarity, he was willing to fight.

Traded to the Comanche during his first year of captivity, Korn
fearlessly squared off against those white settlers and U.S. soldiers
who threatened his new culture. But in 1872, nearly three years
after he was first taken, Korn was "captured" by the U.S. Army and
returned to his parents. To call the reunion less than joyous would
be an understatement. Things had changed drastically since the day
that Adolph Korn had been abducted. The boy was no longer the
son they remembered.

Aftermath

Holding fast to his Native American ways, Korn completely turned
his back on white society. With no luck in turning their son around,
his family eventually let him go. Korn ultimately moved into a cave,
where he lived his odd life as a man white in complexion, but Native
American in spirit. He died in 1900, a castoff from both cultures.

Route 66: Miles and Miles of Texas

For cross-country travelers eager to "get their kicks on Route 66," the Mother Road beckons: More than 150 miles of the original 178 miles of Texas Route 66 remain.

When Route 66 was officially decommissioned in 1985, Interstate 40 took over the job of funneling motorists from east to west and back again across the desolate landscape of the Texas Panhandle. Now, at 70 miles per hour, one could speed in air-conditioned, anonymous comfort across the staked plains and barely catch a glimpse of the unique people, places, and culture that defined the Llano Estacado.

But it wasn't always that way. Once upon a time in the history of cross-country travel, the ride *was* more important than the destination. Travelers made close contact with the places they passed and, as a result, experienced the journey as a part of their trip.

The Mother Road

During the 1950s and '60s, taking a pilgrimage across America—and the Panhandle of Texas—meant that you took the highway designated with the numerals 66. Because it linked towns small and large, Route 66 was at one time referred to as "America's Main Street," a two-lane corridor that allowed the traveler to read the signs up close, smell the barbecue cooking, and hear the music of people who lived and worked along the route.

During its heyday, Route 66 ran a total of 2,448 miles, with the Texas portion grabbing up 178 of them. "(Get Your Kicks on) Route 66" was more than just a song written by Bobby Troup and sung by Nat King Cole: It was an anthem for those itching to hit the open road and "see the U.S.A. in their Chevrolet."

Re-creating the Past

This is an experience that can still be had, as more than 150 miles of the Texas section of the original "Mother Road" remains, much of it the old concrete surface. Drivers pulling off almost any exit ramp will be sure to find the old road waiting for exploration. These days, the crumbling two-lane thoroughfare wanders back and forth to the north and south of the new interstate alignment. Between Texola and Amarillo (except at McLean) the old route can be found just south of I-40. Moving west from Amarillo to Glenrio, the vintage road claims real estate north of the superslab.

Although the road is easy to find, it's advisable that those interested in tracing it pick up a good Route 66 map. Over the decades, the path of Route 66 has seen an endless number of changes, including rerouting and new alignments. And all should be advised: The old road that used to connect Jericho to Alanreed and Adrian to Glenrio is gone for good. So don't even bother looking.

Getting Started

To begin a Texas Route 66 adventure, travelers should start their trip west of Texola, Oklahoma, where the I-40 frontage road pulls directly into the town of Shamrock, Texas. Here, at the corner of North Main and East 12th Street (66), can be found the U-Drop Inn, a former café and Conoco service station, recently restored by the Shamrock Chamber of Commerce. Used as the model for Ramone's Custom House of Body Art in the Disney movie *Cars,* the striking art deco structure is a Mother Road jewel—trimmed with glowing neon.

From town, drivers should continue on 12th to the frontage road, which is the most authentic stretch of Route 66 to be found anywhere. From here, they'll pass through the ghost town of Lela and arrive in McLean, home of the Texas Old Route 66 Association, whose restoration projects include the McLean Phillips 66 filling station, the first in Texas. Offbeat attractions in McLean include the Devil's Rope Museum, where interested parties can learn everything they always wanted to know about barbed wire but were afraid to ask. The 1930s Art Deco Avalon Theater also should not be missed.

The next town up is Alanreed, a forgotten burg whose claim to fame is the oldest cemetery and church along Texas 66. Eldridge cemetery was established in 1888 and includes the graves of Confederate soldiers, freedmen, and other local luminaries. Today, it serves as a sad metaphor for a town killed by progress. Once home to 500 residents, the town is a prime example of what happened to communities after they were bypassed by modern freeways.

Watch Out for the Rain

Next up is Jericho Gap, the infamous spot where Route 66 travelers inevitably got bogged down in the mud. When it rained, the area's rich black soil turned into what some called "black gumbo," rendering the roads impassable. Sandwiched between sections of improved road to the east and the west, it was duly christened "Jericho Gap." Take note: Most of the original Route 66 can't be traveled along this stretch, because it either no longer exists or is located on private property.

On the way to Groom, travelers should keep their eyes peeled for the leaning water tower (which leans because one leg is shorter than the other), a planned tourist attraction that once pulled in customers for the now defunct Britten truck stop and restaurant. In Groom, it's a good thing that people cannot live by bread alone: One of the most impressive sights here is the tallest cross in the western hemisphere, a 190-foot, 1,250-ton inspiration of Steve Thomas. Further west in Conway, trekkers will cross paths with Bug Farm USA, a low-budget, Volkswagen tribute to the more famous Cadillac Ranch.

On the way into Amarillo (the helium capitol of the world), Route 66 once crossed the Amarillo Air Force Base *and* the airport itself. These days, two separate alignments can be explored: the first along Old Third and Sixth, and the second along Amarillo Boulevard. Either way, a plethora of vintage businesses will have cars pulling over to the side of the road for passengers to snap pictures of the local scene. By the time they reach the Big Texan Steak Ranch, travelers will be more than ready for the challenge of the "Free 72-ounce steak."

Farther Along the Road

From Amarillo, the north service road goes out of town, where it runs into Stanley Marsh 3's world-famous Cadillac Ranch, just south of I-40. From there, the old road runs through Bushland and Wildorado and on into Vega (Spanish for meadow), where the crumbling remnants of better days populate the roadsides. Despite the near ghost-town atmosphere, the Vega Motel—an original tourist court built in 1947—is still going strong.

Pressing onward to Adrian, adventurers will come to the official halfway point along the old Route 66 highway. Driving west from here, it's 1,139 miles to Los Angeles; driving east to Chicago, it's the same distance. This midpoint town has also seen better days and is home to about a dozen businesses and only 150 residents. The wonders here are rather low key, punctuated by the local water tower and the Midpoint Cafe, the oldest continuously operating café found along the Texas stretch of the Will Rogers Highway.

Just west of Adrian, the service road comes to an abrupt dead end, where the slab of Route 66 disappears. Don't worry—that's not the end just yet. It resurfaces about a mile or so before Glenrio, the last settlement in Texas before the road crosses over into New Mexico. Here, buildings such as the "First Inn/Last Inn" motel stand like tombstones—stark reminders of what the area was like before the coming of the interstate and the bypassing of what was once billed as America's Main Street.

* * *

- *As he sat on Death Row for murder in Gonzales on March 18, 1921, Albert Howard just had to curse something. He chose the clock in the Gonzales County Courthouse and got to work. Was he successful? Who can say? But to this day, the clock will not synchronize, despite the best professional efforts of clock repairpersons.*

- *The last NFL team to fold outright was the Dallas Texans in 1952. That year, the New York Yanks NFL franchise became the Dallas Texans and went only 1–11. After the team closed down, more than half its players retired.*

- *Two of the three original Angels on TV's* Charlie's Angels *were Texans: Farrah Fawcett from Corpus Christi and Jaclyn Smith from Houston.*

Secede? Seriously?

Texas, the only state to have previously been its own republic, has already left the United States once. Is it so surprising that some in the state periodically call for an amicable separation?

In many ways Texas is a reluctant member of the United States. Before joining the Union, Texas was an independent country, and the affection for independence has never gone away. The ten years of sovereign Texas were filled with war, political strife, and some seriously overdue bills, but independence is independence.

Leave the Union!

One upsurge in secession talk arose in the late 1990s, and the most notorious voice at that time may have belonged to Richard McLaren, a founding member of the militia-allied group the Republic of Texas. Initially, McLaren was simply an opponent of taxation, but in a strange leap into the bizarre, he spent a little too much time reading arcane legal history and concluded that the United States never got the paperwork right when it annexed Texas.

McLaren claimed that because there was no treaty in place between the United States and Texas before annexation (as he interpreted international law to require), the whole state situation was null and void. Set aside for a moment that no one complained about this back when it would have actually mattered—in 1845. McLaren was able to convince a small group of people that his argument was actually a legitimate enough claim for them to assert themselves as the Republic of Texas. The early months of the ROT (an unfortunate acronym if there ever was one) were filled with the usual work of statecraft: figuring out how to get the money to keep things going.

ROT Forever!

McLaren elected himself ambassador and chief legal counsel, and he started issuing liens, judgments for trillions of dollars, and even his own license plates. He lobbied the United Nations for recognition as a sovereign country. He tied up courts for months with "paper warfare" to slow down real estate transactions across the state. To top it all off, he wrote millions of dollars' worth of bad checks, strangely echoing the financial turmoil of the historical independent Texas.

By 1997, the ROT had split into two factions, with McLaren in charge of the smaller and more violent group. On the opposing faction's Web site, the more peaceful members noted that McLaren had "gone off the deep end."

The "Republic" Falls Apart

Things at the ROT began to melt down completely when McLaren decided it was time for a modern version of the Alamo. The group kidnapped two of its neighbors, Margaret Ann and Joe Rowe, reportedly in retaliation for the arrest of two ROT members who were driving without state license plates.

Having recently added armed guards to his staff, McLaren also ordered members of his militia to begin "picking up federal judges, legislators and IRS agents for immediate deportation." This was the last straw for Texas law enforcement. Almost 300 state troopers and Texas Rangers descended on and laid siege to the ROT in the mountain community of Ft. Davis. One member of the ROT was killed, and a hostage was wounded in the standoff. McLaren was sentenced to 99 years in prison for the kidnapping and standoff and an additional 12 years for 26 counts of mail and bank fraud and conspiracy.

Some People Still Have Ideas

Since then, supporters of the idea of an independent and sovereign Texas are still around, although there are fewer attempts to "fire" officials who impose state and federal laws. However, in a strange twist of the kind that could only happen in Texas, one of the state's most prominent officials brought up secession in 2009. At a "tea party" tax protest, Governor Rick Perry addressed shouts from the crowd calling on him to secede.

"There's a lot of different scenarios," said the governor. "We've got a great union. There's absolutely no reason to dissolve it. But if Washington continues to thumb their nose at the American people, you know, who knows what might come out of that. But Texas is a very unique place, and we're a pretty independent lot to boot."

Maybe the door isn't closed on this issue.

Fast Facts

- *The term* maverick *comes from a real person, Samuel Maverick. He was a West Texas rancher back in the mid-1800s, but it's a myth that he refused to brand cattle due to cussedness. He just didn't care. The term stuck anyway.*

- *When Buddy Holly's 1959 Iowa plane crash terminated a promising career, his remains went home to Lubbock. A huge pair of glasses stands outside the Buddy Holly Center, and visitors leave guitar picks at his grave.*

- *The idea of marital community property in U.S. law (which varies by state) came from Spanish Texas. Spanish jurisprudence held that both parties to the marriage should share equally in its wealth. Today, many Western states are community property states. The joint tax return also emanates from this principle.*

- *It's fairly well known that a Texan, Gene Roddenberry from El Paso, invented* Star Trek. *But a lesser-known fact is that Roddenberry was also a decorated World War II veteran B-17 pilot, holder of the Distinguished Flying Cross.*

- Nuestra Señora del Camaro: *In 1993, an Elsa man noticed the Virgin of Guadeloupe in the rust on the bumper of his Camaro. Sanding it off wasn't a viable option for him, so instead he built a garage shrine, which is still open by appointment.*

- *When Heisman Trophy winner Roger Staubach was doing his Navy service before joining the Dallas Cowboys, he kept in shape by running on the beaches at Da Nang in Vietnam.*

- *Texas band ZZ Top, the blues rockers who first hooked up in Houston, turned down Gillette's offer of $1 million to remove their famous facial hair with Gillette hardware. Why? "We're too ugly without 'em," said Billy Gibbons and Dusty Hill.*

- *On San Jacinto Day, April 21, 1942, a few more than two dozen Aggies were among the surviving defenders of Corregidor. As the Japanese shelled and bombed "The Rock," Major General George Moore and the Aggies present conducted Aggie Muster.*

Forty Days on the Rio Grande

*Alonso Álvarez de Pineda was the first known European visitor
to Texas. In 1519, he and his company explored and mapped the
Texas coast, occupying the mouth of the Rio Grande for more
than a month while repairing their ships. Despite his map—Texas
history's earliest document—surprisingly little is known about
Álvarez de Pineda beyond the nature of his grisly death.*

Under orders from Francisco de Garay, the Spanish governor of
Jamaica, Alonso Álvarez de Pineda embarked on a reconnaissance
trip in March 1519. His four ships carried his party of 270 and sailed
from Jamaica to explore the gulf coast in the hope of finding a strait
leading directly to the Atlantic Ocean. Many historians believe
that Álvarez de Pineda's company sailed north along the gulf coast
of Florida before attempting to turn east. If that sounds strange,
it is due to the erroneous reports of earlier Spanish explorer Juan
Ponce De León. In 1513, De León reported a northern passage that
separated Florida from the North American mainland. Therefore,
Álvarez de Pineda fully expected to be the first to prove that Florida
was an island.

Never coming upon a
point at which to turn east,
Álvarez de Pineda's company
instead headed west along
today's Florida panhandle
and Alabama coastline.
While there is some dispute
among historians, it appears
that around the time of the
feast day of Espíritu Santo,
or Pentecost, on June 2,
1519, Álvarez de Pineda became the first European to see the
Mississippi River. He named it Río del Espíritu Santo in reference to
the religious holiday and managed to sail upstream for several miles
before continuing his voyage along the gulf coast.

First into Texas

Álvarez de Pineda mapped the outer islands off the coast of current-day Corpus Christi, Texas, claiming the bay and the land beyond for his king and naming it with the Spanish term meaning "body of Christ." After mapping the entire Texas coastline, Álvarez de Pineda finally made land. His fleet landed slightly south of Boca Chica, at the mouth of the Rio Grande, making his party the first Europeans to set foot in Texas. The Spaniards explored the region for 40 days, the time it took to overhaul their ships and conduct repairs after the extensive voyage. This also means that the Rio Grande was the second place to be visited by Europeans in what is now the United States.

Grisly Demise

Álvarez de Pineda sailed on down the Gulf of Mexico to the mouth of the Panuco River, near where Cortés would later found the town of Tampico, in what is now the Mexican state of Tamaulipas. Here, Álvarez de Pineda's company appears to have suffered a heavy defeat at the hands of the Aztecs. Some reports indicate that Álvarez de Pineda and many of his crew were killed, flayed, and eaten; their skins were then displayed as trophies in the Aztec temples. The Aztecs also burned some of Álvarez de Pineda's fleet; only one ship, under the command of Diego de Camargo, managed to leave successfully.

Álvarez de Pineda's Legacy

Álvarez de Pineda's map of the entire gulf coast made it to safety with Camargo and was presented to Governor Garay, who went on to take all the credit for the expedition and obtain a grant for the territory it explored. Still, it was Alonso Álvarez de Pineda who discovered that there was no strait linking the Gulf of Mexico to the Atlantic Ocean. While many details of his voyage remain shrouded in mystery, there is little doubt that he was the first European to set foot in Texas.

- *Early goths? Men of the Karankawa, an early Gulf Coast civilization, wore cane piercings through their nipples and lower lips. Some of them also wore no clothing most of the time, probably because they spent a good portion of their days in or on the water searching for food.*

Talkin' About Texas

"Honor the Texas flag; I pledge allegiance to thee, Texas, one state under God, one and indivisible."

—Texas Government Code, Chapter 3100, Sections 3100.101–3100.104

"Texas is a state of mind. Texas is an obsession. Above all, Texas is a nation in every sense of the word."

—John Steinbeck, *Travels with Charley*

"My connection to Texas does not stem from deep-rooted ancestry or a fortune made in the oil fields. I came to Texas by chance, but I remain a Texan by choice."

—Lee P. Brown, former mayor of Houston

"Fort Worth is hailed as the birthplace of the washateria. In 1934, as the story goes, J. E. Cantrell installed four washing machines in an empty building. He rented the washers out by the hour to any housewife who couldn't afford an electric washing machine of her own. Cantrell's idea obviously spread to every city and town in the nation."

—Suzanne Martin, author, *Awesome Almanac: Texas*

"The land area of Texas is larger than all of New England, New York, Pennsylvania, Ohio, and Illinois combined."

—Kinky Friedman, musician and author

"Texas is a land of big things, and there are many things in that commonwealth that are different from the rest of the United States."

—Nevin O. Winter, *Texas the Marvellous,* 1916

"This is a place where all things are possible, where the man with a dream, if he works hard enough and dreams well enough, can make it come true.... It is not the oil or the money or the buildings or the growth that makes Texas exciting. It is the attitude."

—David Nevin, author

The Beginning of a Long, Strange Line of Governors

Not every Texas chief executive deserves to be on a list of oddball governors, but more than a few of them should feel right at home. Here are a couple of early examples.

Maybe it's because of Texas's long-standing independent streak, or maybe there's something in the water, but for hundreds of years there has been a parade of eclectic (to put it kindly) characters at the helm of the Lone Star State. In fact, Texas has had a love-hate relationship with independence and impeachment right from the start.

Setting the Standard

Henry Smith

The first American governor of Texas was Henry Smith. Texas was technically part of Mexico at the time, but Texans never were much for technicalities. In 1834, Mexican officials appointed Smith chief of the department of the Brazos, but neither that appointment nor the fact that he'd been deeded his land by the Mexican government quelled his thirst for Texas independence.

Within a year, Smith was heading up the War Party, which set the creation of the independence movement into motion. By the end of 1835, he was named governor of the provisional breakaway government, but perhaps the "War Party" moniker was too literal—he wasn't able to survive political wars with his rivals. No sooner had he attempted to dissolve the provisional government's council than council members fought back by impeaching him.

But, setting a tradition that would be repeated some four decades later, Smith refused to leave office. Texans eventually got rid of him the next year when a new constitutional congress came and created a "do over" for the new Republic of Texas.

A Convoluted Personal Life

Smith's first wife, Harriet Gillette, died in 1820 when they lived in Missouri, seven years before Smith emigrated to Texas. He didn't have to look far for wife number two: In 1822, he married Harriet's sister Elizabeth. But Elizabeth died of cholera in Texas in 1833. Fortunately, Elizabeth had a twin sister, Sarah, who became Smith's third wife. Breaking the curse of the Smith wives, Sarah outlived Henry, who died in 1851 in a mining camp during the California gold rush.

Smith may have had his problems, but he also had a sense of propriety as far as legal documents were concerned. Legend has it that he created what would become the official seal of Texas. As head of the provisional government of Texas in December 1835, he had to seal his first official document, which appointed John Forbes, Sam Houston, and John Cameron as commissioners to negotiate with American Indians in the area. Having nothing official in place for the newly minted state, Smith—still according to legend—took a brass button off his coat, dipped it in some sealing wax, and stamped in the impression of a five-pointed star. It was the beginning of Texas's most common nickname: the Lone Star State.

Leaving Office Is Hard to Do

Giving up the position of governor was definitely not easy for the 14th governor of Texas, either. Edmund Jackson Davis was a Union general in the Civil War and a Radical Republican during Reconstruction. His approach to governing was certainly radical, marked by everything from imprisoning political opponents to suppression and intimidation of newspapers. Not surprisingly, Davis wasn't exactly a popular guy after all this, and he lost reelection in 1873 to Richard Coke by a margin of two to one. Taking a page from Henry Smith, Davis refused to leave the ground floor of the Capitol, locking himself in his office and asking President Ulysses S. Grant to send troops to his aid (Grant refused). Eventually Davis left of his own accord—locking the office door behind him, so Coke's supporters still had to use an ax to break in.

A Lizard for the Ages

Horned toads may be the official state reptile of Texas, but one has gone well beyond its cold-blooded brethren to secure its own spot in Texas history.

In 1897, the cornerstone of the County Courthouse in Eastland was being placed. Among the gathered crowd were County Clerk Ernest Wood and his son, Will, who had a fondness for capturing lizards.

Horned toads, by the way, are lizards, not frogs, and have a rounded body and protrusions around their heads. Some types of horned toads actually squirt blood from the corners of their eyes, something that discourages predators but thrills young boys.

During the placement of the cornerstone, several items were placed in a hollow in the marble cornerstone. County Clerk Wood got a wild hair and added Will's horned toad.

Is It a Miracle?

Thirty-one years later, more than 3,000 people gathered to see the reopening of that cornerstone to check on the lizard. When the old cornerstone was opened and the dusty and apparently lifeless horned toad was held aloft, it began kicking a leg and looking for breakfast.

Dubbed Old Rip, the horned toad lived another year during which it toured the United States and received a formal audience with President Calvin Coolidge. It was also featured in "Ripley's Believe It or Not," and newsreels showed Rip's warty face across the land. Unfortunately, celebrity status proved to be too much. Old Rip returned home and died of pneumonia. But it was carefully preserved in a tiny velvet-lined coffin in a glass case, becoming a miniature tourist attraction.

Even in death, Old Rip continued its adventures. At one point Rip was kidnapped, and at another, its leg fell off due to rough handling by a visiting politician. Old Rip may have been the inspiration for the Warner Brothers cartoon character "Michigan J. Frog," the tap-dancing, singing frog that comes to life when a building is razed.

You Can Thank Texas

Most people have never heard of Jack Kilby, which is a shame because he single-handedly changed the world when he invented the microchip while working for Dallas-based Texas Instruments in 1958. With that discovery, the very foundation of the home computer was born.

Kilby was born in Jefferson City, Missouri, in 1923. He received his Master of Science degree in electrical engineering from the University of Wisconsin and began his remarkable career in 1947 at the Centralab Division of Globe Union, Inc., in Milwaukee, where he developed ceramic-based, silk-screen circuits for consumer electronics.

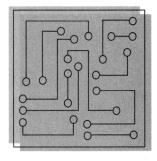

In 1958, Kilby made the jump to Texas Instruments where, later that year, he designed and built the first working electronic circuit in which all components were manufactured in a single, very small piece of semiconductor material. Kilby's creation had numerous military, industrial, and commercial applications, and he quickly set to work making them a reality, heading the teams that built the first military system and the first computer to incorporate integrated circuits.

In 1970, Kilby temporarily left Texas Instruments to pursue some ideas as an independent inventor, including the use of silicon technology for generating electric power from sunlight. In addition, he held the position of Distinguished Professor of Electrical Engineering at Texas A&M University from 1978 to 1984; he was inducted into the National Inventors Hall of Fame in 1982; and, perhaps most prestigious of all, he was awarded the Nobel Prize for Physics in 2000 for his work on the integrated circuit.

Incidentally, the microprocessor was not Kilby's only claim to fame. He also coinvented the handheld calculator (which he called the "Pocketronic") and the thermal printer used in portable data terminals.

So next time, instead of mindlessly surfing the Web, take a moment to thank Jack Kilby—the man who took microchips out of the pages of science fiction and into the home.

The Orange Show

Combine a postal worker's dreams with a love of "clean energy" and oranges, and what's the result? A monument to health, constructed from strange, recycled objects.

The Orange Show Monument—usually called simply "The Orange Show"—has been described as "one man's tribute to the orange." It is a nonprofit arts organization located in sunny Houston. Its creator, Jefferson Davis McKissack (1902–80), was a visionary and an "outsider" artist. His love of oranges and his eccentricities drove him to build one of the most remarkable examples of contemporary American folk art. Today, more than 50 years after McKissack launched his dream, the Orange Show site is in the National Register of Historic Places and inspires thousands of visitors annually.

Try, Try Again

This unique story began in 1956, when McKissack— a Houston mail carrier—started a spare-time building project near his home in Houston's East End. His first idea was to create a worm farm and nursery, which he constructed on two unoccupied lots adjacent to his home, but that project failed almost immediately.

Next, he applied for a permit to build a beauty parlor; McKissack had attended beauty college in the 1940s. But that idea didn't work out either, and he soon typed across his building permit: "Beauty parlors are going out of style. Have a better idea—The Orange Show."

The Round, Healthful Orange

McKissack was driven by his love of oranges, which dated back to the Great Depression, when he worked as a truck driver, distributing the fruit from a Georgia farmers' market throughout the Southeast. He wanted to build a tribute to its health benefits. He believed that hard work and good nutrition were essential to a long and healthy life, and he hoped to share that message through what opened as his "Health Show" and later became known as the Orange Show.

For more than 20 years, McKissack picked up discarded objects as he roamed the Houston area on his mail route. In his free time, he frequented junk shops, antique stores, and the sites of demolished buildings, gathering whatever he found. His collection included tiles and masonry blocks, fire escapes, and fabricated items. There seemed to be no limit to McKissack's imagination as he gathered unwanted objects and gently carried them home.

Bit by Bit

The exterior walls of McKissack's former plant nursery were the beginning of the Orange Show. From there, the project expanded steadily, with a logic best understood by its creator. There were no architectural plans for the site, which simply grew organically, one display at a time.

By the time McKissack died in 1980, his project had become an architectural maze sprawling across nearly a tenth of an acre. Walkways led to quirky exhibits, including beardless Santa Claus figures and store mannequins dressed in bright 1970s polyester. Surfaces were covered with bright colors, mosaics, and handwritten messages about oranges. Balconies jutted out with no rhyme or reason, and colorful flags and banners suggested childhood memories of fantasy castles.

McKissack added an amphitheater using old tractor seats, then a wishing well, a pond, and an oasis. It was a one-person project occupying all of his free time. He described the site as "the most beautiful show on earth, the most colorful show in harmony and the most unique." He believed it was equal to the "Eighth Wonder of the World," the nearby Houston Astrodome.

A Disappointing Debut

His naiveté probably enabled him to create this remarkable site despite Houston's sultry summers and rainy winters. Unfortunately, when McKissack opened the Orange Show to the public in 1979, he truly expected 90 percent of America to visit his display. When they didn't show up, McKissack was crushed. He died of a stroke seven months later, just two days before his 78th birthday. He likely had no idea that his dream would soon be championed by some of Texas's leading artists and art enthusiasts.

In the year after McKissack's death, Marilyn Oshman, of Oshman's Sporting Goods, founded a nonprofit organization to buy and preserve the Orange Show. Twenty-one people—including art collector Dominique de Menil, philanthropist Nina Cullinan, members of the Texas rock band ZZ Top, and East End funerary director Tommy Schlitzberger—donated funds to begin restoration of the site and to maintain it as one of the world's most unique art centers.

In from the Outside

In 1982, the restored site opened its doors to a now-eager public. The *Houston Press* described it as "the Acropolis of folk art sites in Houston." Since then, the Orange Show Center has expanded to include art classes and events such as Houston art car parades, Main Street Drag, and Eyeopener Tours. It is also responsible for the preservation of the Beer Can House, about eight miles away.

The Houston Art Car Parade is typical of the art inspired by the Orange Show. Art cars are often described as "rolling art" and include cars, bicycles, motorcycles, and roller skates. Each art car is decorated with paint and, usually, with objects as well, which can range from toys to beads to holiday lights to... well, almost anything.

Most of the art cars began as older streetcars; their owners have painted them, redesigned and remodeled the interiors, and added themed objects to the exterior surfaces. The results range from whimsical to dramatic, from breathtaking to absurd.

After a humble beginning in 1986 with an exhibit of a mere 11 vehicles, the Art Car Parade became official, and 21st-century events usually include more than 250 rolling works of art. The main route for the first and largest art car parade in the world is along Allen Parkway, about five miles northwest of the Orange Show.

McKissack's original, 3,000-square-foot design is called the Orange Show Monument. It's just a few blocks from I-45, known around Houston as the Gulf Freeway, which puts it about three miles from downtown Houston, a mile from the University of Houston, and a similar distance from Forest Park Cemetery. The monument is open to the public, but its schedule varies with the seasons.

Jeff McKissack described the Orange Show about as well as anyone could: "You could take 100,000 architects and 100,000 engineers and all of them put together couldn't conceive of a show like this."

How Did Texas Hold 'Em Get Its Name?

Tune in to any televised poker tournament, and the game most likely being played is Texas Hold 'Em, a "community" card game where players use any combination of the five face-up "community" cards and their own two "hole" cards to make a poker hand. But where did Texas Hold 'Em come from and get its popularity?

Some historians wager that poker originated in China around A.D. 900 when the Chinese developed many gambling games. Others bet it evolved from a German game called *Pochspiel* or the Persian card game *ganjifa*. The Spanish game *primero* is another possibility. Many historians, however, put their money on the idea that it started in France as *poque*. The French brought *poque* to the United States in the 1700s, where it evolved into the many variations played today.

The Lone Star Variation

The Texas State Legislature officially recognizes Robstown as the birthplace of Texas Hold 'Em, which was probably first played there in the late 1890s or early 1900s. As it spread to big cities such as Dallas in the 1920s, the game became popular with cowboys and miners as saloon entertainment. It was sometimes called Devil's River or Styx, which may explain why the final card in Texas Hold 'Em is traditionally called "the river."

The most popular explanation for Hold 'Em is that it was once called "Hold Me Darling" then shortened to "Hold Me" and finally dyslexically changed to "Hold 'Em." "Texas" was added in 1967 when Texas gamblers Crandell Addington, Doyle Brunson, and Amarillo Slim began playing it in Las Vegas.

In 1970, Benny and Jack Binion staged the World Series of Poker at their Horseshoe Casino in Las Vegas and made no-limit Texas Hold 'Em the main event the following year. With the televising of the World Series, it being featured in the movies *Rounders* and *Casino Royale,* and the advent of online gambling, Texas Hold 'Em has become the most popular poker game in the world.

Dr Pepper: Drink a Bite to Eat at 10, 2, and 4

When someone in Texas asks if anyone would like a Coke, consider the question generic. More often than not, they are talking Dr Pepper, a soda fountain flavor formula born at Waco's Old Corner Drugstore.

Long before carbonated beverages were bottled and branded, the only way that people could enjoy a sip of soda was to visit the neighborhood soda fountain. During the 1800s, soda fountains were often located inside pharmacies, much like today's fast food joints are sometimes paired up with convenience stores. It was a marriage of necessity, as fountains were ornate, imposing edifices that required maintenance and tweaking, and drinks had to be mixed on the spot.

Pulling Double Duty

In Texas, most small towns had a drugstore where the pharmacist was also what in later years became known as a "soda jerk," a name owing to the jerking motion exhibited when he pulled forward on the soda fountain's spigot. The druggist's specialty, of course, was to compound and dispense medicines, so mixing up the sweet syrups, roots, berries, and herbs that flavored sparkling, carbonated water was a natural offshoot for his talents. In fact, many of the earliest soft drinks were actually bitter concoctions, geared toward settling the stomach or treating a particular ailment.

In the town of Waco, a local flavor blend attained a certain measure of fame during these halcyon days. The story began with pharmacist Charles Alderton, an employee of Waco's Old Corner Drugstore. He was fascinated with the idea of the fountain and enjoyed devising new flavors to mix with the carbonated water. He also noticed that customers had a difficult time choosing one taste over another and saw the opportunity to create something special.

Alderton began to experiment with the palette of ingredients stocked at the store, and like a painter, he mixed them in myriad combinations. Drop by drop, sip by sip, through a painstaking method of trial and error, he succeeded in creating a particularly tasty syrup in 1885. Shop owner Wade Morrison tried the formula and approved of its tongue-tickling nuances.

A New Taste Is Born

Further refinements were made to the formula, which was willingly taste-tested by the local patrons. To Morrison and Alderton's delight, a collective "Aaah" of approval was the unanimous response, and Waco residents soon began to request the fountain specialty by name. At the time, however, it was known only as a "Waco." "Shoot me a Waco!" was the call to order, and soon, druggists east and west of the Brazos were hounding Morrison about purchasing jugs of syrup for their own shops.

To satisfy the demand, Morrison and Alderton began to mix up large batches of the syrup by themselves. Unfortunately, that wasn't enough. As the number of soda parlors that served the Waco swelled, the two realized that they needed a more efficient setup. Enter Texas bottler R. S. Lazenby: After some experimentation, he confirmed that the flavor was a prime candidate for large-scale bottling. Eager to ride the Waco's effervescent wave, he formed a new company called the Artesian Manufacturing & Bottling Company with the sole purpose of volume production. Lazenby packaged the drink exclusively for the growing retail market, and by 1891, he transformed what had been a pharmacist's experiment into a sweet gold mine.

A Now-Familiar Name

By then, the Waco nickname was deemed too local in its appeal, so the drink was renamed "Dr. Pepper's Phos-Ferrates." As historians report, this was a moniker inspired by a real Dr. Charles Pepper, who operated a pharmacy in Rural Retreat, Virginia, and had employed Wade Morrison during his early working years. As a tribute to his positive experiences at that pharmacy, Morrison adopted Pepper's surname for his new beverage. Some claim that Morrison was in love with Pepper's teenage daughter, a story long believed to be true but now disputed by Waco's Dr Pepper Museum and the present-day company. As that account goes, Pepper wasn't thrilled with his daughter's paramour and discouraged the romance. Dejected, Morrison said farewell to his love, left the pharmacy, and sought his fortune in the Lone Star State. Years later, when he named his popular drink Dr Pepper, it was in honor of his lost love.

Regardless of which story one might believe, there's no confusion when it comes to how successful Dr Pepper became. From these inauspicious Waco beginnings, the drink joined the pantheon of carbonated beverages to become one of the most adored brands of "pop" (a nickname derived from the sound the crude marble stopper made when the vacuum was released on an early bottle).

When Should One Drink Dr Pepper?

In the 1920s, the legend of Dr Pepper grew even further after Dr. Walter Eddy of Columbia University discovered that the human body experiences a natural energy drop at three key times of the day. He also discovered that if people had something to eat or drink, they could avoid the crash and stay alert. And so, ad men for the soft drink company came up with a campaign to promote Dr Pepper *as* that energy drink. Soon, the slogan "Drink a bite to eat at 10, 2, and 4" was synonymous with the brand. The familiar clock logo was molded into bottles and has remained a part of Dr Pepper iconography up to the present day, though the slogan has been mostly forgotten.

Indeed, Texans know that Dr Pepper—the original energy drink—is good at any hour of the day, especially if it's made with *real* cane sugar. And that's exactly how they make it down in Dublin, Texas, where the oldest Dr Pepper bottling plant in the world (open since 1891) cranks out case after case of high-fructose corn syrup–free Dr Pepper, packaged in eight-ounce bottles or 12-ounce cans. Die-hard fans and wannabees make the pilgrimage from all over the state to sample the "King of Beverages." Then they take home a case and pop the top on an authentic part of Texas history.

* *The name* Dr Pepper *had a period after* Dr *until 1950, when company officials decided the logo looked better without it.*

Fast Facts

- The Japanese bombed Texas twice during World War II. In March 1945, two of 9,000 balloon bombs sent aloft by Japan to start fires in the United States landed in Woodson and Desdemona. Neither harmed anything or anyone.

- Bevo X, the UT Longhorn mascot from 1976 to '81, became very stirred up during games and required cattle meds to stay calm. On one occasion, star UT tailback Earl Campbell ran into the tranquilized, reclining Bevo behind the end zone. Campbell bounded back up, but Bevo didn't even get up, much less charge Earl.

- Explorer Zebulon Pike visited old Béxar in 1807. He was given a warm welcome, but then he insulted the townspeople by saying that their main conversational topics were women, money, gambling, and horses. The Spaniards escorted him to Natchitoches, Louisiana, suggesting that he never return.

- One hand-pulled ferry still operates in the United States: It's at Los Ebaños, traveling between Texas and Mexico with up to three cars plus however many pedestrians can fit. Unfortunately, there's nothing to visit on the Mexican side. The crossing can take four to ten minutes, depending on the pullers' energy.

- Legendary NASCAR and Formula One racer A. J. Foyt of Houston died in a terrible 1965 wreck at Riverside International in California, at least according to the course doctor. Fortunately, fellow driver Parnelli Jones wasn't a credulous man. Seeing signs of life, Jones revived Foyt, who recovered and went on to huge success.

- Dallas-born actor Owen Wilson was once a St. Mark's School preppie. That ended when the exclusive school expelled him for (a) cheating on a geometry test, and (b) refusing to name any of his fellow cheaters.

- The United States was the first foreign country to recognize the Republic of Texas. What was the second? In 1839, France granted Texas most-favored-nation status and appointed a chargé d'affaires.

The Real Bonnie and Clyde

Bonnie and Clyde, Texas's most notorious outlaws, rose to fame during the Great Depression of the 1930s. The pair gained a mythical, Robin Hood–like status, but the real Bonnie and Clyde were very different from the figures portrayed by the popular media.

The early 1930s was a time when businesses folded at an unprecedented rate and plummeting crop prices forced farmers from their lands in record numbers. Men desperate for work trawled city streets looking for jobs, soup kitchens were swamped, and the value of a dollar plunged. When Bonnie and Clyde began their crime spree, the public viewed them as outsiders fighting back against an uncaring system that had failed the working man.

Where They Started

Bonnie Parker was born on October 1, 1910, in Rowena. When she met Clyde Barrow in 1930, she was already married to a man used to being on the wrong side of the law. However, Bonnie was not a typical gangster's moll. She was an honor-roll student in high school who excelled in creative writing and even won a spelling championship. After her husband was sentenced to the penitentiary, Bonnie scraped together a living by working as a waitress in West Dallas. Then Clyde Barrow entered her life.

Clyde was born on March 24, 1909, in Telico, just south of Dallas, and spent more of his poverty-stricken youth in trouble with the law than he did in school. He was arrested for stealing turkeys, auto theft, and safecracking. Soon after his romance with Bonnie began, he was sentenced to two years for a number of burglaries and car thefts. Bonnie managed to smuggle a Colt revolver to him, and Clyde was able to escape with his cell mate, William Turner.

A Life on the Run

Clyde and Turner were soon recaptured and sentenced to 14 years at the Texas State Penitentiary. But Clyde was pardoned in February 1932 after his mother intervened and Clyde had had a fellow inmate chop off two of his toes in order to garner sympathy.

After two months of attempting to go straight, Clyde started a crime spree with Bonnie that stretched from Texas to Oklahoma, Missouri, Iowa, New Mexico, and Louisiana. They robbed gas stations, liquor stores, banks, and jewelry stores. They also captured the public imagination by frequently taking hostages as they made their daring escapes and then releasing them unharmed when they were out of danger. Other outlaws came and went from the Barrow Gang, but it was only after several of the robberies culminated in murder that public opinion turned against Bonnie and Clyde.

In total, the Barrow Gang is believed to have murdered at least nine police officers and several civilians during their robberies. While Bonnie posed alongside Clyde clutching a machine gun for photos, many argue that at no time did she ever fire a weapon, let alone kill or injure anyone. Another popular misconception had her dubbed as the cigar-smoking moll of the Barrow Gang. Again, Bonnie was known to smoke only cigarettes, but she once posed with a cigar in what became a famous photograph.

Bonnie and Clyde Are Finished

The end came on May 23, 1934, along a desolate road in Bienville Parish, Louisiana. The gang had murdered two Texas police officers, so Bonnie and Clyde were on the run again. A posse of four Texas Rangers and two Louisiana officers waited patiently for hours near the gang's hideout. When Bonnie and Clyde pulled up, the lawmen opened fire, pumping 167 rounds into the outlaws' car. So many gunshots hit the pair that the fingers on Bonnie's right hand were blown away. At the time of their deaths, Bonnie was 23 years old; Clyde, 24.

* *The last survivor of the Barrow Gang, W. D. Jones, died on August 20, 1974, in Houston. He was killed in a shotgun barrage following a disagreement. Earlier, after the gang's 1930s crime spree, Jones had served six years in prison.*

Standing Watch

A tribute to ancient Chinese history makes its unlikely home in the suburbs of Houston.

Six thousand terra-cotta soldiers stand silently in the Houston suburb of Katy. Nearby, a very precise 1:20 model of the Forbidden City awes visitors as they stroll beneath a 40,000-square-foot pavilion. Additional exhibits explore 24 Chinese emperors from the 14th century to the modern day.

From Hong Kong to Houston

All this belongs to Ira P. H. Poon, a former teacher in Hong Kong who made his fortune by investing in real estate. After moving to Seattle, Poon wanted to create a tribute to his homeland. He chose the Houston area because it is the home of a huge Asian population and the heat is similar to Beijing.

Poon began his project in 1997, when he spent about $20 million to purchase and develop 80 acres near Houston. The Forbidden Gardens are a 20-year project and will eventually include the Great Wall of China, as well.

Most of the Gardens' replicas are built in China using traditional wood, brick, tiles, and bamboo. Like the originals, no nails are used in construction, only notches and glue. Every detail is accurate, including the north-south orientation of the replica Forbidden City.

Tops for Chinese Tourists

Poon is passionate about his country's history, and his fellow Chinese seem to feel the same way. Texas's Forbidden Gardens are among the top American attractions for visitors from China. After watching a 22-minute video, visitors follow an escorted, one-hour tour. Guests must keep up with their guide. They may not roam the Forbidden Gardens on their own, and they also may not circle back to see the exhibits a second time. Despite these quirky limits, most visitors recommend the Forbidden Gardens. They're a tribute to Chinese history and one man's enthusiasm for his Chinese heritage.

Ludicrous Laws

- Public buildings in El Paso, such as stores, banks, hotels, railroad and bus depots, and churches, are required to supply spittoons for those who chew tobacco (or don't but just need to spit anyway).

- It's against the law in Dallas to throw anything out the window or door of a tall building.

- The Texas Supreme Court allows public funds to pay for utilities and ice for the governor's mansion but not for groceries and personal items.

- Although the law specifically states that "no religious test shall ever be required as qualification to any office," politicians must acknowledge a supreme being to hold public office in the state of Texas. No particular supreme being is identified, however, so all those followers of Zeus, Apollo, Poseidon, and the rest of the Greek pantheon can step right up.

- Elevators must be odor-free in Abilene.

- There can be no late-night parties or Irish wakes in the city cemeteries of Brownsville, as the consumption or possession of alcohol is illegal there. It is, however, legal to bury a bottle of whiskey with the deceased.

- City ordinances in El Paso prohibit "a person from playing ball, shinny [a form of ice hockey] or any other games or skating on or along any street in the city."

- Parking lot owners in Grapevine can be fined for endangering public health and safety and charged with a misdemeanor offense if their lots emit dust, sand, or dirt.

- Love Limburger cheese? Don't try to buy it on Sunday in Houston. It's illegal for stores to sell it.

- It's against the law for someone to drive a horse and buggy through the town square of Temple. But if that same person wants to unhook the buggy and saddle up the horse, it's perfectly legal there to ride that horse into the saloon.

- Keep your hands to yourself! It's illegal to milk someone else's cow.

Swinging the Night Away

It's country music—like Duke Ellington might have played it. Or jazz, played by a Grand Ole Opry star. Mix them together, throwing in a wailing fiddle, a touch of polka, and a bit of blues and folk. Then give it a pop shine, and it becomes one of America's unique musical art forms—Western Swing.

Born in the heart of Texas and still enjoyed throughout the United States, the dance-oriented country-music sound known as Western Swing came out of the honky-tonks and dance halls favored by hard-working Texans in the 1920s and '30s, places that offered a welcome relief from the oil fields and cattle ranches. The music was upbeat, rhythmic, and infectious, and it got people on their feet.

A Familiar Sound

The biggest name in Western Swing is Bob Wills, the Texan who helped invent the stuff and reigned for decades as its most popular performer. Wills, a native of Turkey in West Texas, took up the fiddle as a child. In search of a career in music, he set off for Fort Worth in the early '30s, where he picked up work playing at parties. With a new friend, singer Milton Brown, he landed a job at radio station KFJZ. The

two were hired, along with pianist Alton Stricklin, by the sales manager of the Burrus Mills flour company and dubbed The Light Crust Doughboys, after the company's most famous product.

Forming the Playboys

The Doughboys played a daily radio show, cut a couple of records in 1932 as the Fort Worth Doughboys, and then broke up, leaving three groups in their wake. Wills launched his own band, the Texas Playboys, in Waco, while Brown and his group, the Musical Brownies, continued to rule in Fort Worth. Under new management, The Light Crust Doughboys also continued to flourish. Looking to expand, Wills and his Playboys struck out for fresh territory—Tulsa, Oklahoma, where they became a fixture at a local ballroom named Cain's.

Although personnel shifted several times, the group eventually consisted of Wills, his cousin Johnnie Lee Wills on banjo, fiddler Jesse Ashlock, drummer Smokey Dacus, steel guitar player—a first in country music—Leon McAuliffe, and Wills's old friend, pianist Alton Stricklin. They began to record in 1935, and the rest is history. Milton Brown, who some argue might also have had a claim to the crown of the King of Western Swing, died too young after an auto accident in 1936. The future of Western Swing, then, lay with Wills and the Texas Playboys. The band drew crowds of 6,000 to their nightly performances at Cain's until 1943. They were broadcast regularly across the country over Tulsa's 50,000-watt powerhouse KVOO radio until late in the 1950s, and they had a slew of hit records over the years, such as "San Antonio Rose," "Take Me Back to Tulsa," "Faded Love," and "Milk Cow Blues."

Widening the Music's Reach

In the '30s and early '40s, Western Swing moved to California with Depression-era migrants. By the 1940s, Western Swing had grown a huge following in California, with stars such as Wills playing venues around the state. Among the literally scores of popular West Coast performers were singer Spade Cooley (who later became notorious for viciously murdering his wife), Hank Thompson and his Brazos Valley Boys, Tex Williams and his Western Caravan, and Dude Martin and his Roundup Boys. The Los Angeles County Barn Dance at the Venice Pier drew 10,000 fans to dances in the early '40s.

Western Swing hasn't remained the popular powerhouse it once was, of course, but its influence can be found in the music of dozens of artists, from bands such as Asleep at the Wheel and the Time Jumpers to Elvis, Willie Nelson, Merle Haggard, Lyle Lovett, and George Strait. It's continuing strong today, with young bands still playing Western Swing to appreciative new audiences from California to Nashville—and, of course, in Texas.

Sprechen Sie Texas?

Out-of-staters may not be aware of it, but Texas has been home to a vital German community since before there even was a Texas.

Faced with economic hardships and political unrest, thousands of Germans emigrated to Texas beginning in the 1840s, lured by an early settler's widely circulated reports of fertile soil, great weather, abundant food, and political freedom.

In 1842, a group of wealthy and influential Germans formed the Adelsverein, an organization that encouraged emigration to Texas and purchased three million acres of Central Texas land to help make that happen. By the turn of the 20th century, more than 200,000 German immigrants were in Texas, fully 6 percent of the state's population.

Teutonic Influence

Founding cities such as New Braunfels and Fredericksburg, Germans became one of the largest and most important ethnic groups in Texas history. In the course of that history, their native German language adapted to their new home, in time becoming a unique Texas-German dialect that was widely spoken until the 1970s.

Today, much of that culture survives. Fredericksburg's annual Oktoberfest draws 10,000 people to town, while New Braunfels hosts 100,000 visitors each November for its Wurstfest—both traditional German fall festivals given over to food, beer, music, and fun.

Sadly, the Texas German dialect is fading, no longer passed on from one generation to the next. But a serious effort is underway to preserve it. The Germanic Studies Department at the University of Texas hosts the Texas German Dialect Project (TGDP), which interviews dialect speakers and archives transcriptions and other material in an attempt to save this unique language. It also chronicles Texas German history and gives educational presentations to help keep one of Texas's most unusual traditions alive.

The 1900 Flood: More than Galveston

Many remember Hurricane Katrina with horror, but the 1900 Galveston hurricane and flood did far more widespread damage.

Galveston is an island city that basks in the sun about an hour southeast of Houston. Nearby, vacationing families enjoy the Houston Space Center, Moody Gardens, Armand Bayou Nature Center, Kemah Boardwalk, and the Forbidden Gardens. Every three years or so, Galveston can expect a brush with a major storm. Every ten years, it's likely to receive a direct hurricane hit. Usually, the city breezes through those storms with ease. But September 8, 1900, was another story.

Unprepared and Vulnerable

In 1900, tropical storms and hurricanes weren't assigned names. Galveston residents knew that bad weather was coming, but the U.S. Weather Bureau discouraged use of terms such as *hurricane*. In addition, geographers claimed that the slope of the sea bottom protected the city against harsh ocean conditions. Galveston, the fourth-most-populous city in the state at the time, didn't even have a seawall.

By the time the Category 4 hurricane hit the city, fewer than half its residents had evacuated. In fact, the city was busy with tourists who'd arrived to enjoy the warm gulf waters and watch the eerie, oncoming clouds.

To date, Galveston's 1900 flood, which resulted from that storm, is America's worst natural disaster, killing approximately 8,000 people with a 15-foot storm surge that destroyed roughly half of Galveston's homes and businesses and devastated the surrounding area. The flood has been the subject of books, movies, and songs. In 1904, crowds lined up to see the "Galveston Flood" attraction at New York's Coney Island. Most people don't realize, however, that the storm's damage extended far beyond Galveston.

A Wide Swath

During the 18-hour storm, the winds were so intense that tele-graph lines as far away as Abilene—more than 300 miles from Galveston—were leveled. Between the Gulf of Mexico and Abilene, the 1900 storm snapped trees and crushed houses. On J. E. Dick's ranch near Galveston, 2,500 cattle drowned. Throughout East Texas, cities and towns were destroyed. Katy is just one of them.

Today, Katy is an upscale community about 25 miles west of Houston and 60 miles inland from Galveston. Before the Europeans arrived, it was a winter feeding ground for buffalo and a major hunt-ing ground of the Karankawa. By the late 19th century, settlers had built farms and other businesses there. Katy—or "KT"—was named for the MKT (Missouri, Kansas, and Texas) railroad line that termi-nated in the area.

The 1900 hurricane, however, almost wiped Katy off the map. Only two houses were undamaged when the winds blew through the town's streets and swept homes and businesses from their founda-tions. Today, those two homes—Featherston House and Wright House—are part of Katy Heritage Park.

Houston was also in the storm's path. Much of the area's economy relied on farms and ranches that were ill prepared for the devastation that was coming. Winds and rising waters destroyed almost every barn in the hurricane's path. Waters up to ten feet deep flooded local pastures. Across East Texas, entire forests were crushed. One news reporter observed "no large timber left standing as far as the eye can see."

From there, it's not clear whether the storm headed due north or if it doubled back. Many believe it retraced its path to the Florida Keys and then continued up the East Coast. By the time it reached New York City, the winds were still raging at 65 mph.

Digging Out

In the aftermath of the storm, the Galveston community dredged sand to raise the city up to 17 feet above sea level. The city also built a 17-foot-tall seawall to protect it from storm surges. Likewise, Houston and the cities around it improved drainage and created reservoirs and flood plains to absorb the water from future storms that were sure to come.

Bucks and Brahmas on Blades: The Birth of Hockey in Texas

Athletes attired in helmets and pads, balanced on blades of steel, and lugging lancelike weapons would seem a natural fit in Texas, where success in sport is symbolic with survival. Still, no one could have expected that a hot-air state in the sun-drenched South would embrace a game synonymous with cold, ice, and snow.

The birth of ice hockey in Texas began when Dallas entrepreneur Clarence E. Linz cashed in on the success of two spectacles that were sweeping the nation in the late 1930s. The sport of ice hockey, with its gridironlike physical contact and blazing speed, was gaining popularity from Hollywood to the hinterlands. Even John Wayne had appeared in a hockey movie, which suggested the Duke endorsed the flashing and bashing sport. Also, figure skating princess and movie star maven Sonja Henie and her extravagant Ice Capades shows were selling out across the country. Linz outfitted Dallas's Fair Park Arena—the home of the state fair pig races—with a regulation-size ice surface to promote hockey and Henie.

Overexpansion?

Linz was also instrumental in helping establish a hockey franchise in Fort Worth. Both the Dallas Texans and the Fort Worth Rangers joined the American Hockey Association in 1941. The fledgling sport was advertised as "the most dangerous game in the world...murder on ice...with flashing blades and crashing bodies." After a four-year hiatus because of World War II, hockey returned to Texas with a third Texas team from Houston. Rising costs and travel expenses, however, caused all three clubs to fold after the 1949–50 season. Hockey didn't return to the state until 1967, but it has exploded in popularity since then. Today, the number of professional teams in the state of Texas—including the Texas Brahmas and Loredo Bucks—extends into double digits.

Cadillac Ranch

Although it's no longer on Route 66, the Cadillac Ranch has become almost as famous an icon as the old highway itself, symbolizing America's continuing love affair with the automobile, the freedom of travel it affords, and whatever excesses the journey might bring.

Paris has the Eiffel Tower; Rome, the Colosseum; and China, its Great Wall. In West Texas, Amarillo's claim to fame is the Cadillac Ranch, an impressive roadside monument to motoring that's caused passing cars to stop and wonder for more than 30 years now.

Ironically, the curious car-sculpture-turned-tourist-attraction came to life in 1974 at the height of the Arab oil embargo, when gasoline dried up at service stations nationwide. While car owners fumed in long gas lines waiting for their ration of fuel, Texas helium mogul and millionaire Stanley Marsh 3 (he thought Roman numerals pretentious) commissioned a San Francisco artists group (which called itself the Ant Farm) to create the ostentatious sculpture for his Amarillo ranch. The medium? Cadillacs—real automobiles. The canvas was a dusty wheat field.

The Ant Farm Goes to Work

Artists Doug Michels, Chip Lord, and Hudson Marquez jointly labored on the project, collecting both running and derelict Caddies from around the panhandle area. Models representing the "Golden Age" of American automobiles from 1949 through 1963 were chosen. It's no coincidence that this span highlighted the birth and death of the tail fin, the Cadillac's most defining feature. After all, the tail fin represented America, the space race, and the nation's emergence to prosperity during the 1950s. It was the perfect symbolism for a sculpture constructed with full-scale automobiles.

To anchor the cars, massive eight-foot holes were dug into the Texas prairie. The vehicles were put to rest, nose down, and were positioned so that they would face west, at the same angle as the Great Pyramid of Cheops in Egypt.

Location, Location, Location

Because Marsh's homage to the Cadillac was located directly along America's famed "Main Street," U.S. Route 66, there was no shortage of gawkers speeding past. The Stonehenge-esque assemblage quickly gained a loyal following. Photographs were taken of it, articles written about it, songs sung about it, and movies made that featured it. If you planned to motor west on Route 66, making a pilgrimage to see the fins was a must.

Relocation, Relocation, Relocation

In 1997, Marsh became worried that Amarillo's urban sprawl would endanger his beloved Caddies, so he had the pop art homage to Detroit steel quietly moved two miles further to the west, along Interstate 40 (which replaced the original Mother Road in Texas). The only evidence left behind at the original site was ten huge holes. It was an eerie reminder of the death of Route 66 itself, decommissioned a dozen years earlier.

Today, Cadillac Ranch continues to draw the curious. Although located on private property, it's easy to access: Just drive along the frontage road, and enter the pasture through an unlocked gate. Part of the ritual of visiting Cadillac Ranch is to leave a personal touch on the decaying cars with spray paint, a practice that Marsh doesn't seem to mind. Be sure to bring along a can.

As the seasons change and the travelers come and go, the Cadillacs mutate through a range of colors and messages—left by modern-day explorers out to discover the off-the-wall attractions that bring life to the roadside carnival.

• *Many people fought over barbed wire in Texas back in the old days. Along old Route 66 at McLean, there's a Devil's Rope Museum, named for one of the kinder epithets used to describe the wire.*

Top Texas Snake Legends

Snakes are a favorite topic when Texas storytellers tell tall tales by the campfire. Here are a few stories that may not be entirely true, but Texans will assure campers that they're darn near factual.

Eternal snakes: The Karankawa people lived along Texas's Gulf coast and believed that some snakes never died. According to their lore, rattlesnakes do not grow old and, unless deliberately killed by a human or animal, will live forever.

The fatal boots: A Texas cowboy wore his new snakeskin boots to court the prettiest girl in town, but he died days later. He left his boots to his best friend, who also died after wearing them with the same young lady. When a third victim died, the coroner found a venomous rattlesnake fang embedded in the lining of the boots.

The 50-rattle rattlesnake: According to legend, settlers along Texas's Colorado River killed a rattlesnake more than ten feet long with 50 rattles on its tail.

The longest rattlesnakes in Texas: In the summer of 1877, a Dallas newspaper reported an 18-foot snake in a rural area northwest of San Antonio; its tail had 37 different rattles.

The fattest rattlesnake: In the mid-1840s, a tiger hunter was touring Texas and sat down to rest on what he thought was a fallen tree. That "tree" turned out to be a rattlesnake about a foot and a half across and 17 feet long.

The second-fattest rattlesnake: Around 1840 near the Nueces River, explorers found a rattlesnake as big around as the thigh of an average man and at least nine feet long.

Flying snakes: Texas's flying snake legends date to before Europeans arrived in North America. In June 2008, a flying snake appeared in video footage from a security camera in Lajitas.

Urban legend: In 2005, a rattlesnake caught in Fritch reportedly weighed 97 pounds. Critics claim that it weighed "only" 34.25 pounds.

Bragging Rights

Dallas Cowboy Stadium: Texans love football and many are especially proud of Dallas's NFL team, the Cowboys. In fact, this love was proved in 2009 with the opening of the new three-million-square-foot stadium in Arlington. The largest NFL venue ever built, the arena boasts the largest column-free room in the world, measuring a quarter mile in length. The expansive retractable roof is also the world's largest and measures 660,800 square feet. It is supported by two arches soaring 292 feet above the playing field. If that isn't enough, the stadium also has the world's largest end-zone doors, comprised of five 38-foot panels. A one-of-a-kind video display board hangs 90 feet above the field, and its largest panels measure 72 feet tall and 160 feet wide. The stadium site covers 73 acres, just enough for Cowboy fans. The arena is the ultimate in Texas grandeur.

Brewster County: The biggest county in Texas is located out west in the Trans-Pecos region. It covers more than 6,000 square miles, 42 times the area of the smallest county, Rockwall, and five times the area of Rhode Island. The county has been home to the mercury-mining industry and cattle ranching since the 1800s. It is home to Big Bend National Park and boasts many of Texas's native flora and fauna. The Great Camel Experiment caravan traveled through Brewster County on its way to finding sites for building forts. Today, visitors enjoy the area's natural scenery and laid-back lifestyle.

Port Lavaca Fishing Pier: The 3,200-foot pier, which formerly served as a causeway across Lavaca Bay, is the centerpiece of a 1.8-acre park in Calhoun County and the longest pier in the United States. Another bridge was built across the bay in the early 1960s, and the old bridge was turned over to the Texas Department of Parks and Recreation. The park at the base of the pier offers a boat ramp and picnic facilities, and the main pier has been joined by two smaller versions. The length and width of the span and the additional lighting added by the parks department make the pier the perfect destination for day and nighttime fishing.

The *Belle* Shipwreck

*Mired in gook for more than three centuries, a 17th-century
shipwreck provides a unique window into Texas's past.*

In 1995, a team of researchers led by the Texas
Historical Commission found a sunken vessel
in the mud of Matagorda Bay. This in itself
was not unusual. The area had given up
scores of wrecked ships in the past,
each a slowly rotting testament to the
ravages of the sea. But this one was
different. It dated back to 1687 and was
remarkably intact. Better still, it was one of
four vessels sailed by French explorer René-Robert Cavelier Sieur de
La Salle. Although the adventurer's goal to start a coast colony never
materialized, the archaeological bonanza left in the ship's wake proved
to be worth its weight in gold.

Stroke of Luck

While a tale of accidental discovery would surely add to the drama,
the *Belle* was not found by chance. The Texas Historical Commission
knew that the ship rested somewhere in Matagorda Bay; a Spanish
map drawn up in 1689 hinted at its location. But it wasn't until
1995 and the advent of geographical positioning systems that the
ship was finally unearthed—quite literally—from the gooey seabed.
Ironically, it was this muck encasing the *Belle* that had saved it from
bacterial attack, thus preserving the vessel and its priceless artifacts.

Treasure Trove

Pottery, glass beads, bronze cannon, hawk bells, and other items were
recovered alongside organic materials such as bone, wood, rope, and
cloth. Even the skeletal remains of an unlucky crew member came up
with the eclectic treasure trove. In all, over one million pieces were
recovered in what is considered one of the most important shipwrecks
ever discovered in North America. A vast number of *Belle* artifacts are
displayed at the Texas State History Museum in Austin.

Fast Facts

- When looking for examples of how to do business, one could do no better than Ninnie Baird. This Fort Worth baker grew a small operation into a large, thriving multicity company, making Mrs. Baird's Bread synonymous with quality and generous philanthropy—and a great Texas tradition.

- The only Texas Aggie to win the Heisman Trophy was John David Crow in 1957. Coach Bear Bryant said that if Crow didn't win the Heisman, they ought to stop giving it out. When A&M's chancellor called Crow with the invitation, modest John's first thought was that he was in big trouble.

- One of the early unsung Texas oilmen was Luis de Moscoso Alvarado, who found black gold on the water off the Texas coast during a storm in 1543. Unfortunately for Luis, his expedition only found it useful to caulk their flatboats. If he'd just built an offshore rig…

- Robert E. Lee's much-loved Texas Brigade (1st, 4th, and 5th Texas Infantry regiments) was never all Texan. At various times it included regiments from Georgia, South Carolina, and (for the entire second half of the Civil War) the 3rd Arkansas Infantry.

- Jerry Hunt of Waco showed some early signs of his future electronic/occult music ways. He was only 14 when he joined the Rosicrucians, a mail-order spiritual house based in San Jose, California. Before long he was advertising "the path of the infinite" by mail order in the local paper.

- The message of the Mineral Wells Washing Machine Museum: Don't take those convenient appliances for granted. More than 50 antique machines, including old washboards, are on display. Gaze upon the way they did it old school, and respect great-grandma.

- Singer Janis Joplin came from a very conservative religious family in Port Arthur. No doubt her mother, who taught Sunday school, knew something was wrong when young Janis started preferring Southern Comfort over spiritual comfort.

When Cattlemen Party

*Working cattle can be an extremely tough job—anyone who's
not sure should try it sometime. And hard workers need a way
to let off some steam. Cattle barons need balls of their own.*

Television viewers who watched *Dallas* in the 1980s—and that was
just about everyone, wasn't it?—will recall the Oil Baron's Ball as
one of the show's annual high points. Whether it was Cliff Barnes
biting J. R. Ewing during fisticuffs in the midst of the black-tie
event, or J. R. announcing Bobby and Jenna's wedding while Bobby's
ex-wife Pam looked on in horror, the ball was always the scene of big
melodrama, big diamonds, and big hair.

The Cattle Baron's Ball

In fact, the Oil Baron's Ball was a Hollywood
version of a long-standing Dallas charity
event, the Cattle Baron's Ball. A fixture
on the Dallas social scene since 1974,
the ball is the nation's single largest one-
day fund-raiser for the American Cancer
Society and the inspiration for nearly two
dozen other Cattle Baron's Balls around
the country.

   While the Ewing family and friends
(and enemies) were decked out in black
tie and ball gowns, the Cattle Baron's Ball is
all about open collars, designer jeans, custom
cowboy boots, and ten-gallon hats that cost more than a horse.

   Why the informality? One of the founders, Jacque Wynne,
recalls that way back in 1974, she and her friends went door to door
with baskets to solicit donations for cancer research. A party seemed
like an easier way to go, but her husband suggested a non–black-tie
event as a sure way to enlist the support of Dallas men. She had her
doubts—"Cowboy wasn't cool back then," she says—but he proved to
be correct.

The first ball, to which only the city's elite were invited, was a huge success, and the event has only grown in stature and profitability over the years. Now, thousands of well-heeled—if casually dressed—Dallas socialites attend one of the city's premier social events, chugging long-necks, slurping barbecue, swaying and stomping to country music, and spending freely, very freely, at an eye-popping live auction—a hoe-down that in true Texas tradition is proudly over the top.

Bigger and Better

The party is legendary for its big budget—in 2007 organizers spent $1.5 million—and its big ticket price. The 2007 party required one entire 18-wheeler full of liquor and another full of 1,200 cases of beer. Couples shelled out $2,500 to attend. And that's not even counting what they bid on: such trinkets as a $58,000 diamond neck-lace, a $143,000 Mercedes, and a visit to football training camp with NFL great Roger Staubach. That year, the ball gave $3.16 million to the American Cancer Society.

In 2008, the numbers were even bigger (hey, this is Texas). Four thousand merrymakers descended on Southfork Ranch (yes, *that* Southfork, a major tourist destination in Dallas even after all these years) for the 35th annual gala, which raised more than $4 million for cancer research.

Forget society dance bands—two-steppers at this party danced to tunes provided by the Country Music Association's Duo of the Year, Sugarland, on one of two stages erected for the party. In addition to a silent auction, a live auction netted big proceeds from an evening of poker, steaks, and cigars with Troy Aikman, Emmitt Smith, Daryl Johnston, Michael Irvin, and Jay Novacek ($60,000); an Iron Chef barbecue event with the city's finest chefs ($50,000); a single-malt Scotch package tour of Scotland ($22,500); and dinner with the Trumps in New York ($20,000).

Planning for the next ball begins before the sound trucks have packed up and the decorations have come down from the most recent one. A virtual army of volunteers works year-round on the high-profile event, and a full schedule of subsidiary parties are planned throughout the year. You're really a Texan, they say, when you've gone to a Cattle Baron's Ball. And if you're asked to chair a Cattle Baron's Ball commit-tee, then you've really arrived in Dallas society.

A Few Favorite Texas Sayings and Adages

An adage is a brief saying that lingers in the memory long after it's spoken. Here are some of Texas's best.

- A squeaky wheel gets the grease, but a quacking duck gets shot.
- You can put your boots in the oven, but that don't make 'em biscuits.
- Just because a chicken has wings doesn't mean it can fly.
- Only a fool argues with a skunk, a mule, or a cook.
- Don't worry 'bout the mule, son, just load the wagon.
- The bigger the mouth, the better it looks when shut.
- Don't call him a cowboy 'til you've seen him ride.
- Kicking never gets you nowhere, unless you're a mule.
- The cowboy that straddles the fence gets a sore crotch.
- It's time to paint your butt white and run with the antelope.
- You can't stomp a snake with both feet in the bucket.
- If you lie down with dogs, you get up with fleas.
- If you can't run with the big dogs, stay on the porch.
- Give him an inch and he'll take a mile—and you'll pay the freight.
- Don't hang your wash on someone else's line.
- Don't wet on my leg and tell me it's rainin'.
- Dance with the one that brung you.
- She's happy as a puppy with two tails.
- It's hotter than hell with the lid screwed down.
- I'm hungry enough to eat a cast-iron skillet.
- He doesn't have the sense God gave a monkey wrench.
- She's as nervous as a politician on Judgment Day.
- That's as rare as fangs on a duck.

Texas Timeline

Continued from p. 87)

March 19, 1840
In what will come to be known as
the Council House Fight, more
than 30 Comanche are slaugh-
tered while attempting to negotiate a prisoner exchange in San
Antonio.

December 29, 1845
Texas becomes the 28th state to
join the United States of America.

February 21, 1846
Former president and army commander General Sam Houston
is elected to the U.S. Senate,
becoming one of the first to represent the new state.

April 23, 1846
Mexico declares war on the United
States four months after Texas is
annexed.

February 2, 1848
The Mexican-American War ends
with the signing of the treaty of
Guadalupe Hidalgo, whose terms
require Mexico to cede much
of what is now the American
Southwest to the United States.

December 24, 1852
The *General Sherman* becomes
the first locomotive in Texas when
it chugs into Galveston along
the newly constructed tracks of
the Buffalo Bayou, Brazos, and
Colorado Railway Company.

August 9, 1857
The first stagecoach employed to
carry mail from Texas to the West
Coast leaves San Antonio bound
for San Diego.

September 2, 1858
Firth, Pond & Company copyright
"The Yellow Rose of Texas." The
song is recorded in the 1950s
and reaches #1 on the Billboard
charts.

March 2, 1861
Texas secedes from the Union
after citizens vote overwhelmingly
to join the Confederacy.

September 12, 1866
Lyne Barret and the Melrose
Petroleum Oil Company are the first
to strike oil in Texas. The well, which
finds oil at a depth of 106 feet,
produces ten barrels a day.

February 11, 1869
The *Mittie Stephens,* a 300-foot
sternwheeler plying the waters of
Caddo Lake, catches fire. In all,
some 63 passengers drown, get
trampled, or are crushed by the
paddle wheel in an attempt to flee
the flames.

March 30, 1870
President Ulysses S. Grant signs
a bill readmitting Texas to the
Union, with the provision that the
state ratifies the 13th, 14th, and
15th amendments. Texas is the
last Confederate state readmitted
into the United States after the
Civil War.

November 24, 1874
Illinois resident Joseph Glidden
receives a patent for barbed
wire. Glidden's invention will soon
be strung across the length and
breadth of Texas, as well as much
of the Southwest.

Continued on p. 165)

The Macabre Museum to the JFK Assassination

The Texas School Book Depository and Dealey Plaza carry a certain amount of baggage in some circles. And they're open for visitors.

The assassination of John F. Kennedy was one of the most significant events of the 20th century, and its site is one of the most visited spots in North Texas. More than six million visitors have come to downtown Dallas to learn more about the event or relive memories of that unforgettable day. Some are lured by the macabre nature of the exhibits and the conspiracy theories surrounding the assassination.

Very quickly after Kennedy was assassinated, evidence was found that shots had been fired from the sixth floor of the Texas School Book Depository building by Lee Harvey Oswald. As time passed, it only seemed natural to memorialize the location with a museum dedicated to the life, times, death, and legacy of JFK.

Planning the Museum

In 1972, the idea to locate the museum in the School Book Depository building was met with mixed reactions. Many felt that the memories were too painful and that the building should be torn down altogether. Others were concerned that the museum would be viewed as a memorial to an assassin rather than JFK. Conover Hunt, the founding director, continued to lobby for the museum despite public outcry. Just as it looked as if the city council was going to give its approval in 1981, John Hinckley attempted to assassinate President Ronald Reagan. Hinckley had grown up in Dallas, and the local ties begged comparison to Oswald. The museum was delayed again.

The Dream Is Realized

Finally, on Presidents' Day 1989, the Sixth Floor Museum was opened as a direct response to the number of visitors coming to learn more about the assassination and see the sites where the events took place. Exhibits were designed to highlight the impact of

Kennedy's death on the nation and the world. Two key areas where evidence was found were restored to their 1963 appearance.

On Presidents' Day 2002, the museum expanded to include a gallery for temporary exhibits, special events, and public programs. The current collection holds 35,000 items including manuscripts, documents, photographs, film, audio recordings, newspapers and magazines, and oral histories. These are a few of the most popular exhibits:

- The Abraham Zapruder Collection, which contains the world-famous silent, 8mm film of the Kennedy motorcade just before, during, and after the shooting.

- The Orville Nix Collection, containing his film of the motorcade shot from Dealey Plaza, the opposite angle of the Zapruder film.

- The Jay Skaggs Collection, consisting of 20 slides taken by an amateur photographer in Dealey Plaza just before and immediately after the shooting.

- The Phil Willis Collection, representing the most extensive record of the day's event in Dealey Plaza with 30 color slides, including a single photo of JFK as he was shot that has been studied by investigators and researchers.

- The KDFW, KTVT, and WFAA collections that include 250 hours of news coverage related to the assassination.

- The Parkland Hospital Collection, including medical reports, doctors' summaries, administrative reports, and employees' recollections of the events the day of the assassination.

- The JFK Funeral Ephemera Collection, featuring invitations, menus, place cards, escort badges, and programs.

Museum visitors are led through the exhibits by an audio tour that incorporates excerpts from historic radio broadcasts and the voices of the reporters, police officers, and witnesses commenting on JFK's legacy. The narrator is Pierce Allman, the first journalist to broadcast from the Texas School Book Depository on that fateful day.

The museum is nonprofit and receives all its revenue from ticket sales. And despite its macabre exhibits, the museum continues to be the second-most visited historical site in Texas behind the Alamo, proving that the legacy of JFK and the public fascination with the circumstances surrounding his death are eternal.

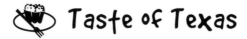

Taste of Texas

Just the facts on Tex-Mex:

- Tex-Mex originated hundreds of years ago when Spanish and Mexican recipes combined with Anglo European fare. As modern Americans know it, Tex-Mex is a 20th-century phenomenon. Food historians note the first printed use of the term was in the 1940s. The contemporary Tex-Mex fad began in the 1970s, when Diana Kennedy published her popular cookbook *The Cuisine of Mexico.*

- Chili is a truly Texan invention, undoubtedly arising from the ample supply of beef in the state. The dish was unknown in Mexico.

- Nachos are another Tex-Mex original, supposedly first served at a concession stand at Dallas's State Fair in 1964.

- Fajitas were introduced at Ninfa's restaurant in Houston on July 13, 1973, as tacos al carbon. Food experts aren't sure when the name *fajita*—which means *girdle* or *strip* in Spanish—began to be used.

- The debut of Frito Pie may not have come immediately on the heels of the introduction of Fritos, but it didn't miss by much. Both were invented in Depression-era San Antonio. In 1932, C. E. "Elmer" Doolin discovered home-fried corn chips in a Mexican café. He borrowed $100 from his mother, Daisy Doolin, for the chip's recipe and the right to market it. Fritos were soon being sold throughout the South. Daisy Doolin poured chili on a bed of the corn chips and invented Frito Pie—a Texas favorite at cookouts, tailgating parties, and even trendy restaurants for more than half a century.

- Not all Tex-Mex recipes have gone on to wide popularity. A dish from West Texas, *morcilla,* involves cooking pig blood inside the animal's cleaned-out stomach, then frying it with chile, chopped onions, and tomatoes, and seasoning with garlic and oregano. An older recipe calls for adding raisins and nuts.

- Not all Tex-Mex comes from Texas. The burrito was first sold in Los Angeles at the El Cholo Spanish Café in the 1930s and spread southwest some 20 years later, eventually going worldwide.

Texas's Beauty Queen

Mary Kay's empire helps make the whole world gorgeous.

Mary Kay Ash was a businesswoman's businesswoman. By developing a quality line of reasonably priced cosmetics and touting direct sales as a great way for women to create their own home businesses, she built a beauty empire that spans the globe.

Hands-on Sales

Ash—known simply as Mary Kay to her international legion of fans—started her direct sales career in the 1930s. For many years she represented Stanley Home Products, demonstrating the company's merchandise at convenient "home shows" in customers' living rooms. As an independent contractor, she purchased the items directly from Stanley and sold them herself, an arrangement that offered tremendous freedom. Her first year with Stanley was a bit slow, but things picked up quickly, and before long she was one of the company's most successful salespeople.

Mary Kay's business acumen came to the fore early on. She started recruiting other women as sales reps because Stanley paid a commission to recruiters for the sales of each person they brought on board. Within a few years, Mary Kay had nearly 150 women working under her.

Stanley asked Mary Kay to move from Houston to Dallas to work her entrepreneurial magic in that untapped market. Although she reluctantly made the move, she ultimately left the company in 1959. Soon after, she took a sales position with World Gift Company and quickly became its national training director, only to leave in 1963 following a disagreement.

The Future Is Cosmetics

Eager to set out on her own, Mary Kay decided to form her own direct sales company. This sales method, she knew, would be very appealing to women because it would allow them to set their own hours. For her merchandise, she chose a line of skin-care products to which she had been introduced while working for Stanley. The products had been developed by a cosmetologist who based them on a leather tanning solution created by her father. The woman marketed the cosmetics to friends and neighbors, but at that time she had only experienced moderate success. When the cosmetologist died, Mary Kay purchased the formula from her daughter, invested her life savings of $5,000 in manufacturing—and Beauty by Mary Kay was born.

From the beginning, Mary Kay's business was a family affair. Her sons, Richard and Ben, and her daughter, Marylyn, all pitched in to make the company a success. Beauty by Mary Kay kicked off in September 1963 with a line of products manufactured in Dallas and sold through a national network of salespeople that the company called "beauty consultants." Sales representatives purchased an initial "Beauty Showcase" kit and received training in scheduling and conducting Mary Kay "parties" in customers' homes. Sales reps purchased products at 50 percent of the retail price and resold them at a comfortable profit. Best of all, they received a commission on the sales of everyone else they recruited.

Developing the Mary Kay Technique

Mary Kay knew the secret to successful sales and actively worked to instill all of her beauty consultants with the lessons she had learned over the years. For example, "hard selling" at home parties was a big no-no—the emphasis was always on educating customers, not strong-arming them into buying something. Home parties were limited to six customers, and on-the-spot payment and delivery was the rule. Mary Kay also wisely limited her product line so that salespeople could remain knowledgeable without being overwhelmed.

Motivating its beauty consultants has always been a key to the company's success, and toward that goal it instituted a unique incentive program in 1967 that included the use of a pink Cadillac for its top sales directors. The program proved so successful that five Cadillacs were awarded in 1968, and ten in 1969. By 1970, Mary Kay Cosmetics was annually doling out 20 pink Cadillacs, a vehicle that eventually became one of its most recognizable symbols. In the years that followed, Mary Kay Cosmetics stopped awarding pink Caddies only to its top sellers and started giving them to every sales representative who achieved a preset sales level. By 1993, a whopping 6,300 reps were driving the bubble gum–colored cars.

Equally motivating are the company's annual conventions, which are held to recognize sales achievements and inspire the masses. The conventions have something for everyone in the Mary Kay Cosmetics family, including workshops for the husbands of sales reps on how to be supportive of their spouses' careers.

Skyrocketing Success

As a result of Mary Kay's business prowess and ability to fire up her sales reps, the company saw more than $198,000 in sales and 318 salespersons during its first full year. Two years later, nearly 850 women around the country were promoting Mary Kay's line of cosmetics.

Flush with success, Mary Kay briefly flirted with the idea of franchising to reach a wider market. She ultimately dismissed the idea, however, because she realized that it would require women to reach outward for financing, which went against the concept of female independence that she had worked so hard to cultivate. Instead, she took the company public in 1967 and used the monies raised through the initial public offering to finance expansion. As a result, Mary Kay Cosmetics became the first company chaired by a woman on the New York Stock Exchange.

The company grew by leaps and bounds in the years that followed, especially after it boosted compensation rates for its sales reps. In 1969, Mary Kay Cosmetics built a new 275,000-square-foot manufacturing plant in Dallas, then followed it with four regional distribution centers. By 1993, the manufacturing facility was the size of three football fields.

Mary Kay Cosmetics saw some ups and downs during the 1980s and '90s, including a slump in sales due to the growing number of women entering the national workforce and a failed bid to acquire its archrival, Avon. But today, Mary Kay Cosmetics is selling strong with more than 200 products, including traditional cosmetics, unique skin-care products, sunscreens, and fragrances (none of which is tested on animals, the company is proud to note).

It's a remarkable success story that started with one dedicated Texas woman who had a special knack for getting people to buy—and sell.

A Few More Strange Governors

*Texas didn't run through all its oddball governors in the
1800s. The 1900s certainly had its share, as well.*

It may just be that a certain flair is necessary to run for office in
Texas. These state executives had flair, all right.

If You Liked Me, Wait Till You Meet My Wife

Impeachment should spell the end for most political careers, but Jim
Ferguson found a way not only to survive but to thrive after being
impeached. Given that Ferguson was run out of Austin in 1917 during his second term with accusations of misappropriation of funds
and embezzlement, not to mention that it was illegal for a successfully impeached governor to ever run for office again, there was no
way that he would regain the governorship. Well, it may have been
impossible for *him,* but it wasn't illegal for his *wife* to run.

With Jim's guidance in 1924, the genteel and highly educated
Miriam Ferguson was rebranded "Ma" on the campaign trail. Her
new image was carefully crafted with pictures of chicken coops and a
bonnet someone borrowed along the way. Inexplicably, Ma won, and
she and her husband returned to Austin triumphant.

The second woman governor in the United States, Ma Ferguson
had her husband's desk placed right next to hers in the governor's
mansion and would reportedly ink over documents Jim had written in pencil. A number of significant laws were passed during her
administration, such as one attacking the Klu Klux Klan by banning
the wearing of masks in public. She also prohibited smoking and
drinking in the governor's mansion—a policy that was quietly overturned the minute she was gone. Ma Ferguson ran again and won in
1932, giving the Fergusons a total of three and a half terms in office.

Football and Politics Don't Mix

Texas's well-known passion for football actually led to the demise of
one governor. Nowadays, Governor Rick Perry, who took office after

the previous governor, George W. Bush, was elected to the presidency, is the longest-serving governor in Texas history. But before him, William P. Clements held that distinction. He served two nonconsecutive terms, from 1979 to 1983 and again from 1987 to 1991. Clements's tenure was particularly surprising because of his garish taste in sports coats—plaid in a number of colors (it *was* the '70s, after all). But he is perhaps most notorious for his involvement in a pay-for-play scandal at his alma mater, SMU.

Needing to clean up its image after a series of NCAA football recruiting violations, SMU brought Clements in to head its board of governors. Although the football program was sanctioned and promised to clean up its act, nefarious goings-on continued behind the scenes. During the 1970s, the school had begun paying cash to athletes to attend and play football at SMU, a direct violation of NCAA rules. Clements and other university officials believed they'd made a commitment to these players and continued to pay them.

Two months into his second term as governor, Clements held a press conference to come clean. The NCAA, needless to say, came down even harder on SMU, imposing a "death penalty" and shutting its football program down completely for 1987; SMU officials decided themselves to extend that condition through the 1988 season. This was too much for even the most rabid college football fan. Although he had almost his entire second term in front of him, Clements may have decided then and there that he could not run for reelection.

Painful Truths

In the category of "also-rans" stands Stanley Edward Adams, who ran for office in 1990, perhaps with the impression that Texas's bar for high office was rather low. He actually listed his occupation as "alleged white collar racketeer," winning a tongue-in-cheek "truth in advertising" award from the *Washington Post*.

Adams was infamous for his involvement with one of the larger Texas savings and loan failures in 1988 and was implicated in everything from shady real estate deals to money laundering for arms dealers. He had applied for permission to open up a branch office of Lamar Savings and Loan Association on the moon, with the stated purpose of serving the needs of individuals there and on other celestial bodies.

Happy Juneteenth!

*Taking root in Galveston, an obscure holiday
has become anything but a trivial affair.*

If asked to name an important holiday that falls in the month of
June, some might suggest Father's Day. If not that, a few people
may be able to pull Flag Day out of their minds. Anything more?
Unfortunately, many people might find their memories dry by this
point. But Texas has a significant holiday in June: Juneteenth (a combined term for June 19), which originated in Galveston in 1865. It
predates both Father's Day (1910) and Flag Day (1885), but it is not
as widely known as either. If other states begin to follow the Lone
Star State's lead, however, this holiday could end up as a major day
of remembrance.

Roots

On June 19, 1865, two months after
the Confederacy had surrendered
in the Civil War, an interesting foot-
note occurred at Galveston. Without
telephones to deliver news from the
various fronts or a timely communications network to relay news from
Washington, important information often arrived slowly. When a
contingent of Union soldiers rode

into the city with news that President Abraham Lincoln had issued
an Emancipation Proclamation freeing American slaves, it is not
clear how much they were spreading news and how much they were
enforcing a law that had been kept secret from the slave population. Were slaves surprised by the development, or had they become
impatient with what had already been declared their due? Either
way, never before had an American president gone firmly on record
with such a proclamation, and never before had slaves been promised a legitimate end to their suffering.

First Celebrations

As the oldest nationally celebrated commemoration of America's end to slavery, it's surprising that the holiday dwells in such obscurity. Originating as Emancipation Day on that pivotal date of June 19, 1865, the holiday is currently celebrated by various states in a rather loose fashion, with different dates set aside for its observance. Texas became the first state to proclaim Juneteenth an official state holiday on June 3, 1979. Since that time, the holiday has become firmly entrenched in Texas culture, and the celebration of slavery's end is gaining ground in other states as well. Washington, D.C., holds its observance on April 16 each year, the very day that President Lincoln signed the Compensated Emancipation Act of 1862. More than half of the 50 U.S. states have established Juneteenth as a holiday or a special day of recognition.

Current Celebrations

Mimicking the joy that slaves felt when they first learned of their freedom, Juneteenth revelers manage to cut loose and have a good time. In Texas, many families host elaborate family reunions to coincide with the holiday, and the mid-June date generally assures good weather for outdoor cookouts. From there, the sky's the limit. The day has been used to play, visit friends, unwind, and relax, but most importantly it's a time to reflect: "Juneteenth is arguably one of the most important days in our country's history, as well as African American history," opined Congresswoman Corrine Brown in praise of the holiday. Galveston, to its immense credit, got that ball rolling.

- *Jack "The Galveston Giant" Jackson faced off against James L. Jeffries in a 1910 Reno boxing match that amounted to a race war with gloves. The big African Texan stomped the Yankee Jeffries, which brought on race riots all over the nation.*

- *Was Satchel Paige the greatest Negro League pitcher in history? Some think it was Cyclone Joe Williams from Seguin. He posted a 20–7 record in exhibition games against all-white teams. At the age of 44 in 1930, he struck out 27 Kansas City Monarchs in 11 innings.*

Fast Facts

- Born in Spur and buried in San Antonio, Marshall Herff Applewhite started the Heaven's Gate cult, whose practitioners killed themselves in 1997 while wearing new tennis shoes. It was an act, they claimed, that would earn them a ride on Comet Hale-Bopp.

- What do Survivor Colby Donaldson, singer John Denver, AFL star E. J. Holub, WNBA great Sheryl Swoopes, first female DEA administrator Karen Tandy, former Panamanian president Demetrio Lakas, Litton Industries founder Charles Thornton, and 60 Minutes journalist Scott Pelley have in common? The scarlet and black of Texas Tech.

- Ohioan Anthony Banning Norton (who emigrated to Texas in 1855) publicly vowed in 1844 not to shave or cut his hair until Kentucky's Henry Clay was elected president of the United States. Clay ran several times without winning, and Norton—a white-maned and colorful soul—kept his vow for the last 49 years of his life.

- "I'll have my snake medium rare, thanks." So someone might say at the Sweetwater Rattlesnake Roundup and Cook-Off, held every March. It's not hard to estimate the size of the Sweetwater snake population when it's learned that most years the roundup yields around two tons of snake meat—so eat hearty.

- At Baylor Medical Center in Waco, hand surgeon Adrian Flatt has assembled dozens of bronze casts of famous people's hands. The collection includes numerous athletes, actors, and presidents. Jimmy Carter refused to remove his wedding ring for the casting, explaining that he never took it off.

- Tom "The Hammer" DeLay was once a bug exterminator in the Houston area with unique political motivations. He decided to run for Congress when the federal government banned a fire ant pesticide named Mirex, which proved too persistent in soil. He worked his way up to House majority leader, but after one scandal too many, he resigned his seat in 2006.

Dino-mite!

Dinosaur Valley State Park provides a trip back in time.

For anyone who loves all things prehistoric—and who doesn't?—a trip to Dinosaur Valley State Park in Somervell County should be at the top of the list for gotta-see vacation destinations. Located just north-west of tiny Glen Rose, just past the Creation Evidence Museum, Dinosaur Valley State Park is the Lone Star State's answer to Jurassic Park, complete with a life-size *Tyrannosaurus rex* and Brontosaurus (*Apatosaurus*). The only difference is that these are fiberglass models rather than real-life, attorney-munching behemoths.

Dinosaurs to Spare

The statues, located at the entrance to the 1,500-acre park, are relics from the Sinclair Oil Company's 1964 New York World's Fair display. In fact, Sinclair Oil had a whole menagerie of leftover dinosaurs, which it offered to the Smithsonian Institution when the World's Fair ended. The Smithsonian didn't want them, however, so the prehistoric beasties found new homes across the country. *Ankylosaurus* ended up at the Houston Museum of Natural Science; *Corythosaurus,* in Independence, Kansas; *Stegosaurus,* at the Dinosaur National Monument in Vernal, Utah; *Struthiomimus,* in the Milwaukee Museum—and *T. rex* and Brontosaurus at Dinosaur Valley State Park.

Walk Where Dinos Walked

The faux monsters set the stage for the park's most impressive attrac-tion: approximately 100 actual dinosaur footprints preserved in the bed of the Paluxy River. At 113 million years old, these are some of the best-preserved dinosaur tracks in the world. They have become both a popular tourist attraction and a scientific boon; over the years, the tracks have shed great insight into how dinosaurs walked.

The tracks are visible only when the water is low, so it's a good idea to call ahead to check on current river conditions before a visit. If the tracks aren't easy to spot, however, a replica of them is also available.

That's Just Like...

To talk like a real Texan, one has to get a handle on the art of crafting clever "rhetorical tropes." Heck, it's not as hard as it sounds—it's only comparative similes and metaphors. What are those? Simple: catchy statements that describe something as *being* or being *equal to* something else in some way. Here are some examples.

- He's so scared his skin jumped up and crawled all over him.

- That woman's so old the spring has gone out of her chicken.

- They're bad enough to be locked up under the jail.

- He's so big, you could split him in half and still have enough for two people.

- She had calluses from pattin' herself on her own back.

- He'd fight a rattlesnake and spot it the first bite.

- They're as brave as the first man who ate an oyster.

- It's so cold the wolves are eatin' the sheep for the wool.

- That's as cold as an ex-wife's heart.

- That dog looks as confused as a woodpecker in a petrified forest.

- If you put his brain in a sparrow, it would fly backwards.

- It's deader 'n a lightin' bug in a milk pitcher.

- That's as hard as pushin' a wet noodle through a keyhole.

- She's so dishonest she'd play cards with a politician.

- My brother's so drunk that he couldn't tell wet from windy.

- If brains were bacon, she wouldn't even sizzle.

- He's so ignorant that when he tells you howdy, he's told you all he knows.

- This job is as easy as catchin' fish with dynamite.

- She lives so far away that her and the horizon are buddies.

- That kid's as useless as a water bucket without a well rope.

Famous Cattle Drives and Trails

Before there were railroads, 18-wheelers, or refrigerated trucks, cattle made it out to market the old-fashioned way—on their own four feet.

In the days of the Old West, the "drive" in cattle drive came from cowboys on horses who "steered" hundreds of thousands of animals from Texas ranches to markets in California, Kansas, and other states with large-scale holding and butchering facilities and access to railroads. Although the heyday of the cattle drives  spanned less than 50 years in the late 1800s, the routes, called "trails," endured in the cattle towns established along them and the Western movies that romanticized them. Here are a few of the best-known cattle drives and trails.

The Chisholm Trail

While not the first, the Chisholm Trail was the biggest and best-known of the Texas cattle drive routes. The Chisholm Trail ended in Abilene, Kansas, where in 1867, Joseph G. McCoy built pens and loading docks next to the Kansas Pacific railroad line, which could deliver cattle to markets in the East. Purchasing 2,400 head of longhorns in San Antonio in 1867, O. W. Wheeler drove them to Abilene. He was partly following tracks blazed a few years earlier by Jesse Chisholm, a trader who transported and sold goods to Native Americans from what is now Wichita, Kansas. The trail had various names, such as the Kansas Trail, the Abilene Trail, and McCoy's Trail, but eventually Texas cattle drivers began referring to the entire route from the Rio Grande to Abilene as the Chisholm Trail. Texas towns along the trail included San Antonio, Austin, Waco, and Fort Worth. At its peak in 1871, 600,000 head of cattle followed the

Chisholm Trail and, by the time it closed in 1885 when barbed wire fencing ended the open range, it had been traveled by more than five million head of cattle and a million mustangs.

The Shawnee Trail

The Shawnee Trail is generally considered to be the earliest Texas cattle drive route. Drivers in the 1840s began guiding herds through Austin, Waco, and Dallas, and then crossing the Red River into Oklahoma and heading to Missouri and Kansas. The trail's name comes either from a Shawnee village on the Red River near the crossing or from the Shawnee Hills in Oklahoma where the trail crosses the Canadian River. The Shawnee Trail was used until 1859, when pressure from Missouri farmers, who believed their own cattle were dying from a tick fever spread by Texas longhorns, forced the territorial government to block Texas cattle from entering the area. The trail went unused during the Civil War. An attempt to resurrect it in 1866 failed because of tick fever fears, so cattle drivers switched to the new Chisholm Trail.

The Goodnight-Loving Trail

The Goodnight-Loving Trail began in 1866 when Charles Goodnight and Oliver Loving drove a herd of longhorns from Young County, Texas, to Fort Sumner, New Mexico, following the Pecos River. This trail eventually extended to Las Vegas, Nevada; Denver, Colorado; and Wyoming. Charles Goodnight invented the chuck wagon for carrying and cooking food on cattle drives, naming it after himself. The Goodnight-Loving Trail was used until the early 1880s when it was replaced by railroads.

The Western Trail

John T. Lytle started the Western Trail in 1874, driving 3,500 long-horns from South Texas to Fort Robinson, Nebraska. Sometimes called the Dodge City Trail or the Fort Griffin Trail, the Western Trail became the main route for Texas cattle destined for northern markets. The Western Trail grew as a number of smaller trails fed into it. Like other Texas trails, the Western Trail ended in 1893 when the open range was closed by barbed wire fencing, frontier developments, railroads, and the spread of tick fever.

Aluminum Siding

Back in the day when the greening of America meant dabbing the decks with emerald-colored paint, and long before recycling was routine, Houston householder John Milkovisch decided to put the empty beer cans that constantly clogged his closets and garnished his garage to good use.

Most people with an excess of beer cans cluttering their house would take the consumed containers to the nearest salvage storehouse. Not Houston's John Milkovisch, though. He crushed the canisters and paneled his palace with the aluminum.

Rethinking and Reusing

Milkovisch, an upholsterer for the Southern Pacific Railroad, initially began his unique home makeover project in 1968. Tired of mowing the lawn, he re-worked the grounds around his suburban residence by replacing the grass with concrete inlayed with designs made of marbles, rocks, and metal. A cold libation or two not only helped temper his thirst, it also provided the budding artist with the raw materials needed to accomplish his next assignment: covering the outer walls of his residence with flattened, empty beer cans.

Over the next 20 years, Milkovisch cut, crushed, compacted, and compressed more than 50,000 beer cans and mortared them to the outside of his home until he had completely covered it from ceiling to cellar with aluminum empties. Do beer cans provide effective insulation? Apparently not. But with the walls finished, Milkovisch started using lids and pull-tabs to make curtains and fences for shade, and even windchimes. Milkovisch's energy bills dropped.

One might wonder how the woman of the house felt about all this, but Mary Milkovisch remained living there for more than a dozen years after her husband passed away, until her own death in 2001. In 2008, the Beer Can House became a legitimate tourist attraction, opening its doors to the public for tours and visits.

George, by George: The Odd Odyssey of George Foreman

Part shaman, part huckster, and wholly Texan, George Foreman went from back alley thug to Olympic gold medal winner to the heavyweight champion of the world before he found his true calling at the pulpit of the people. Whether he's praising the rewards of religion or promoting the glory of grilling, Foreman is formidable, forceful, and full of fun.

One of the most feared fighters to ever stride inside the roped ring, George Edward Foreman was blessed with a hammer for a fist, troubled with a tempestuous temper, and burdened by a Texas-size chip on his shoulder. Born in the tiny hamlet of Marshall and raised on the hard streets and back alleys of Houston, big George spent most of his youth looking for trouble and finding it.

Foreman's father left the family home and his seven children when George was young, leaving his mother Nancy to raise the entire brood by herself. A hardened street fighter, petty thief, and common criminal, the troublesome teenager dropped out of high school at age 16. After one extremely intense encounter with the law that saw him hide inside a sewer pipe to escape the police dogs nipping at his heels, Foreman decided to turn his life around. Enticed by an advertisement for President Lyndon Johnson's Jobs Corps and its slogan, "If you have dropped out of school and want a second chance in life, then the Job Corps is for you," Foreman signed up. He eventually relocated to California, where he met counselor and boxing coach Doc Broaddus, who fine-tuned Foreman's raw brawling skills and helped turn the criminal chump into a heavyweight champ.

The Sweet Science

Once he stepped inside the square circle, it was clear Foreman had the potential to become a formidable fighter. In addition to his natural instincts, pure power, and athletic prowess, he also had an intimidating stare and an aggressive ring presence that often pole-axed his opponents before a single punch was thrown.

Foreman shot up the amateur rankings and earned a spot on the 1968 Olympic boxing team. He accompanied the squad to Mexico, where he easily pummeled his way to the gold medal. When he accepted his award, he wrapped himself in an American flag, a display of patriotism in stark contrast to the raised black fists of protest by fellow African American medal winners John Carlos and Tommie Smith. He returned home a hero.

Within four years of turning professional, Foreman was the top-ranked contender for the heavyweight title with 37 consecutive victories notched on his belt, most of them by knockout. On January 22, 1973, Foreman decked champion Joe Frazier in two rounds to capture the heavyweight crown. He successfully defended his title twice before agreeing to meet former champ Muhammad Ali in Zaire in what would become known as "The Rumble in the Jungle," perhaps the most famous fight in the history of the pugilistic pursuit.

Foreman had been able to use his brute strength, menacing mug, and pistonlike jab to neutralize every opponent he had faced. But Ali, a shrewd, skillful, and strategic showman, could not be bullied. The former champ allowed Foreman to pound him at will in the early rounds, carefully protecting his head while letting his body absorb the blows. The maneuver, dubbed "rope-a-dope," fatigued Foreman, which allowed Ali to reclaim his crown by knocking out the champion.

Waking Up

That loss changed Foreman forever. Although he continued to fight, it was clear his spirit was exhausted. Retiring from the ring in 1977, he dedicated himself to more humane causes. He became an ordained minister and began preaching on the same streets he'd prowled as a kid in the poverty-ridden haunts of Houston. In 1984, he founded the George Foreman Youth and Community Center, a nondenominational facility that provided kids with a safe haven that Foreman himself had needed but couldn't find. By 1987, with his ministry and youth center in need of a monetary boost, Foreman returned to the ring, shocking scribes of the sweet science by winning 24 consecutive bouts. In 1994, at the age of 45, Foreman floored Michael Moorer to win the IBF and WBA heavyweight titles, becoming the oldest boxer in history to capture the crown and the only fighter in history to go a full two decades between title victories.

Retirement for Real

Big George hung up the gloves for good in 1998. By this time, the once scowling scrapper had become a smiling symbol of success. His transformation has been miraculous. Foreman has gone from a monosyllabic menace to a well-spoken and highly regarded humanitarian, Christian, and caregiver. He is also a very wealthy entrepreneur and TV marketer, using the airwaves to hawk everything from mufflers to clothing to his world-famous George Foreman grill. He also tried his hand at situation comedy, starring in the short-lived TV series aptly titled *George.* Unfortunately, like many of the opponents who stood toe-to-toe with him, it flopped.

In other endeavors, he has published a series of best-selling cookbooks and spiritual testaments. He also authored an inspirational guide to fatherhood, another subject in which he is an expert. The father of ten children, he is renowned for naming all five of his sons George, although to avoid obvious confusion in the Foreman household, they are known by their nicknames: Monk, Red, Joe, Big Wheel, and Little George.

He continues to publish, preach, guide, and teach, and he still calls the Houston area and the Lone Star State home.

* *If Western movies about Texas cowboying were more accurate, a larger number of the cowboys would be black. And small wonder African Texans were attracted to ranching; while prejudice was never entirely absent, on horseback a person's skills spoke a lot louder than that person's melanin.*

* *Believe it or not, the molding pit of the original Liberty Bell still survives. Liberty, Texas, has a replica of the bell that was cast from the old gear. Since this one isn't cracked, the townspeople use it to ring in the new year and on July 4.*

You Can Thank Texas

Mechanical typewriters long ago went the way of the dinosaur, cast aside in favor of various kinds of newfangled word processors. But back in the day, typewriters were the best friend of anyone who had to put words on paper. Even more time-saving than a manual machine was the electric typewriter, which was invented by a finger-weary Texan named James Field Smathers.

Smathers was born in Valley Spring on February 12, 1888. Upon graduating from business school, he taught shorthand and typing for a year then took a job as a typist, accountant, and credit manager with a company in Kansas City, Missouri.

Typing was an integral part of Smathers's job, and he found it both time-consuming and tiresome. An electric typewriter, he reasoned, would do the job much more quickly, so he set to work creating one, and by the fall of 1912, he had developed a working model. Smathers applied for a patent as he perfected his invention, and in 1914, he produced a model that worked with stunning proficiency. In that instant, the lives of secretaries everywhere became much easier.

In 1923, after improving his electric typewriter even further, Smathers was approached by the Northeast Electric Company of Rochester, New York, which offered him a royalty contract for his revolutionary invention. However, it wasn't until 1930, when Electric Typewriters, a subsidiary of Northeast Electric Company, began marketing its Electromatic model that American businesses truly embraced the electric typewriter.

International Business Machines, better known today simply as IBM, purchased Electric Typewriters in 1933 and made it the cornerstone of its new Office Products Division. Smathers, meanwhile, was awarded the Edward Longstreth Medal by the Franklin Institute in Pennsylvania for "ingenuity in the invention of the electric typewriter." He joined IBM as a consultant in 1938 and remained employed by the company until his retirement in 1953.

Take It to the Limit

Television's longest-running concert music program, Austin City Limits, has been expanding the boundaries of musical diversity since it first hit the airwaves in 1975. Featuring a Texas-tempered stew of styles, a potpourri of performers, and an erudite eye for distinct, innovative talent, this exhibition of melodious magnificence has no limits.

The distinct and diverse musical history of Texas has always been prominently displayed on the city streets and in the concert halls, city bars, and community centers of Austin. The ascendancy of the state capital from a town with "room enough to caper," as Billy Lee Brammer described it in his novel *The Gay Place*, to self-proclaimed "Live Music Capital of the World" began in the early 1970s. A versatile variety of performers such as Willie Nelson, Jerry Jeff Walker, Jimmy Dale Gilmore, Guy Clark, Townes Van Zandt, and Joe Ely relocated to Austin and basked in the city's rich mix of culture, politics, and laissez-faire attitude. Soon, a plethora of nightclubs and bars, such as Armadillo World Headquarters, the Soap Creek Saloon, and the Broken Spoke were established to provide a stage for this unique collection of singer/songwriters to ply their craft and harvest their creative juices.

On to Television

It was amid this eclectic atmosphere that the seeds for the program that would eventually become *Austin City Limits* were planted. The show itself was the brainchild of Bill Arhos, a Public Broadcasting System veteran who had worked at Austin's PBS affiliate KLRU since 1962. Together with coconspirators Paul Bosner, Bruce Scafe, and Joe Gracey, Arhos envisioned a live concert series that would serve as a platform to introduce Austin's multifarious musical tapestry to a nationwide audience. Two practice performances were taped in 1974 with B. W. Stevenson and Willie Nelson taking center stage at the KLRU production facility. Unfortunately, so few patrons attended the Stevenson taping that the producers decided not to present it to the PBS brass, because it "looked like a party where half the guests decided not to show up." Willie had a much wider following, and his show was taped in front of a raucous full house. This was the episode that was presented to the PBS network executives.

Arhos and company didn't even have a title for their show as they prepared their pitch. They originally dubbed the show *Travis County Line* before it was decided that the moniker was too similar to the title of the movie *Macon County Line,* so a compromise was reached, and the name *Austin City Limits* was born. The concept appealed to PBS, and the network agreed to broadcast 13 episodes beginning in 1976, although the actual performances were taped in 1975. Asleep at the Wheel and the grandfather of the Texas swing sound, Bob Wills, were the first performers in the show's inaugural season. Other acts that year included Doug Sahm, Townes Van Zandt, Charlie Daniels, and B. W. Stevenson, who finally got the opportunity to showcase his talents to the nation.

Picking Up Steam

In the show's earliest incarnation, the audience was seated on bleachers behind the stage and on a rug-covered floor in front of the performers. Soon, however, the bleacher seating was extended to surround three sides of the stage, with tables and chairs supplanting the rug. The now familiar and famous Austin city mural was added for season seven.

Since its inception, hundreds of acts featuring musical styles as diverse as folk, cajun, zydeco, Tex-Mex, refried blues, country honk, and straight-ahead rock 'n' roll have been showcased on the series stage. The program has highlighted the well-known talents of performers such as Ray Charles, B. B. King, Johnny Cash, and Loretta Lynn while introducing the country to the abilities of new acts such as the Drive-By Truckers, My Morning Jacket, Rilo Kiley, Franz Ferdinand, Femi Kuti, Iron and Wine, Bloc Party, and The Swell Season. The times may have changed, but the edict of introducing and emphasizing eclectic music of all types has not.

- *On October 1, 2009, the* Austin City Limits *studio was named a rock and roll landmark by the Rock and Roll Hall of Fame and Museum.*

When Hell Came to Texas

The Texas City explosion was one of the worst industrial accidents in history.

Texas has seen its share of devastation over the years, most of it caused by massive hurricanes or killer tornadoes. But on April 16, 1947, the residents of Texas City experienced a disaster unlike any other, a bizarre shipboard explosion that killed hundreds and set the Galveston County port town ablaze.

Instant Devastation

That morning, just before 8 A.M., longshoremen were loading ammonium nitrate fertilizer into Hold 4 of the French Liberty ship SS *Grandcamp* when smoke suddenly started billowing from the ship's belly. After a series of failed attempts to get the fire under control, including the use of pressurized steam that succeeded only in blowing off the hatch covers, the Texas City Fire Department was called.

The town's entire contingent of 28 firefighters was struggling to douse the blaze when, at 9:12 A.M., the *Grandcamp* suddenly exploded with a fiery blast that was felt 100 miles away in Port Arthur. The devastation was horrifying: The entire dock was destroyed, along with the nearby Monsanto Chemical Company, grain warehouses, and several oil and chemical storage tanks. In addition, more than 1,000 residences were damaged or destroyed. Adding to the chaos, flaming debris rained down over the area, igniting a series of smaller explosions and fires, while columns of thick, oily smoke blackened the sky.

The explosion killed all 28 firefighters and annihilated the town's firefighting capability. Also killed were numerous ships' crews and scores of curious bystanders drawn by the fire earlier that morning. The explosion's shockwave was so intense that it knocked down buildings and caused deadly metal shrapnel to rain over the community. A wave of water estimated to be 15 feet tall swept inland, grounding a 150-foot steel barge. The receding water then carried debris and many of the dead and injured back out to sea.

Unprepared for the Aftermath

Because Texas City was relatively small, it had no municipal hospital and only three clinics, which were immediately overwhelmed by the large number of burned and injured. But within hours, hundreds of doctors and nurses began arriving from nearby cities and military bases, working together to establish temporary hospitals and morgues.

Unfortunately, Texas City's problems weren't over just yet. The *Grandcamp* explosion had also damaged the SS *High Flyer,* which was in dock for repairs and, like the *Grandcamp,* was loaded with thousands of tons of ammonium nitrate fertilizer. These chemicals ignited, as well, but it was several hours before rescue workers realized the danger. Tug boats were dispatched from Galveston to tow the *High Flyer* away from the dock, but they were unable to maneuver the ship, and as the flames grew higher and higher, the tugs pulled back. Not much later, the *High Flyer* also exploded, causing more damage to the waterfront area and starting fresh fires among the port's petroleum storage tanks. Luckily, casualties were minimal because the area had already been evacuated.

Among the Worst Ever

The explosion of the SS *Grandcamp* remains one of the worst industrial accidents in U.S. history. It's unknown exactly how many died during the event, given the force of the explosion and the intensity of the resulting fires. However, a monument lists 576 persons killed, with 398 positively identified and 178 listed as missing. Many of the dead were never recovered.

In addition, an estimated 3,500 people were injured—nearly a quarter of the town's population. Property loss was believed to be around $100 million, in addition to the loss of nearly 1.5 million barrels of petroleum. A third of Texas City's homes were condemned, leaving nearly 2,000 residents homeless.

But while Texas City was down, it was not out. Residents and businesses immediately turned to the task of rebuilding, invigorated by insurance money and aid donations from individuals and corporations. Some companies, such as Monsanto, even expanded their operations as a sign of their commitment to the community.

Houston's Astrodome

The first covered baseball and football stadium—nicknamed the "Eighth Wonder of the World"—is a tribute to American ingenuity.

The story of the Astrodome began in 1962 when Major League Baseball expanded to include the Houston Colt .45s, owned by Houston Judge Roy Hofheinz. The city's subtropical weather made scheduling difficult—extreme heat and humidity were a challenge for players, and tropical downpours were always a risk.

What About a Roof?

However, after a trip to Rome's Colosseum, Judge Hofheinz had an idea. He'd learned that the original Colosseum had a retractable fabric canopy called a *velarium*. With more modern 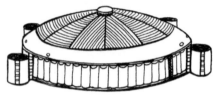 technology, Hofheinz speculated, a modern sports arena could be enclosed within a dome and air-conditioned.

In November 1964, his dream became a reality as the Harris County Domed Stadium was completed. It stood 18 stories tall and covered nearly ten acres of land, about six miles from downtown Houston. The ceiling was made of clear Lucite plastic; sunlight lit the interior well enough that the playing field could be natural Bermuda grass, bred for indoor use.

Around the world, Houston's domed stadium was acclaimed as an engineering miracle. Almost immediately, other cities launched plans to enclose their existing stadiums or build entirely new ones based on the Houston design.

The Space Age

Hofheinz soon renamed the stadium the Astrodome to highlight Houston's connection with the space industry. At the same time, the Houston Colt .45s became the Astros. During an exhibition game, Mickey Mantle hit the first home run in the Astrodome. Everything seemed perfect, until the first official games in the new dome.

Players complained that they couldn't see fly balls due to glare from the Lucite panes in the ceiling.

Two sections of the panes were painted white, but the grass died when it couldn't get enough sunlight. For most of the 1965 season, teams played on dying grass and dirt that had been painted green.

Installing the Astroturf

Researchers at Monsanto invented artificial grass, which they called *ChemGrass,* that same year, but it wasn't in full production at the start of the 1966 baseball season. So, although most of the infield was covered with the ChemGrass—soon renamed *AstroTurf*—the outfield remained painted dirt until more AstroTurf arrived in July.

The stadium continued to adapt to challenges, and its popularity grew with fans and teams alike. In 1968, the Houston Oilers football team made the Astrodome their stadium, following the arrival of the annual Houston Livestock Show and Rodeo in 1966. Basketball games were also featured at the Astrodome, including the 1971 NCAA Final Four games and the 1989 NBA All-Star Game. In 1973, the Astrodome was also the site of the famous Battle of the Sexes tennis match in which Billie Jean King beat Bobby Riggs.

Declining Fortunes

However, by 1996, the age of the Astrodome became evident. The Oilers demanded a new stadium, but when Houston turned them down, owner Bud Adams moved the team to Tennessee. Next, the Astros insisted on a new ballpark or they'd leave the city as well. In 2000, a new park, now called Minute Maid Park, was built in downtown Houston. And this ballpark has a retractable roof.

In 2002, Reliant Stadium opened next to the Astrodome, as the home of Houston's new NFL team, the Texans. Like Minute Maid Park, it features a retractable roof.

The Astrodome became known as the "lonely landmark" due to the fact that so few events have been scheduled there since the new stadiums were built. The stadium did, however, serve one more noble act of kindness in 2005, when its doors were opened to welcome displaced survivors of Hurricane Katrina. For two weeks, more than 13,000 people found shelter inside the Astrodome, which once again became the focal point of world headlines and applause.

Oil Is Well in Texas

The Texas petroleum industry began in 1901 with the discovery of oil in the Spindletop salt dome formation south of Beaumont. That discovery helped start Gulf Oil and Texaco, now parts of Chevron Corporation, and eventually established Texas as the heart of the world's oil and energy industries.

Texas currently has 5 billion barrels of known petroleum deposits, about a quarter of the known reserves in the United States. Oil is continuously pumping from the largest Texas oil deposits, and the actual total sizes and amounts of reserves left are often kept secret by the companies removing the oil. These are the top ten largest Texas oil fields ranked by proven reserves estimated from recent data. Included in this list are the year each field was discovered, its size in acreage (when known), and its estimated production volume in barrels (42 U.S. gallons) in 2007.

- **Wasson Field, West Texas.** Discovered in 1937, covers 62,500 acres, 23.6 million barrels

- **Spraberry Trend, West Texas.** Discovered in 1949, covers 500,000 acres, 28.1 million barrels

- **Slaughter, West Texas.** Discovered in 1937, covers 100,000 acres, 11.3 million barrels

- **Levelland, West Texas.** Discovered in 1945, 8.0 million barrels

- **Seminole, West Texas.** Discovered in 1936, 7.5 million barrels

- **Goldsmith, West Texas.** Discovered in 1935, 5.8 million barrels

- **Yates, Southwest Texas.** Discovered in 1926, covers 22,500 acres, 9.9 million barrels

- **Cowden North, West Texas.** Discovered in 1930, 5.0 million barrels

- **Giddings, South central Texas.** Discovered in 1960, 6.5 million barrels

- **Kelly-Snyder, West Texas.** Discovered in 1948, 10.1 million barrels

Fast Facts

- During the Vietnam era, the 111th Tactical Recon Squadron, Texas Air National Guard became known as "Air Canada" for the number of Vietnam-dodging VIPs who served there. That's how politicians' sons or Dallas Cowboys avoided walking point in the A Shau Valley.

- Seven-time Academy Award nominee (and one-time winner) Greer Garson (1903–96), born in the British Isles, was one of Hollywood's most glamorous stars in the 1940s. After she married a Texan, she soon showed she had a Texas-size heart: The generous actress funded a theater facility at SMU.

- Back in 1971, Tom Moore decided to prove that his colleagues in the Texas legislature didn't even read the bills before voting, so he introduced one honoring Albert DeSalvo (aka the "Boston Strangler") of Massachusetts for his population control and psychology work. It passed unanimously.

- Every major river in Texas except the Red is either Spanish-named or has an English name translated from Spanish.

- On June 16, 1986, Texas Rangers pitcher Charlie Hough took a 1–0 no-hitter against California into the bottom of the ninth. A three-base outfield error, a base hit, a passed ball, and a dropped third strike wrecked his no-hitter, shutout, and victory—and hardly any of it was Hough's fault.

- In 1881, a faith healer named Don Pedro Jaramillo settled near Falfurrias, and a number of people seemed to get well after trying his mudpack and water treatments. He passed on in 1907, and his grave remains a popular shrine today.

- The second largest cross on the continent (second only to the one the taxpayers must bear) stands 190 feet tall with a 110-foot crosspiece, near Groom. A man named Steve Thomas wanted people to think about Jesus, so he built it in 1995. His prayers have probably been answered.

The Secret Life of Big Tex

*What was the original purpose of this beloved
state fair mascot? Think North Pole.*

Every year since 1952, Big Tex, a 52-foot, 6,000-pound cowboy
standing at the entrance to the "Million Dollar Midway," greets
attendees of the Texas State Fair. But Big Tex has a big secret: He
started out as Santa Claus in 1948 in the small town of Kerens.

Making Christmas Shopping Fun

Howell Brister, secretary of the Kerens Chamber of Commerce, was
concerned that the citizens of Kerens were traveling the 70 miles all
the way to Dallas to shop for Christmas. He needed a gimmick to
encourage the locals to spend their money closer to home, and he
finally decided on a 49-foot Santa Claus made of iron-pipe drill cas-
ing and papier-mâché. The statue was outfitted with a Santa suit and
hat and a beard created from 7-foot lengths of unraveled rope.

The promotion proved a huge success during the 1948 holiday
shopping season, but the novelty quickly wore off. In 1951, the Texas
State Fair purchased the giant Santa for $750,000 and transported
him to Dallas. Santa was transformed into a cowboy and dubbed
"Big Tex" on time to make his debut at the 1952 State Fair.

Santa's Makeover

To achieve the transformation, his nose was straightened and his eyes,
which appeared to be winking lasciviously, corrected. The H. D. Lee
Company donated a plaid shirt and denim jeans, and a pair of size
70 boots and a 75-gallon hat completed the ensemble.

In 1953, Big Tex was installed with a device that allowed his
mouth to move automatically, and over the years, seven different people have performed the booming "H-O-W-D-Y" that is his
signature greeting. Jim Lowe, a pioneer broadcaster in Dallas, was
the voice of Big Tex for most of the last five decades. In 2009, the
seventh voice of Big Tex was Bill Bragg, who took over the job on
Big Tex's 50th birthday in 2002. Bragg broadcasts from a small booth
60 times a day for the 24 consecutive days that the fair runs.

Improvements over the Years

Additional updates have made Big Tex stronger and given him more character. His original papier-mâché head was ultimately replaced with one made of fiberglass. In 1997, his body was rebuilt with a cagelike skeleton of 4,200 feet of steel rods. In 2000, a mechanical arm was installed so that Big Tex could wave at visitors, and animatronics were added to allow him to move his head.

Big Tex has to be a snappy dresser, and his clothing has also undergone changes over the years. He has worn special outfits to commemorate events and local culture. In 1965, he donned a 300-pound, 15-foot-by-60-foot Mexican serape. In 1975, Big Tex greeted visitors in a candy-striped shirt for the Yankee Doodle Dandy–themed fair. And in 1982, he showed his school spirit by sporting an orange University of Texas T-shirt.

The current cowboy outfit sported by Big Tex was specially designed by the Williamson-Dickie Company of Fort Worth. It took a team of eight employees to assemble it. The custom shirt covers Big Tex's 30-foot chest and 181-inch arms with room for his 100-inch neck. The buttons are three and a half inches in diameter, and the shirt is made of 70 yards of blue denim and 80 yards of awning material. It is 600 times larger than the Dickie's shirts found in western wear stores. Tex's matching denim pants are size 284W with a 200-inch inseam, a 56-inch fly, and rivets three and a half inches in diameter. These hefty jeans weigh 65 pounds. This outfit is completed with a 75-gallon hat measuring five feet and size 70 boots measuring seven feet and seven inches.

Each year, Big Tex is lifted into position at the start of the fair by a crane and a crew of seven people. Once he's set, the crew actually climbs inside Big Tex to disconnect the crane and attach him to his standing platform. This hot job is made cooler by the fans that have been installed inside his body to provide circulating air for the workers.

So when fall arrives and the fair kicks into gear at its 50-acre park in Dallas, listen for the booming voice of Big Tex calling out "Howdy" to all fairgoers and visitors. And don't forget to wave.

Taste of Texas

Texas cuisine is well documented in the canon of American cookbooks. These are a few standouts in the field.

- In 1972, Diana Kennedy started the Tex-Mex craze with *The Cuisines of Mexico.* While the title doesn't mention Texas, Kennedy ventured deep into its heart, making distinctions between dishes from Mexico's interior and the "mixed plates" north of the Rio Grande. The cuisine was embraced by the world, and tortilla chips, margaritas, and chili con carne became part of the global food culture.

- Frank X. Tolbert's chili cookbook, *A Bowl of Red,* declines to offer the recipe used at Tolbert's Restaurant in Grapevine—a family secret. Chili guru Tolbert, who helped make chili the official Texas state dish, offers a different but no less tasty version instead. Key ingredient: 3–6 ancho chile pods—boiled 5 minutes, cooled, stemmed, seeded, and chopped.

- Famous for his barbecue, C. B. "Stubb" Stubblefield's entry, *The Stubb's Bar-B-Q Cookbook,* details not only standouts such as "Shortcut" Pulled Pork, Wicked Jezebel Ribs, and Smoked Beef Brisket, but bold zingy side dishes, such as his robust Capers 'n' Creole Deviled Eggs, featuring fresh lemon juice and coarse-grained mustard.

- Tom Perini's *Texas Cowboy Cooking* offers 75 recipes from the Perini Ranch Steakhouse. Combining culinary art and chuck wagon traditions, his recipes include oven-roasted beef brisket, green chili hominy, and calf fries, a regional delicacy made from beef testicles. Perini also shows the diversity of Texas cuisine with such recipes as the J. B. Hawkins Ranch's Hot Crab Spread. Located in coastal Matagorda County, the ranch has a crab wharf just behind the main house.

- *Texas Home Cooking,* by food and travel writers Cheryl Alters Jamison and Bill Jamison, documents their two years traveling the back roads talking to master chefs, cooks at food festivals, cattle ranchers, fishers, farmers, and a lot of everyday Texans. Their book's 400 recipes cover the breadth of the Texan palate, from the trinity of Lone Star spices—cumin, oregano, and garlic—to canning recipes to assorted Tex-Mex treasures.

Texas Timeline

(Continued from p. 133)

December 15, 1881
The nation's second transcontinental railroad is completed as the Texas and Pacific Railroad meets the Southern Pacific Railroad in West Texas.

July 4, 1883
Hands from three Pecos area ranches compete in the world's first rodeo.

September 13, 1886
Apache leader Geronimo stands trial in San Antonio. He spends the rest of his life as a prisoner, dying in Fort Sill, Oklahoma, in 1909.

March 23, 1893
The Fort Worth Stockyards are incorporated adjacent to the Texas and Pacific Railroad, soon becoming the Southwest's largest livestock market.

February 14, 1895
A highly unusual weather pattern leaves the cities of Galveston and Houston buried under some 20 inches of snow.

February 20, 1895
A massive dust storm blows across the panhandle, turning day into night and leaving as much as a foot of dust in some areas.

September 15, 1896
Two die and dozens are injured from flying debris during a staged train wreck north of Waco. The head-on collision of two Missouri, Kansas, and Texas Railway Company locomotives was a promotional stunt.

June 1899
The Brazos River overflows its banks during a period of virtually nonstop rain over several days. Nearly 300 people drown in the floodwaters.

September 8, 1900
Some 10,000 lives are lost as a category four hurricane slams into Galveston, flooding the city in as much as 15 feet of water.

March 3, 1910
The people of Dallas see their first airplane as stunt pilot Otto Brodie performs tricks over Fair Park.

May 10, 1911
Lieutenant George Kelly crashes his aircraft near San Antonio, becoming the first military pilot to die in a plane crash.

May 31, 1919
Conrad Hilton purchases the Mobley Hotel in Cisco, launching what will become a global hotel empire.

March 7, 1923
An earthquake measuring an estimated 4.7 on the Richter scale rattles El Paso and northern Mexico.

May 14, 1923
Killer tornadoes rip through Howard and Mitchell counties, claiming 23 lives and injuring more than 100 others.

July 30, 1923
Roy Mitchell, convicted murderer of six, is hanged in Waco, the next-to-last public hanging in Texas.

(Continued on p. 211)

The Late, Great Buddy Holly

*One of the first rock 'n' rollers, Buddy Holly shone
brightly but for only a very short time.*

Named after a Texas Ranger who was a
Confederate colonel during the Civil War,
home of Texas Tech University, and center
of the largest contiguous cotton growing
region in the world, Lubbock is a pure West
Texan city on the South Plains. The city will
always be known as the hometown of Buddy
Holly—a local boy who became a rock 'n' roll
legend and whose life was tragically cut short.

Charles Hardin Holley was born in Lubbock on September
7, 1936. The fourth child of Lawrence and Ella Holley, he was
nicknamed Buddy by his mother. Although he only lived to age
22, Buddy Holly was one of the most influential musicians of early
rock 'n' roll, and many of his songs have become American classics.

Early Promise

The Holleys were a musical family, and as a boy Buddy learned to
sing and play several instruments. By the time he entered seventh
grade in 1949, he could hold his own on the guitar, the banjo, and
the mandolin. At J. T. Hutchinson Junior High School, he began
playing together with another seventh grader, Bob Montgomery.
They were inspired by the country music they heard on radio shows
such as *The Grand Ole Opry* and *Louisiana Hayride* and started
several bands while still in junior high. In high school, Buddy and
Bob had their own music show on Lubbock's KDAV radio station,
and they started listening to black rhythm and blues musicians and a
young new star named Elvis Presley.

Presley barnstormed through Lubbock in early 1955, and after
seeing him perform, Holly decided that music was his life's ambition.
Buddy and Bob opened for Presley when he returned to Lubbock in
October 1955. Later that month, the duo performed with Bill Haley

and His Comets at another local concert. A Nashville talent agent was in the audience, and shortly afterward, Buddy Holly signed a contract with Decca Records. The record company misspelled his last name as "Holly," which became his stage name.

The Hits Start Coming

Holly left Lubbock for Nashville and later New York, forming a band he named The Crickets. Sales of their early recordings were disappointing, but in May 1957, Buddy Holly and The Crickets released a single, "That'll Be the Day," which topped charts in the United States and Great Britain. In December of that year, the band performed their first hit and another, "Peggy Sue," on *The Ed Sullivan Show.*

Holly's music was sophisticated for early rock 'n' roll, and he was a masterful lead and rhythm guitarist and lyricist. He was one of the first rock stars to write, produce, and perform his own songs, and The Crickets set the template for the standard rock 'n' roll band: two guitars, bass, and drums.

International Influence

In March 1958, the band began a 25-day tour of England, an event that many rock historians consider a turning point in popular music. Holly was wildly popular in Britain, and his performances directly inspired musicians who would lead the "British Invasion" of the United States a few years later. Paul McCartney recalls watching The Crickets perform live on London television. Keith Richards, who would become lead guitarist for The Rolling Stones, attended one of the concerts. Even Holly's fashion choices—black horn-rimmed glasses and Ivy League three-button jackets—would influence early English rock.

During the last year of his life, Holly recorded and toured constantly. He returned to Lubbock in August 1958 to marry Maria Elena Santiago, a receptionist at a New York music company, who he had met two months earlier—he proposed on their first date.

Under the pressures of the road, Buddy Holly and The Crickets parted ways after a final tour in the fall of 1958.

An Unexpected End

In January 1959, Holly, with a new band behind him, started a three-week group tour across the Midwest with other young stars on the bill, including Dion and the Belmonts, Ritchie Valens, and J. P. "The Big Bopper" Richardson. The weather was frigid, and the tour buses had continuous problems—one of Holly's band mates had to be hospitalized for frostbite. On February 2, they performed in Clear Lake, Iowa, a last-minute addition to the schedule. Eager to avoid another long bus trip in the cold weather, Holly chartered a private airplane to fly him to the tour's next date. The plane crashed soon after take-off, killing Holly, Richardson, Valens, and pilot Roger Peterson.

Holly's funeral was held on February 7, 1959, at the Tabernacle Baptist Church in Lubbock, and he was buried at the City of Lubbock Cemetery in the eastern part of the city. His headstone uses the correct spelling of his last name, Holley, and features a carving of his Fender Stratocaster guitar.

In Memory Of...

Holly remains Lubbock's most famous native son. Hutchinson Junior High School and Lubbock High School have several tributes to the late musician on their campuses. A life-size statue of Holly playing his Fender guitar is the centerpiece of Lubbock's West Texas "Walk of Fame," an outdoor tribute to the region's artists and musicians.

In 1997, the city of Lubbock purchased a renovated train station downtown and started the Buddy Holly Center, a museum dedicated to Holly's life and music, as well as more general Texas art and music. The center houses an extensive collection of Buddy Holly memorabilia, exhibits on other West Texas musicians, and a fine art gallery. Displays include Holly's Fender Stratocaster, songbooks, photographs, fan mail, posters, stage clothing, and a hand-tooled guitar strap he made as a teenager. Personal items from Holly's boyhood in Lubbock include a pair of his glasses, a wooden slingshot, his report cards, and his collection of 45 rpm records. The Holley family home in Lubbock is a private residence and is not open for tours.

Music is a big part of Lubbock and West Texas culture. Other notable West Texans who are honored at the Holly Center and on the Walk of Fame include Mac Davis, Waylon Jennings (who was in Holly's band on that last tour), Delbert McClinton, Jimmie Dale Gilmore, Butch Hancock, Joe Ely, Dixie Chicks singer Natalie Maines, and Glenna Goodacre. The city also sponsors the annual Lubbock Music Festival.

The Top 5 Most Haunted Places in Texas

- **The Alamo, San Antonio:**
  It's probably no surprise that Texas's most famous fort and battle site also reports Texas's most hauntings, from General Santa Anna to John Wayne. Since 1836, visitors and passersby have noticed eerie lights and ghostly figures here, day and night.

- **Texas Governor's Mansion, Austin:** Across the street from Texas's state capitol, the governor's mansion has been the site of drama, victory, tragedy, and hauntings. According to legend, former governor Sam Houston haunts the mansion, where he's hiding from his third wife. She tried to reform Sam into a sober, churchgoing man. He'd rather spend his afterlife without her.

- **Market Square, Houston:** Downtown Houston may be haunted by 19th-century madam Pamelia Mann. According to staff and patrons at establishments such as La Carafe, the late Ms. Mann is a nightly visitor. Dressed in a white Victorian gown, she has reportedly been seen outside on Congress Avenue and inside some of the buildings. She checks the ladies' rooms on the Market Square block where her brothel once stood.

- **The Jail at La Grange:** Many people know La Grange for "the best little whorehouse in Texas." Nearby, Fayette County Jail is known for tales of the ghost of Marie Dach, who starved herself while on death row. Today, the jail is the La Grange Chamber of Commerce, and the gaunt figure of Mrs. Dach haunts her former cell. Ironically, it's part of the chamber of commerce's kitchen.

- **Driskill Hotel, Austin:** For celebrity ghosts in an elegant setting, look no further than Austin's downtown Driskill Hotel. Some say that former U.S. President Lyndon Baines Johnson is among the hotel's famous ghosts. The spirit of LBJ appears around the hotel mezzanine, where he used to celebrate on election nights.

Old Presidents Never Die...

...They just go home to Texas, where they build libraries.

Three U.S. presidents preserve and display their personal papers, public documents, and memorabilia in Texas. The libraries of Lyndon Johnson, George H. W. Bush, and George W. Bush give the Lone Star State more presidential libraries than any other state.

Under the aegis of the National Archives and Records Administration in Washington, presidential libraries officially began with Franklin Roosevelt's donation of his papers to the federal government. Today, there are 13 such facilities in operation or in the planning stages. Six other presidential libraries are operated by other government agencies or organizations.

Regardless of any specific political sympathies one might have, a visit to the George Bush and Lyndon Johnson centers is a Texas must-do for kids and grown-ups alike (George W.'s library has not yet opened). In both, visitors will find fascinating historical documents and exhibits, of course, but also rare automobiles, planes, boats, clothing, artwork, and just plain weird stuff.

LBJ's Legacy

The Lyndon Baines Johnson Library and Museum in Austin was established in 1971. Considering the historical sweep of this institution, one can't help but be amazed at what Johnson lived through and what he personally touched in world history—three major wars, the nuclear age, civil rights and other social-change movements, and the Cold War. The collection here reflects that drama; it is, he remarked at the library's dedication, "the story of our time—with the bark off."

The library houses 45 million pages of historical documents—all of Johnson's papers and those of many colleagues—and primarily caters to scholars. But the museum is open to the public year-round.

In addition to serious historical memorabilia, such as his White House daily diaries, visitors can linger over an animated, life-size figure of Johnson that's dressed in a Western shirt and cowboy hat and tells jokes; a 1910 Model T Ford donated by Henry Ford II; art and gifts from foreign countries, including a Diego Rivera painting and a wooden Senegalese ceremonial headdress; a replica (in seven-eighths size) of the Oval Office; and an audio recording of LBJ and Ladybird's love letters read by Helen Hayes and Kirk Douglas.

George H. W. Bush's Bequest

Not to be outdone, the George Bush Presidential Library and Museum on the campus of Texas A&M University in College Station boasts 43 million pages of documents, thousands of audio and video recordings, and two million photos, in addition to more than 100,000 artifacts related to the Bushes.

The voices of Bush and First Lady Barbara guide visitors through exhibits spanning Bush's long public life, including his days as a decorated Navy pilot; his tenure as a congressman, ambassador to the United Nations, U.S. liaison to China, and director of the CIA; and on to the presidency. Don't miss the restored World War II TBM Avenger, which is just like the plane Bush flew during the war, or the flight simulator that allows visitors to "land" on the deck of the carrier *San Jacinto*.

View a 12-foot piece of the Berlin Wall, which fell during Bush's administration, his beloved speed boat, and a re-creation of the White House Situation Room. Look for a replica of Barbara's three-strand pearl necklace in the museum shop.

Plans for George W.

While the younger Bush's library and museum won't open to the public until 2013, plans for the center, in the heart of the Southern Methodist University campus in Dallas, should put the facility in good company with his father's and LBJ's enormous institutions.

The George W. Bush Presidential Center, designed by Robert A. M. Stern and Associates, will house the usual millions of pages of official documents, photos, and memorabilia. It will also be home to the George W. Bush Policy Institute and a presidential museum that promises to provide "an understanding of the historic events that occurred during the Bush presidency and case studies of key decisions made by the President that promoted the fundamental governing ideals of freedom, opportunity, responsibility and compassion."

Where Eagles Dare: The Abilene High School Eagles

Steeped in tradition, determined with discipline, and bolstered by the state's oldest high school marching band, the Abilene Eagles have won six state championships and appeared in the semifinals a record 11 times. Guided by some of the most legendary names in high school history, the Eagles have achieved gridiron greatness through talent, perseverance, and courage.

Abilene High School is one of the oldest educational institutions in Texas, founded more than 150 years ago in a modest landlocked enclave of 160,000 people located almost smack-dab in the middle of the great state of Texas. As in most communities in Texas, high school football is the sport that garnishes the most attention and produces the wildest rivalries.

Early Greatness

The gridiron program at Abilene first attracted statewide attention in 1920 when the fledgling football team reached the semifinals of the state championship under the tutelage of renowned coach Pete Shotwell. He took over the program's reins in 1917 after serving as head coach at Cisco High School. Although the Eagles failed to advance to the championship match, the team's determined and dogged defense  served notice to anyone paying attention that the school would be a dominant fixture on the range for some time.

In 1923, Shotwell's squad ran the table, winning all 12 games they played, including a 3–0 victory over Waco, which had not allowed an opponent to score a single point in almost three full seasons. Once again it was the assertive and aggressive "D" that enabled the Eagles to smother their opposition, surrendering only one touchdown the entire season and capturing the state championship.

Retrenchment

After leading the school to the title, Shotwell moved onto the collegiate ranks, taking the head-coaching job at nearby Hardin-Simmons University. The Abilene athletes struggled after Shotwell's departure, failing to make the playoffs for the next three seasons.

In 1927, Dewey Mayhew became the Eagles' head coach, joining the school staff after a successful stint with the Marlin High Bulldogs. Under Mayhew, the Eagles returned to the lofty heights they had achieved under Shotwell, winning a pair of state championships in 1928 and 1931. Mayhew departed as the school's winningest coach in 1941. His successors—including the legendary Shotwell himself, who returned in 1946—could not match Mayhew's unparalleled success. Then Chuck Moser arrived, and Abilene's ascent into the legend began.

A New Commitment

By all accounts, the team Moser inherited in 1953 was just an ordinary group of high school kids. But Moser used the school's tradition for excellence as a moral building block and molded a program based on discipline, dedication, and determination—both on and off the turf. Over the course of the next seven seasons, Abilene captured the attention of the entire state with their precise procedures on the field and their well-respected discipline off the gridiron.

From 1954 to 1957, the Eagles won 49 consecutive games, including three consecutive state championships. In Moser's seven years pacing the sidelines, Abilene won 78 games and lost only 7. Those explosive exploits were impressive enough to earn the Eagles the title Texas High School Football Team of the Century.

Since Moser left the school in 1959, the Eagles have not been able to match the accomplishments they achieved under his rule. While they have reestablished themselves as a championship contender in the 21st century, they have made only one semifinal appearance in the last 50 years. Despite the recent drought, the mention of the name Eagles still invokes proud memories of the days when Abilene boasted the biggest little team in Texas.

Lone Star Lexicon

- **crusty:** Used to describe a tough or ill-tempered man, woman, horse, or species of livestock. "He's a *crusty* old coot, I'll tell you what, more ornery than a bag full of rattlesnakes."

- **all swole up:** A pouty, brooding, close cousin to *agger-vated*, with a healthy smidgen of proud, obstinate, and self-absorbed behavior thrown into the mix.

- **catty whompus:** One of many *whomp*-based descriptions, this term is used to describe something that is out of alignment: "Cletus had a conniption and kicked in the door. Now, it's *catty whompus* in the frame."

- **whompy jawed:** A subtle variation of the more precise *catty whompus*, this term describes something that does not fit properly, e.g., "Be sure you screw down the lid on the barbecue sauce. Don't leave it all *whompy jawed*!"

- **fit to be tied:** Used to describe someone who is extremely upset, either experiencing a conniption or hissy fit, the type of reaction that can be controlled only by hog-tying someone like a rodeo calf.

- **tank:** What would otherwise be known as a pond. The majority of *tanks* are constructed by people (via bulldozers) on farms and ranches and used to store water for livestock.

- **lit out:** Used to describe someone who took off, absconded, or quickly started out across some terrain, e.g., "When she saw that rattlesnake, Bobby Sue *lit out* over the hill and didn't turn back."

- **go ahead on:** Instead of saying, "You go ahead, I'll catch up later," this Texas phrase falls right in with the Texan's habit of obfuscating the obvious with superfluous, incoherent language.

- **over in through there:** Another confusing directional phrase that is typically understood only by Texas locals, most likely a throwback to the days before real roads and highways.

- **slaunchways:** Geometric description describing a piece of wood that was sawed on an angle. Not to be confused with *catty whompus* or *whompy jawed*.

Bragging Rights

- **The World's Largest Military Barbeque:** The Abilene Civic Center is home to this annual event. Established in 1965, the event arose as a community thank you from the citizens of Abilene to the men and women stationed at the nearby Dyess Air Force Base. Volunteers from the Military Affairs Committee of Abilene dish up thousands of pounds of barbecue beef and a truckload of coleslaw and baked beans. More than 10,000 people share in this day of tribute and camaraderie each year.

- **The Big Event:** In 1982, Joe Nussbaum, the vice president of student government at Texas A&M University, created the Big Event to say thanks to the communities of Bryan and College Station for supporting the students. The unique one-day service project pairs students with citizens who need tasks completed around their homes. Students paint, fix, landscape, clean, and build for the recipients in need of these services. In the 27 years since its inception, the Big Event has grown to become the largest one-day, student-run service project in the nation.

- **Padre Island:** The 600-mile Texas Gulf coastline is home to a string of barrier islands that includes the longest barrier island in the world. These islands, some of which may be no more than 3,000 years old, likely formed due to a combination of currents, tides, and waves working on ocean sediment. Padre Island measures 113 miles in length, which makes it the longest barrier island in the world.

- **The Texas Pterosaur:** In 1971, Doug Lawson, a student archaeologist working at the Texas Memorial Museum, discovered a pterosaur skeleton in Big Bend National Park. The pterosaur, *Quetzalcoatlus northropi,* had a wingspan of nearly 40 feet. The giant dinosaur soared over the tropical landscape 65 million years ago but fell to earth and sank into the ooze of the jungle floor. That ooze gradually turned to stone, fossilizing these remains until Lawson found them. Currently the pterosaur stands as the largest flying animal yet discovered.

What Is a Cowboy?

It seems that there are as many ideas of what a cowboy really was as there are John Wayne movies in which he played one.

The cowboy is probably the most recognized and beloved symbol of the Old West, of Texas, and perhaps even of the United States itself. But what did cowboys really do? What were their responsibilities? What made them cowboys?

An Unexpected Origin

The first surprise may be that the American cowboy can trace his roots to the young men who herded cows on the haciendas, or ranches, in Spain. The task of herding cattle began in that country in medieval times. The Spanish word for cow is *vaca,* and those who herded them on horseback were called *vaqueros,* a name that eventually evolved into the American term *buckaroo.* Because the hours were long and the work was physically demanding, boys were best suited to be vaqueros.

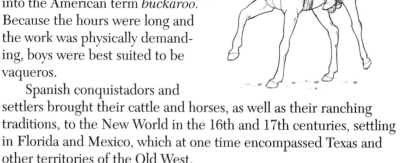

Spanish conquistadors and settlers brought their cattle and horses, as well as their ranching traditions, to the New World in the 16th and 17th centuries, settling in Florida and Mexico, which at one time encompassed Texas and other territories of the Old West.

American Traditions

Many customs of the vaqueros became part of the American cowboy tradition. They used the lariat or lasso to rope cattle. The vaqueros put saddles on their horses, although the Spanish horse saddle didn't have a horn in the middle—that was added later by early American cowboys who wanted an anchor to tie the lariat to. Branding a cow's hide with a hot iron as a means of identifying the owner also came from Spain, and the Mexican sombrero was an ancestor to the cowboy hat. Spurs (for prodding a horse to run faster), chaps (leather over-pants to protect the legs), and the rodeo (Spanish for *roundup*) are also vaquero contributions.

Settlers from the newly formed United States began moving west in greater numbers in the early 1800s, bringing with them English riding and ranching customs that would eventually blend with those of the vaqueros. The real heyday of the American cowboy came after the end of the Civil War, when former soldiers from both sides moved west in search of opportunities. At the same time, demand for beef in the East increased. Ranchers taking advantage of the huge open ranges in Texas needed scores of cowboys to tend their herds, round up cattle, and drive them to the markets in rail centers such as Abilene, Kansas, to be loaded onto trains.

Because of their experience, many Mexican cowboys were hired by the Texas ranchers. In addition, because the huge demand for ranch workers generally won out over racism and discrimination, a large number of African Americans freed from slavery were hired as cowboys. Native Americans were also sometimes hired as cowboys, often as part of government programs to "assimilate" them into American culture.

The Daily Grind

The lifestyle of real cowboys was far from romantic. Their pay was around a dollar a day, but food and beds were free, with sleeping quarters usually in a large one-room bunkhouse. Besides herding cattle, cowboys also had to herd horses, both tame and wild, to keep themselves supplied with the three to four fresh mounts each needed every day. Wild horses were "broken" by riding them until they settled down, a practice known as "bronco-busting." Before the annual cattle drives, cattle herds had to be rounded up for branding and castration, tasks done by the cowboys. Calves were chased and roped, and cattle were herded using special horse skills known as *cutting*. Many of these activities and skills can be seen today in cowboy rodeo competitions.

Life on a cattle drive gave us the image of what we might call the "lonesome cowboy." The Chisholm Trail was 1,000 miles long, and cattle would only be driven 15 miles a day, which meant that a drive could last as long as two months. Singing, telling stories, and other campfire activities were the cowboys' primary forms of entertainment, along with listening to the sounds of indigestion from the meat, beans, and bread served by the chuck wagon cook. While Mexican cowboys carried lariats and knives, American cowboys who were Civil War vets preferred rifles and handguns for hunting, scaring off varmints, and defending themselves. Due to cowboy demand, the Colt company developed the famous Colt .45 six-shot revolver, another symbol of the Old West.

Cowboy Fashion

The fancy clothes worn by popular cowboy singers of today and the past had no place in real life. Working cowboys wore wide-brimmed hats that combined features of the Mexican sombrero and the hats worn by both sides in the Civil War. The popular Stetson hat was made by the John B. Stetson Company in—not Texas—Philadelphia! Cowboys wore cotton bandannas to wipe off sweat and protect their eyes and nose from dust. Leather cowboy boots had pointed toes to help slip easily into stirrups, high heels to keep them in the stirrups, and high tops to guard the cowboys' calves while riding. The standard cowboy pants were jeans with a smooth seam on the inside to protect from blistering while riding. Leather chaps worn over the jeans gave added protection.

Although modern observers may wish it were not the case, there's usually not much mention of "cowgirls" in cowboy history. Some women, however, usually wives and daughters of ranchers, worked on the ranches and occasionally owned them.

The life of the true Texas cowboy, herding cattle and working the trail drives in the mid- to late-1800s, was much tougher, much more boring, and much less romantic than the version generally seen in the movies. Modern cowboys are better paid and still perform some of the traditional duties, although horses have been replaced by pickup trucks, all-terrain vehicles, and sometimes even helicopters. Helicopters? That sounds like something cowboy John Wayne might even like.

Fast Facts

- At Tenison Glen in East Dallas, where golf met gambling and lost its polo shirt, Lee Trevino used to win money betting that he could beat people with a Dr Pepper bottle as his club. They say he got a pretty good backspin with that bottle.

- The history of livestock branding in Texas dates back to 1778, when Comandante General Teodoro de Croix realized that cattle could provide a good source of tax revenue. He decreed that ranchers had four months to brand their animals (and pay tax on that brand) or they would revert to the Spanish Crown.

- As coach of the Oilers, Jerry Glanville often left complimentary tickets at Will Call for dead celebrities such as Elvis Presley or Buddy Holly. It's not clear whether any of these tickets were picked up.

- Ah, those wacky developers in Lake Jackson. One of its housing developments has the following streets: This Way, That Way, Parking Way, and even Any Way. Naturally, This Way and That Way intersect, as do That Way and Any Way.

- Back in the 1870s, a drifter named John St. Helen got sick and confessed to being John Wilkes Booth. He recovered and lammed for Oklahoma, where he died in 1903 under another name. His claim being entirely unverifiable, entrepreneurs did the logical thing: put his body on tour and charged admission.

- Álvar Núñez Cabeza de Vaca and three of his party were the only known survivors of a 300-strong expedition that left Florida in 1528 to explore Texas. The expedition finally met other Spaniards again in 1536. Cabeza de Vaca kept detailed notes and is a primary source on the native cultures he met.

- Texans used to be called New Filipinos. Martín de Alarcón, who was governor from 1705 until '08 and again from '16 to '19, called himself "Governor and Lieutenant Captain General of the Provinces of Coahuila, New Kingdom of the Philippines Province of the Texas."

Howard Hughes: Oddball!

*Here are a few fascinating—and possibly unexpected—
facts about the wacky, Texas-born recluse.*

When it comes to bizarre behavior, few people can match the antics of billionaire Howard Hughes. Born in Houston on Christmas Eve in 1905, Hughes was a shrewd businessman whose personal interests ranged from aviation to motion pictures. But Hughes also had a dark side—brought on by mental illness—that ultimately overshadowed his many important accomplishments. Here's a glimpse:

There was evidence as far back as the 1930s that Hughes wasn't quite right in the head. Associates reported, for example, that he was obsessed with the size of peas, one of his favorite foods, and even created a special fork so he could sort them on his plate.

During the making of 1941's *The Outlaw,* a biography of Billy the Kid that Hughes produced, Hughes became fixated on a perceived flaw in Jane Russell's bras, which he insisted made it look as if she had two nipples on each breast. This problem so vexed him that he designed a steel underwire bra for her to wear during the shoot.

The Spruce Goose

During World War II, Hughes was given $18 million by the U.S. military to build three "flying boats" for use in transporting troops and supplies. The contract stipulated that the planes be ready within three months, but Hughes saw that as merely a suggestion. He ultimately delivered one plane—his infamous "Spruce Goose"—in 1947, two years after the war had ended. That plane was flown only once, by Hughes himself, and then mothballed.

Becoming More and More Eccentric

Hughes was phobic about germs and went to extraordinary lengths to protect himself from contamination. Everything he touched had to go through a rigorous cleansing process that involved four separate scrubbings with soap and water. The item then had to be wrapped in a tissue or a paper towel and handed to him by someone wearing white cotton gloves. Plus, Hughes hired only Mormons to serve on his personal staff because he believed they were more hygienic than non-Mormons.

In 1966, Hughes traveled to Las Vegas and booked two floors at the Desert Inn for ten days. Then he refused to leave. He bought the hotel and turned the ninth floor into his private home.

Television was a like a drug to Hughes, who in later years kept the TV on at high volume 24 hours a day. He bought the Las Vegas CBS affiliate and dictated which shows would run and when. However, Hughes often took so long in making up his mind that the station was unable to release a reliable schedule to the public.

It's the Little Things

Hughes was an inveterate writer of memos—hundreds, perhaps thousands of them penned over the years to his highly paid team of lackeys. But rather than focus on the intricacies of his business empire, many of these missives dealt with the ridiculously mundane, such as the volume of the commercials on his Las Vegas television station. One three-page, single-spaced memorandum detailed, step by step, how canned fruit was to be prepared for him.

He was also a not-so-secret racist. He coveted the ABC television network and intended to purchase it for $200 million, but he canceled that plan after viewing an episode of *The Dating Game* in which a black man went on a date to Rome with a white woman.

Hughes refused to get rid of anything that belonged to him—including his own urine, which he collected and kept in capped jars. But today, that's viewed as just one more Hughes eccentricity.

At the time of his death on April 5, 1976, Hughes was virtually unrecognizable. His frame was skeletal, his hair long and matted, and his fingernails and toenails grotesquely long. He had lived as a recluse for so much time that officials had to rely on fingerprints to confirm his identity.

Unusual Texas Road Names

That quintessential Texan Willie Nelson is known for singing "On the Road Again," but he may have thought twice about promoting road travel if he knew about some of these Texas streets, byways, and highways with strange and unusual names.

- Purgatory Road is in New Braunfels. If you're looking for it, it connects Heaven and Hell Streets.

- A neighborhood in San Antonio has streets named after famous movie stars and popular movie and television characters. A quick trip through it will take you across Danny Kaye Drive, Dean Martin Drive, Lon Chaney Drive, Gary Cooper Drive, Edie Adams Drive, Ernie Kovacs Drive, Charlie Chan Drive, Gomer Pyle Drive, Errol Flynn Drive, George Burns Drive, and John Wayne Drive.

- Tater Peeler Road in Lebanon might be a good place for a restaurant serving French fries.

- Those into jewelry may find happiness in Garland on Bronze Street, Silver Street, Gold Street, or Platinum Street. Anyone who already has a lot of those metals might be more likely to live on Easy Street, also in Garland.

- Abilene fans of Geoffrey Chaucer's *The Canterbury Tales* can live on Chaucer Drive, Nun Court, Parson's Road, Pardoner's Road, Reeves Street, Squires Road, or Lawyers Lane.

- A particular former U.S. president might want to avoid an uncomfortable trip down Clinton Drive in Houston, which intersects with Fidelity Street.

- *Gone with the Wind* fans will feel comfortable in a neighborhood of Pharr on streets named Rhett Drive, Gable Drive, Scarlett Drive, and O'Hara Drive.

- Fans of Western movies will definitely feel at home in a neighborhood of Austin where the streets are named Gun Fight Lane, Six Gun Trail, Shotgun Lane, Shootout Court, and Gatling Gun Lane.

Too Hot to Handle

In a state where largeness is almost a birthright, students at Texas A&M University regularly increased the size of their annual bonfire. As the stack of logs grew taller and potentially more dangerous, size limitations were implemented. But in the end, such safety measures were for naught.

Traditions

Texas A&M University features a number of long-standing traditions. *Muster* provides an opportunity for A&M students, alumni, and faculty (all of whom are known more commonly as Aggies) to gather together around the world. *Silver Taps* is a solemn affair that honors students who have passed away. *All-U-Night* is the first cheer and yell practice of the school year, firing up incoming first-year and returning students for the football season. But in the annals of the university no tradition has scored quite as successfully or garnered nearly as much notoriety as the annual A&M Bonfire. Ironically, this megapopular event also produced the school's greatest tragedy.

A Roaring Start

Ask a group of Aggies to name their chief nemesis, and without hesitation they will answer the University of Texas (or *t.u.*, as they derogatorily call it). To symbolize their burning desire to vanquish the Longhorns at their annual football game, the Aggies began setting large stacks of wood ablaze. The first pile, hastily thrown together before the big game in 1909, was little more than a disorganized heap. Over the years the students became more creative, and the pile grew more sophisticated.

In 1942, the Aggies embraced a new "teepee" design that permitted the bonfire to grow from 25 to 50 feet. But even with this increase, they weren't finished. In 1969, students built their bonfire to an astounding height of 109 feet. The conflagration was not only visible for miles around, it earned a berth in Guinness World Records as the world's largest bonfire. Fearing that such outlandish heights might one day invite disaster, however, the university eventually limited the bonfire's height to 55 feet. Nearby campus buildings were also equipped with sprinkler systems as a just-in-case measure. But even the best-laid plans can sometimes go awry, as history bears witness. The Aggies learned this truism the hard way.

Tragedy

By the 1990s, construction of the bonfire had grown into a monumental task. Although the wood stack was shorter than it had been in previous years, it was still undeniably huge. And its latest wedding-cake design ensured that it would still be visible for miles around. Local landowners donated more than 8,000 logs to the cause, and 5,000 students toiled for a combined 125,000 hours to make each bonfire a reality.

Early in the morning of November 18, 1999, all was going according to plan. Successive "layers" of the cake design had taken form, and the stack had risen to 59 feet; four more than the university's limit. But suddenly, something went horribly wrong. As 58 workers stood on and around the pile, the structure began to twist. In one horrific instant, the massive assemblage came down, pinning many beneath it. A total of 12 students and graduates lost their lives, and 27 were injured. Students and faculty mourned their dead comrades and began to ask the same question: Why did this stack tumble when others, substantially taller and more elaborate, had not?

Embers

A five-member task force investigated the accident. Chairman Leo Linbeck Jr. cited excessive internal stresses and inadequate containment strength within the structure as the two primary factors for the collapse. He added that the tragedy stemmed from faulty decisions made by university officials and students in lieu of "adequate physical or engineering control." As a direct result of the tragedy, 1999 became the last year that A&M officially staged the bonfire. A proud 90-year tradition had collapsed. An unofficial off-campus bonfire—not sanctioned by the university—has since arisen to take its place.

In 2004, a Bonfire Memorial was dedicated on the disaster site. It contains 12 portals—one for each student killed in the tragedy—plus 27 stones for each person who was injured.

Talkin' About Texas

"I have travelled near five hundred miles across Texas, and am now enabled to judge pretty near correctly of the soil, and the resources of the Country, and I have no hesitancy in pronouncing it the finest country to its extent upon the globe."

—Sam Houston

"Every man has a chance, no matter what his past has been. The Texans care not especially what a man has been, or what his fathers were before him; they accept him for what he is, and value him for what he can do."

—Nevin O. Winter, author, *Texas the Marvellous*

"Don't Mess with Texas."

—Texas Department of Transportation Anti-Litter Campaign, 1986

"There is very little that binds us here in Texas. We may talk about music, cowboys, big cars, big hair, boots, open landscapes, and forests, but each of these reflects only a part of Texas, very little about its glue. About the closest thing one can say that makes us Texan is our pride *in being* Texans."

—David Taylor, editor, *Pride of Place*

"Friendship"

—Texas State Motto

"Texas is a place where dreamers go, a place where dreamers are born. It is a place where you can find out who you are, where you came from, and where you are going."

—Jory Sherman, "What Texas Means to Me"

"No matter where I am, in my heart I'll always be a Texan."

—Gale Storm, actress

"One's feelings in Texas are unique and original and very like a dream or youthful vision realized. Here, as in Eden, man feels alone with the God of nature, and seems, in a peculiar manner, to enjoy the rich bounties of heaven, in common with all created things."

—Mary Austin Holley, Journal, December 1831

Proof Positive?

Did dinosaurs and humans walk the earth simultaneously? The Creation Evidence Museum has the proof—the Cretaceous, fossilized footprints of humans and dinosaurs literally crossing paths.

What if dinosaurs and humans walked the earth at the same time? Sounds far-fetched, but some people believe the fossilized proof may exist. This controversial relic is housed at the little-known Creation Evidence Museum in Glen Rose, a nonprofit educational museum chartered in 1984 for the purpose of researching and displaying scientific "evidence for creation."

The museum's founder and director, the Christian evangelist Dr. Carl Baugh, is a vocal proponent of the "creation model," a framework of information in which the universe and its living systems are explained as having been designed and sustained by God. These days, creationism versus evolution is quite the hot topic in Texas and nationwide, as school boards across America debate the merits of teaching children both theories.

The Evidence Itself

Stephenville residents Alvis Delk and James Bishop may not have been thinking of upsetting the educational apple cart when they were hunting for fossils near Glen Rose in July 2000. It was there in the Cretaceous limestone along the Paluxy River where Delk flipped over a small slab of rock and discovered the pristine footprint of an *Acrocanthosaurus.*

At the time, Delk claims, he didn't realize the full significance of his find, and the stone collected dust in his living room. In 2007, however, a serious accident landed him in the hospital, and the medical bills began to pile up. He decided to turn some of his fossil collection into cash and began preparing the stones for sale. To his amazement, he discovered a human footprint embedded in that Paluxy River dinosaur imprint, hidden for all these years by dry clay!

Delk's amazing find was later sold to Dr. Carl Baugh, who realized that, quite possibly, this specimen was the Rosetta stone equivalent for creationism. He had established his Creation Evidence Museum in 1984. Delk's one-of-a kind stone was exactly the kind of evidence Baugh intended to feature—displaying it for the general public and preserving it for posterity.

A Close Examination

Baugh also predicted that skeptics would line up to dispute the authenticity of the fossil, so he embarked on a campaign to have it tested by a professional laboratory. Roughly 800 X-rays were taken in a CT scan procedure, and the mysteries of the rock were probed. Technicians clearly verified compression and distribution features, dispelling claims that the fossil's crystalline outer layer had been artificially gouged out. Distinct high-density areas were found in the rock, both underneath and surrounding the tracks. These "compression layers," they argued, were features that only true fossilization over time could create.

Nevertheless, the pundits roundly dismissed the find as a fake and maintained that the tracks had been carved. Yet, carving out the tracks would have cut through the harder surface layer, and evidence of such activity was missing. Some claimed that acid was used to etch the rock to hide tool marks. But there was no reduction at all in the surface density of the rock.

A Little Respect?

Despite the many tests, the Delk fossil and the Creation Evidence Museum haven't garnered much respect in the larger scientific community. Instead of joining in the spirit of discovery and quest for truth, critics focus only on Dr. Baugh's credentials, disparaging his zeal for the Christian faith and his penchant for saving souls. The stone, they argue (if they acknowledge it at all) is a fake.

But salvation isn't all that's at stake here. If accepted as genuine, the Delk fossil would validate the creationism model and strengthen the argument that humans and dinosaurs at one time lived on the earth together. More important, this topsy-turvy sequence of fossilized imprints would ignite a paradigm shift in the way science views how life on earth began. Much of the argument based in evolutionary theory would be cast into doubt, rendered moot by a small slab of rock found in Glen Rose.

Order of Sons of America

The struggle for civil rights in Texas often focused on Mexican Americans. One organization came together to join the battle.

In the early 20th century, Mexican Americans were subject to prejudice, abuse, and mistreatment by American citizens. Many felt that this was their lot in life—an unchangeable constant they'd simply have to endure. Historical journals are rife with factual accounts of prejudices and mistreatments visited upon Mexicans by the very group with whom they wished to assimilate. Like any minority lacking for power, most who suffered through such hardships kept their heads down and prayed for the best. More often than not, however, their prayers went unanswered. A smaller number of individuals took a more proactive approach. And a select few of these managed to change the world. Thirty-seven men bonded together to form the Mexican American civil rights organization *Orden Hijos de America* (Order of Sons of America). Texas would never be the same.

A Grand Stand

In the early 1920s, Ramon H. Carvajal operated a barbershop in San Antonio. As in other such establishments, banter of all types was casually traded back and forth. A favored topic among haircutters and customers was politics. While many Mexican Americans differed on the preferred path toward their emancipation, most agreed that something had to be done.

Rather than merely dream of pie in the sky, one group of determined men decided to take concrete steps to aid their people. On October 13, 1921, they banded together to form a new Hispanic civil rights organization that became one of only a handful of such groups then operating in Texas. The Order of Sons of America (OSA) would meet Hispanic oppressors head on, fighting the good fight against anything or anyone that it deemed abusive.

This was no small task, of course. Bigotry, ignorance, and preconceived notions about Hispanics had a firm grip on many Texans. A change in accepted norms would require a stiff, uphill battle.

The Prevailing Climate

To appreciate what the OSA was up against, it helps to have a feel for the period. Texas during the 1920s was a land fraught with divisiveness and distrust. A mighty wave of some 219,000 Mexican immigrants arrived in the United States between 1910 and 1920, doubling the state's Hispanic population. These people came predominantly for the mining, railroad, and agriculture work that was being offered in the Southwestern states. The intense demand for low-wage physical labor offered an answer to hungry Mexicans fleeing a country rife with economic instability.

When World War I drew to a close at the end of the decade, however, an economic recession produced a severe backlash against Mexican immigration. With only so many jobs to go around, newcomers were sometimes viewed as interlopers. And Mexican immigrants were no exception. Serving to inflame the situation, an estimated 500,000 Mexicans entered the United States during the mid-1920s. Like the group who had come before them, the majority found jobs in physical labor. Not surprisingly, long-brewing resentments soon reached a fever pitch.

A Mob Mentality

A number of Texans feeling displaced and powerless by the ever-increasing migration north decided to push back. And push they did. Ethnic slurs against Mexican Americans became commonplace. Mob violence and intimidation increased sharply. By the late 1920s, an estimated 600 Mexican immigrants had been lynched.

Even the Texas Rangers played a role in the repression of Mexican Americans. It is estimated that hundreds, if not thousands, were killed outright by the famous law-enforcement agency. And such abuses had a snowball effect. Mexican Americans were quickly losing whatever small significance they had, becoming politically disenfranchised from the land that they'd hoped to call their home. Clearly, something needed to be done.

The Seed Grows

Founders John C. Solis, Francisco and Melchor Leyton, and Santiago G. Tafolla Sr. turned their idea of establishing a political organization into reality by first obtaining a state charter in January

1922. The OSA pledged to use its "influence in all fields of social, economic, and political action in order to realize the greatest enjoyment possible of all the rights and privileges and prerogatives extended by the American Constitution."

A charter, first drawn up in English and later in Spanish, added that the OSA would function as a mutual aid society, a civic group, and a pro-labor machine. Chapters began to spring up in numerous Texas towns, with each concentrating in specific areas of expertise. The Corpus Christi and San Antonio chapters, for instance, were most active in civil rights activities.

The OSA quickly went to work righting wrongs. In Corpus Christi, it fought to erect a new Mexican school. As a direct result of its efforts, the Cheston L. Heath School opened in September 1925. In 1926, the organization helped desegregate the all-white Palace Bath House. In 1927, it managed to seat the first Mexican American on a jury in Nueces County. Later that year it won the right to remove a blatantly prejudicial "No Mexicans Allowed" sign from North Beach. There seemed to be precious little that the OSA couldn't accomplish when its members put their minds to it. But their days were numbered. Change was blowing in the air.

The OSA's Legacy

Despite winning scores of battles for Mexican American citizens, however, the OSA was short-lived. Splinter groups that began forming only a few years after the OSA's inception would eventually weaken it by siphoning off key members. By 1929, *Orden Hijos de America* had all but dissolved. Eventually, it would be displaced entirely by other civil rights organizations, the majority of which would morph into the League of United Latin-American Citizens, commonly known as LULAC. That organization, more than 150,000 strong, thrives to this very day. It owes its existence to the Order of Sons of America and those 37 brave souls who had the audacity to proclaim "enough is enough."

- *The earliest Spanish-language newspaper definitively known to have been published in Texas was the Nacogdoches* Mexican Advocate *in 1929. One side was printed in Spanish, with English on the other.*

Fast Facts

- *Not all Texans sided with the Confederacy. One group of German immigrants meant to head for the Union via Mexico, but few survived attacks by Rebel partisans en route. After the war, the survivors retrieved and interred their fellows' bones at Comfort.*

- *Willie Shoemaker, who was born in 1931 in Fabens and stood 4'11", was once told he was too small to be a jockey. He weighed only two and a half pounds at birth and never really caught up—except on horseback, where he won four Kentucky Derbys, two Preaknesses, and five Belmont Stakes.*

- *Alvin Ailey, a native of Rogers who grew up picking cotton, went on to become one of the world's most renowned dancers and choreographers. In 1970, when Ailey's troupe played Leningrad in the Soviet Union, the culture-loving Russian audience gave them a 20-minute standing ovation.*

- *The difference in annual rainfall between Texas's eastern and western extremes is profound: 56 inches along the lower Sabine compared to only 8 inches around El Paso. More than half the state gets 24 inches of rain or less per year.*

- *Outside Groom, there's a Leaning Tower of Water. A truck stop owner thought that a leaning water tower would get people to stop and look (and spend). Although the leaning tower remains, the truck stop does not.*

- *Nudist resorts aren't rare, but nudist apartment complexes are. In the 1970s, Austin's Canyon Villa had a waiting list as long as the Colorado River. Some of its residents may well have also participated in Austin's Naked Motorcycle Club.*

- *H. L. Hunt was a Texas oil millionaire and outspoken supporter of right-wing causes (even though he supported John F. Kennedy and Lyndon B. Johnson). He also authored a utopian novel called Alpaca. Why? To promote his concept of the "perfect constitution" to world leaders, none of whom adopted it.*

The NoZe Brotherhood: Not Your Ordinary Frat Boys

Merry collegiate pranksters? Badly behaved ruffians with no respect for authority? Yes—and yes. The NoZe Brotherhood, sometimes the scourge of Baylor University in Waco and sometimes the silly providers of campus comic relief, have been described as both.

Founded in 1924, which makes it one of the very oldest Baylor campus organizations, the NoZe Brotherhood has had its moments of greatness as well as its dark days. It's been banned from campus several times (it's currently in Baylor's good graces—for the time being) and criticized for its often tasteless practical jokes and withering—if funny—criticism of Baylor's administration, Baptists, religion in general, and whatever campus pomposity is reigning at the moment.

But the NoZe Brothers have also endowed a $50,000 scholarship and have bestowed "ornery membership" (some might call it "honorary") upon such incongruously assorted luminaries as Bill Cosby, Leon Jaworski (a Baylor alum), Kinky Friedman, Bob Hope, President George W. Bush, John Glenn, Dan Rather—and the 12th and 13th presidents of the university. All of them have deemed it an honor to be inducted into the club, which, after decades, has earned a certain measure of prestige.

The Nose Knows

Why the name? Popular wisdom has it that the group, originally known as the Nose Brothers, was inspired by a student, Leonard Shoaf, around whose prominent proboscis, it is said, students decided they could form an entire club.

Members have taken on fake "nose" names, and ever since the club was tossed off campus the first time in 1965, secret identities. Wearing outlandish costumes and Groucho Marx–style phony noses and glasses in public on campus is also traditional NoZe behavior.

Membership in the group (renamed the NoZe Brotherhood upon its reinstatement in the '60s), originally only for men, is now open to women as well. The group publishes its own newspaper, *The Rope*, a take on the official campus paper, *The Lariat*. But most importantly, the Brotherhood pulls off fantastic pranks.

Feats of Daring

The NoZe Brothers have presented the campus chaplain with a ping-pong paddle during chapel—and then released 4,000 ping-pong balls. In 2007, a different chaplain was given a donkey, Hot Damn, on stage. They've painted various campus landmarks, including a bridge and a fountain, pink—their official color. One version, possibly apocryphal, has it that the NoZes actually burned the bridge.

In 2004, the Brotherhood staged a Race for the Pure, in which the three competitors—dressed as Jesus, a rabbi, and a Muslim—carried a cross, an eight-foot Star of David, and a crescent moon, respectively. In August 2005, members removed toilet seats from restrooms in the university's new science center and screwed them onto *The Lariat*'s distribution boxes. In 2009, students found their cars tagged with phony—but very real-looking—parking tickets, noting offenses such as "inverted tailpipe" and "automobile loitering." At least twice a statue of Jesus was moved, once winding up in front of a campus Christmas tree (bearing a warning against idol worship).

Not Always Rosy

Thrown off campus again in 1978 for being, as Baylor president Abner McCall said, "lewd, crude and grossly sacrilegious," the Brotherhood returned but ran into trouble and was bounced again in 1999, after publishing a parody "African American Culture Survey," which many on campus found racist. Readmitted to campus in 2002, the group seems to be on an even keel with Baylor these days.

"I think Baylor needs some of the ribbing the NoZe Brotherhood provides in a clean, fun sort of way," said Dr. William B. Long (Brother Short Nose), a member who wrote a book on the brotherhood. "It adds flavor to the campus."

And, really, how bad can they be? After all, as Bro. Aristopha-NoZe once noted, "The reason for the NoZe Brothers has consistently been campus beautification and Bible study."

Pride of the Lone Star Pitmasters

Barbecue has emerged as a culinary art form in Texas—as serious as religion and as controversial as politics. Anyone and everyone has an opinion about what it takes to make good barbecue and what it means to be called a legend.

Ask any group of typical Texans about how barbecue got started in the Lone Star State, and they'll answer back with as many different stories as someone can slice cuts of meat from a 1,600-pound Black Angus steer.

Some historians cite that the Texas tradition of barbecuing meats began during the 1850s, when German and Czech immigrants first settled the "German Belt," a swath of land stretching from Houston all the way to the rolling Hill Country. As they did in their homeland, the immigrant butchers sold their fresh meat in a storefront market and cooked the less savory cuts in smokers out back.

The lesser-quality meat provided cheap eats to itinerant African American and Hispanic cotton pickers who took advantage of the bargain. No sooner had they purchased a hunk of smoked pork loin or sausage link than they set  upon devouring it, directly out of the butcher paper it came wrapped in. For them, this was "barbecue," much to the astonishment of the butchers.

Alternate Theories

Others claim that African Americans imported barbecue-style cooking from the traditional American South. After Texas joined the Union as a slave state in 1845, Southern cotton planters eyed it as a place to buy cut-rate land. Of course, the wealthy plantation owners moving into the area brought their large slave families with them. After slavery was abolished in 1865, the freedman's knack for turning inferior cuts of meat into mouth-watering fare influenced backyard cooks far beyond the plantation.

Still others date the beginnings of Texas barbecue to the 1800s, when the Anglo cowboys and Mexican vaqueros of the Rio Grande Valley cooked game such as rabbit, squirrel, and venison in open pits out on the range. In the tradition of Mexican *barbacoa,* they wrapped the meat in agave leaves and buried it under coals, where it slowly cooked for hours. So tender was the final product that it was said to have reduced hardened range riders to tears.

A Pillar of Texas Cuisine

Whatever the origins, one thing is certain: Barbecue has emerged as a culinary art form in Texas—as serious as religion and as controversial as politics. Every Bubba and Bobby Joe has an opinion to offer.

Should it be beef, pork, chicken, or turkey? Brisket, ribs, or sausage? Sauce or no sauce? Serve it with white bread? What type of side orders should be served with it, if any? What type of wood should it be cooked over? How low and how slow should it be cooked? A traditional pit or a smoker box? Prepackaged rubs or homemade? Some barbecue aficionados will even argue over whether a fork and knife should be used . . . or if people should just go natural by eating with their hands.

Rules of the Road

Although there is no universal agreement on these and other aspects of Texas 'cue, there are a few accepted standards that have emerged. First and foremost is the way the meat is cooked, and that means always over real wood or coals. Texas pitmasters who hope to pass off electric or gas-fired barbecue had better watch their backs. In some areas hereabouts, they still ride people out of town on a rail . . .

Second, any true Texan knows that beef is the meat of choice. Brisket—the normally tough cut of meat that's taken from the lower chest of the cow—is the common commodity of most pitmasters of this region. Locally prepared sausage (from Elgin) is also a favorite, made with beef, including the tripe, with natural casings. Texas pit bosses cook up a fair amount of beef ribs, too—something a pitmaster in Memphis or North Carolina wouldn't even consider (in those regions, pork rules).

Location, Location, Location

So, where can people find the best Texas barbecue joints? Sage advice suggests a drive straight to Lockhart, the nerve center of the state's barbecue scene. Located just 30 miles south of Austin off Highway 183, the town's quartet of BBQ restaurants serves more than 5,000 visitors each week and more than adequately answers the question, "Where's the beef?" In the fall of 2003, the Texas state senate even passed a resolution proclaiming Lockhart "The Barbecue Capital of Texas."

The town square should be a first stop, where Smitty's Market sets the standard for the stereotypical meat-market format. According to *Texas Monthly* magazine, Smitty's serves some of the best barbecue in Texas and, by the magazine's count, is at least in the top five barbecue restaurants in the state. Brisket, pork chops, and sausage are among the daily fare, with pork ribs on the weekend. There's a large dining area at one side of the store, and out back, visitors will find an area where pitmasters toil over massive stone pits, covered by metal lids. The pits are well seasoned, thick with years of smoke, as are the restaurant's walls.

If their appetites remain up to the task, culinary explorers should head over to Kreuz Market next, another legend in the making spun off by a Smitty's family member. For barbecue lovers, this is the Disneyland of smoked fare, a cavernous building that houses immense wood-fired smokers packed with every imaginable cut of meat. Learned pitmasters—armed with an impressive arsenal of butcher knives—slice the meat by the pound, putting on a show that is eclipsed only by the taste of the mouth-watering food. Here, forget the sauce and the utensils. It's a communal food fest, with diners elbowing up to each other on long tables outfitted with copious rolls of paper towels.

Those into a more intimate setting should seek out Black's Barbecue. Owned and operated by the Black family since 1932, it's billed as Texas's oldest major barbecue restaurant continuously owned by the same family. Here, they smoke meats over hardwood for hours to create a flavor that *Gourmet* magazine touted as "the best BBQ in the heart of Texas, and therefore the best on earth." It's definitely a friendly, family atmosphere here, with knotty-pine paneling, gingham table cloths, and food that will make diners swear off the chain joints.

Chisholm Trail Lockhart Bar-B-Q & Hot Sausage completes the foursome of Lockhart classics, an up-and-comer that started operations in 1978. Here, diners will be happy to find the usual standards, including brisket, beef and pork ribs, pork chops, chicken, ham, and turkey. The fajitas and the sausage from the restaurant's own recipe are also worth a try. Unlike some of the other local barbecue eateries that are light on sides, Chisholm Trail lays it on thicker than any of the other contenders. To wit, they feature a large cafeteria-style hot food bar with everything one might want—including pinto beans, green beans, fried okra and squash. There's also a salad bar with traditional coleslaw, potato salad, and numerous special salads.

It's All Good

The truth of the matter is that those who make the trip to Lockhart and taste for themselves the stuff that barbecue legends are made of really won't care if Texas barbecue originated at the early butcher shops, from inventive slave cooks, or from vaqueros. The only thing on their minds will be the wonderful taste, the intoxicating smell, and scheduling the next opportunity to swing through town again to sample more real Texas 'cue: the pride of the Lone Star pitmasters.

* *Early Texas explorer Álvar Núñez Cabeza de Vaca's last name means* head of a cow *in Spanish. Why? One of his ancestors left a cow's head at a mountain pass to guide Christian forces trying to attack the Moors in the 13th century.*

* *For more than 30 years, Lufkin has hosted the Southern Hushpuppy Cookoff. Past recipes have included such nontraditional ingredients as shrimp, crabmeat, onions, vegetables, chili, and even whiskey.*

* *Anyone who follows Tejano music at all has heard of San Antonio's Flaco Jiménez. His sub-genre,* conjunto, *has long been the music of the Tejano working class, and his five Grammys attest to his success.*

You Can Thank Texas

Few television shows have influenced popular culture as much as *Star Trek* has. And the Star Trek empire would never have happened had it not been for a Texan named Gene Roddenberry.

Roddenberry was born in El Paso on August 19, 1921. He spent his boyhood in Los Angeles and studied to be a police officer before transferring to aeronautical engineering. Roddenberry volunteered for the U.S. Army Air Corps in 1941 and flew B-17 bombers in the Pacific Theater during World War II.

After the war, Roddenberry continued flying until he got his first taste of television. He quickly realized the amazing potential of the new medium and strove to break in as a writer. But openings were few, so he instead took up his fall-back position: He joined the Los Angeles Police Department.

Roddenberry eventually broke into Hollywood by working on and selling freelance scripts to a variety of shows, including *Dragnet, Naked City, Dr. Kildare,* and *Have Gun—Will Travel.* Once established, he turned in his badge to pursue writing full time.

In 1966, Roddenberry gave the world *Star Trek,* a science fiction series he once described as "*Wagon Train* to the stars." The voyages of the starship *Enterprise* and its grandiose captain, James T. Kirk (William Shatner), struck a chord with science fiction aficionados, but poor ratings caused the series to be canceled after three years. Die-hard fans were heartbroken and kept the series alive via fanzines and regional Star Trek conventions.

In 1979, the concept of Star Trek was resurrected as a movie: *Star Trek: The Motion Picture.* After that, Captain Kirk, Mr. Spock, and the rest of the *Enterprise*'s valiant crew were rarely out of the public eye. Four *Star Trek* television series followed (*Star Trek: The Next Generation, Star Trek: Deep Space Nine, Star Trek: Voyager,* and *Star Trek: Enterprise*), in addition to at least 10 more motion pictures.

Gene Roddenberry died on October 24, 1991, but his most famous creation continues to live on, both on the screen and in the hearts of millions of fans.

Lone Star Lexicon

- **dang it, dad gum it, dad blame it, dag nab it:** Euphemisms commonly substituted in the place of more graphic expletives to allow Texans the use of colorful, expressive speech without having to resort to "cussing."

- **go to the house:** Another wonderful catch phrase used when someone wants to go back to their home base for lunch, dinner, supper, or any other kind of scheduled meal.

- **sorry:** An essential Texas adjective meaning worthless, no-count, useless, or bad. To make this descriptor more emphatic, the user applies just the right amount of verbal emphasis, or spin.

- **wore out:** A term that describes someone who is completely fatigued or exhausted. Can also be used to describe machinery or mechanized contraptions that are "worn out."

- **all choked up:** To be overcome with emotions when deeply moved by sadness (such as when the Dallas Cowboys lose a football game) or the thoughtfulness of others.

- **fixins:** Generally refers to the side dishes and condiments that do not comprise the main course. With barbecue, *fixins* are the potato salad, sauce, beans, cornbread, coleslaw, and other side vegetables.

- **calf-rope:** Uttered during an argument, rassel, or any sort of contest to acknowledge the superiority of one's opponent; usually issued as a last resort (similar to "crying uncle").

- **place:** Rural usage, refers to an individual's farm, ranch, or abode, sometimes even long after the person has left or moved out. "Yessir, it's past the old Johnson *place,* you can't miss it."

- **norther:** A storm that blows in from the north overnight, turning 90 degree temperatures to freezing. *Blue norther* is the amplified state, often with freezing rain or snow.

- **tump:** A hybrid of *tip* and *dump*, used to describe something that has been spilled or dumped over, i.e., "Dang it, that dad-blamed mutt *tumped* over my Shiner Bock!"

The Real Babe

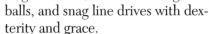

The greatest female athlete to ever tear down the track, lope across the links, compete on the court, or dash round the diamond may have been born Mildred Ella Didrikson, but throughout her acclaimed and admired sporting life, she was known simply as Babe.

Is it fitting that Texas should produce the greatest female athlete to ever lace up a pair of running shoes? Mildred Ella Didriksen—she later changed the spelling—was born in Port Arthur in 1914 or 1911, depending on which source one believes. In her autobiography, Babe claimed to have been delivered onto this mortal coil in 1914, yet her tombstone and baptismal certificate assert she was born in 1911. While there may be a dispute over that date, there is no argument over the accomplishments she achieved on the playing field.

Skills on the Diamond

A natural at every pursuit she attempted, Didrikson excelled at basketball, diving, swimming, tennis, bowling, and lacrosse as a youngster. As talented as she was at this wide array of athletic aspirations, she made her first headlines and acquired her moniker playing the male-dominated sport of baseball. She could throw a baseball with alarming accuracy from astonishing distances, snare hotshot ground balls, and snag line drives with dexterity and grace.

It was her ability with the bat, however, that opened eyes and slackened jaws. She was so adept at hammering the horsehide that she drew instant comparisons to George Herman Ruth, the New York Yankees' Sultan of Swat who was known worldwide as the Babe. Didrikson's success with the stick earned her the same nickname, and she adopted the appellation with pride.

Although her greatest athletic achievements would come on the track and golf course, she continued to play baseball whenever and wherever the opportunity presented itself. In 1934, she spent the summer with the esteemed House of David baseball team, an amateur group with tremendous ability that toured the country playing—and often defeating—some of the best professional teams in the land.

Athletic Diversity

As adept as she was on the diamond, Babe was also a standout on the basketball court at Beaumont High School. The Employers Casualty Insurance Company of Dallas noticed her star status and enlisted her to play for the company's industrial league team, the Golden Cyclones. Between 1930 and 1932, she guided the team to the Amateur Athletic Union (AAU) national championship and was voted All-American each season. Her exceptional athletic versatility prompted the company to expand its women's sports program into track and field. The company sponsored Babe's involvement in the 1932 AAU championships, which served as an Olympic-qualifying tournament for the upcoming games. Babe competed in eight of ten events, winning five gold medals while setting world records in the javelin, 80-meter hurdles, high jump, and baseball throw.

That performance earned her a berth on the U.S. Olympic team, and she represented her country with distinction at the 1932 summer games in Los Angeles. Though technically a novice—she had never even seen a track and field meet until 1930—her competitive desire and prodigious prowess allowed her to overcome her inexperience with astounding results. Didrikson won Olympic gold in both the javelin and the 80-meter hurdles, breaking her own world records in the process. She also set a world record in the high jump, but her effort was downgraded from gold to silver-medal status because of a technicality: She cleared the record height by diving headfirst over the bar—a method so revolutionary that Olympic officials refused to award her a gold medal.

Hitting the Links

Following her unprecedented Olympic success, Didrikson didn't exactly settle into civilian life. She continued to barnstorm around the country, speaking on the rubber chicken circuit, appearing as a vaudeville novelty act playing harmonica while running on a treadmill, and playing basketball and baseball. She also pursued a new passion, the game of golf. After only a few months of practice, Babe deemed herself competent for competitive play and won the second tournament she entered—the Texas Women's Amateur Championship in April 1935.

Didrikson went on to record 82 career amateur and professional victories—including 10 major titles. She captured a trio of U.S. Open crowns in 1948, 1950, and 1954 and strung together a remarkable and unprecedented 17 consecutive wins from April 1946 to August 1947, a feat no other duffer of either gender has been able to equal.

Didrikson was a founding member of the Ladies Professional Golf Association (LPGA) and continued to win tournaments with uncanny ease until 1954, when she was diagnosed with colon cancer. Fourteen weeks later, she returned to the links and won the U.S. Women's Open. Though noticeably slowed by her illness, she captured another pair of titles before succumbing to the disease in September 1956.

In 1950, the Associated Press named her the female athlete of the first half of the century and, in 2000, *Sports Illustrated* magazine anointed her as the second-best female athlete of all time, behind heptathlete Jackie Joyner-Kersee.

* *Tetsuo Okamoto, of Japanese heritage and Brazilian birth, won Brazil's first Olympic medal ever (swimming in 1952). He was also a Texas Aggie—in fact, a four-time All-American Aggie swimmer.*

* *When basketball eccentric and defensive bastion Dennis Rodman tried out for high school hoops in Dallas, he didn't make the team—he was only 5'11" upon graduation. He went to work as a custodian at DFW Airport, had a massive growth spurt, and tried hoops again—this time more successfully.*

* *Brad Corbett, who owned the Texas Rangers from 1974 to 1980, knew how to throw piles of money at mediocrities, has-beens, and never-weres. When Corbett wasn't making players' agents happy, he was getting hosed in trade after trade by other owners.*

Fast Facts

- Horses and cattle brought mesquite farther inland in Texas, but not in wagons. The tree is native only to the coast, and deep grass will strangle it. When grazing lowered the grass, the drought-tolerant mesquite was able to propagate inland. It may even have been helped along by seed pods in horse and cow manure.

- In 1966, Astros hurler Claude Raymond posed for his Topps baseball card with his fly open. Okay, anyone can goof up once, but it takes effort to repeat the mistake (or joke)—Raymond's pants were also unzipped in his '67 photo.

- Country legend Roger Miller of Fort Worth joined the Army as an alternative to Stripe City after he stole a guitar. He had a sense of humor about his Korean War days, which is no small feat. As his education, he claimed: "Korea, Clash of '52."

- Some French diehards in 1818 hoped to set up a base on the Trinity River, "liberate" New Spain, and then go spring Napoleon from his St. Helena exile. Note to diehards: Don't neglect the basics. A colony must flourish before it can be used to liberate anyone, and theirs fell apart after about six months.

- Marene Johnson, who ran the Eastland post office in the early '60s, decorated that building with a huge mural comprised of more than 11,000 stamps from countries around the world. Appearing in the mural are the United Nations emblem and a map of Texas.

- On September 21, 1969, Cowboy punter Ron Widby tried for too much hang time. He sent a punt at too vertical an angle into a high wind, and it blew backward, landing in the Dallas backfield and bouncing straight back to him. He fell on it for a net punt yardage of -7.

- Mardi Gras in Galveston? It's a major event. Visitors can get a hint of the occasion from the 26-foot cornet mounted on struts in front of Old Galveston Square. It looks sharp, mainly because its front tuning slide is all the way in.

The High-flying Jacob Brodbeck

Jacob Brodbeck isn't very well known outside of the Lone Star State, but to many Texans he is the father of American aviation.

When it comes to American aviation history, folks from Fredericksburg and Gillespie County consider Orville and Wilbur Wright's accomplishment at Kitty Hawk in 1903—lauded as the first successful piloted flight of a powered, heavier-than-air aircraft—to be no big deal. They boast that their local Jacob Brodbeck achieved that feat some 38 years before the Wright Brothers even got off the ground.

A Born Inventor

Born in Württemberg, Germany, in 1821, Brodbeck had an innate propensity for invention. According to some accounts, he tried inventing a self-winding clock; others claim he fashioned a watch that didn't need winding for months and was insulted when the kaiser of Württemberg offered him the cash equivalent of one cow for it.

In 1847, Brodbeck packed up his timepieces and belongings and made his way to Fredericksburg. Once settled on the Texas frontier, Brodbeck took teaching positions in various Gillespie County schools, married, and fathered 12 children. Yet he still somehow found time for inventing: He purportedly designed an ice-making machine and lessened Mrs. Brodbeck's domestic load by building her a windmill-powered washing machine.

Brodbeck embarked on a project in the 1860s that literally took his inventiveness to new heights. He envisioned what he called an "airship," a self-propelled flying machine that could carry a passenger and, potentially, replace the wagon and stagecoach—not a bad idea considering the Fredericksburg–San Antonio stagecoach was frequently robbed. It may have seemed like a pie-in-the-sky notion, but in 1863 he built a small prototype model sporting a rudder, wings, and a propeller powered by a coiled spring (similar to a clock spring) that wowed people at local fairs. Determined to make his airship idea fly, Brodbeck secured financial backing from some San Antonio businessmen and set about building the real thing.

Flying High in Luckenbach

By September 1865, Brodbeck's full-size airship was ready to take flight. The larger machine mirrored Brodbeck's earlier model, but it also contained a fuselage for the "aeronaut" (to use Brodbeck's term) and a boat propeller in case of an unexpected wet landing. On September 25, Brodbeck brought his airship to a field outside Luckenbach for its maiden voyage. Accompanying Brodbeck were his nervous investors, a handful of local newspaper reporters, and some curious onlookers.

Brodbeck climbed aboard the machine, engaged the spring-powered propeller, and in seconds, the airship was off the ground. Witnesses reported that Brodbeck piloted his airship for approximately 100 feet at a height of about 12 feet. For a few fleeting moments, Brodbeck's dream was a reality.

But everything literally came crashing down for Brodbeck when he was unable to rewind the spring coil, which caused the propeller to stall. The airship crash-landed into a chicken coop.

Unfortunately for Brodbeck, he had no photographic equipment in place to capture his airship in flight for posterity, and the press scribes deemed the debacle a nonstory. Worse, Brodbeck's financial backers bailed on him, leaving him without the cash needed to assemble another airship.

The Aftermath

What happened after is a matter of debate. Some say a despondent Brodbeck destroyed the wreckage of his airship and all his drawings. Others contend that he took his drawings to the 1900 St. Louis World's Fair seeking investors to bankroll the building of another airship—only to have the drawings stolen.

No drawings, photos, or written accounts remain to verify Brodbeck's aeronautic achievement—only the faded word of long-dead eyewitnesses. But in Gillespie County, where a man's word is as good as gold, that's proof enough.

Texas Towns with the Most Unusual Names

Not only is everything bigger in Texas, it's weirder too, especially when it comes to the names of small towns and communities. If you get bored driving through Texas, a map can provide plenty of laughs, especially when you find towns such as Nameless, Cut and Shoot, and Ding Dong.

- **Dime Box:** A local practice gave Dime Box its moniker. The town was originally called Brown's Mill after a local mill. Until it had a post office, residents put their mail and a dime in a box at the mill's office for a weekly pickup. An official post office eventually opened, only to close a few years later. When it opened again, the mail carriers sometimes got confused between Brown's Mill and Brownsville, so the old ten-cent practice gave the town a new and unique name.

- **Guy:** Ironically, Guy is named after a girl. The town was named for a young crippled girl, Una Guy Rowland, whose father Orr was its first postmaster.

- **Oatmeal:** It doesn't appear that Oatmeal was named after the hot breakfast dish. One story is that it's named for a German family named Habermill because "haber" is a German word for oats. Another claims it's a variation of the name of a Mr. Othneil, who owned the area's first gristmill or flour mill.

- **Nameless:** An act of frustration gave Nameless its unusual name. After having six potential town names rejected by the post office, residents reportedly sent a letter that said: "Let the post office be nameless and be damned!" A devilish postal worker took them seriously and awarded them the name Nameless.

- **Twin Sisters:** Not named for twins, sisters, or even girls for that matter, Twin Sisters got its name from a local landmark—two matching hills that are visible for miles.

- **Cut and Shoot:** Local lore says that this East Texas town got its unholy name from a church dispute. Though it's not certain whether the church people were arguing over land claims, the design of the church steeple, or who should be allowed to preach there, the name was coined when a boy reportedly offered to settle the disagreement by saying he would cut around the corner and shoot through the bushes.

- **Ben Hur:** There's no record that settlers came to this north central Texas area in chariots rather than covered wagons. But according to local lore, the town's name—originally called Cottonwood—was changed to Ben Hur by A. T. Derden, a resident who was apparently a big fan of the book.

- **Bug Tussle:** An unusual name such as Bug Tussle has more than one theory behind its origin. The local favorite is that it memorializes a bug invasion upon a local church's ice cream social. More interesting but less flattering is the explanation that the name comes from the fact that there was nothing else to do at the church's Sunday school picnics but watch bugs tussle. A similar theory has it that two longtime residents arguing over a name took a break to watch ... that's right ... bugs tussle.

- **Ding Dong:** Two bells gave this community its name—Zulis Bell and Bert Bell. These early settlers opened a store and hired an artist, Cohn Hoover, to paint a sign with two bells and the words "Ding Dong" coming out of them. The community that grew up around the store adopted that as its name.

- **Fly Gap:** A battle between settlers and Native Americans may have given this town its name. According to legend, a band of settlers being chased by Native Americans tied up their horses and hid in a gap in the nearby Kothmann Mountains. When they returned to their horses, the animals were covered with horseflies, giving the location its name.

The National Museum of Funeral History

This Houston site takes visitors "six feet under" with style and panache.

The fate that befalls human beings after they leave this mortal world is, of course, a matter completely open to faith and conjecture. There are perhaps as many theories about the big "dirt nap" as there are people, and nothing conclusive, one way or another, appears on the horizon.

But even though people possess scant knowledge of the after-world, there's no reason that they shouldn't still plan to leave this life with a modicum of dignity and style. Glomming onto this form of self-expression, funeral directors have long answered this most basic human desire. From no-frills pine boxes to elaborate diamond-inlaid caskets, from simple funeral handcarts to highly stylized hearses, these keepers of the deceased merrily ply their macabre trade and turn a tidy profit for their efforts. Celebrating the art of the final send-off, Houston's National Museum of Funeral History (NMFH) covers nearly all.

Dearly Departed

Perhaps the NMFH couldn't exist if survivors didn't feel a pressing need to memorialize their loved ones. When Uncle 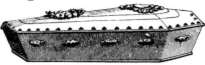 John passes on, for instance, what loving family would commit his earthly remains to a potter's field when a full-blown mausoleum with a polished granite vault was within their grasp? The NMFH examines nearly every form of such loving expression, from the simplest coffin to the most elaborate burial box.

A Deadly Combo

Some 25 years in the making, Robert L. Waltrip's museum was envisioned as a place that would "educate the public and preserve the rich heritage of the funeral industry." In 1992, Waltrip's dream became a reality at a 20,000 square-foot site in Houston.

Packed to the rafters with caskets, coffins, hearses, and other items associated with the post-death process, the space has eventually grown to some 35,000 square feet. Because of its vast size, the NMFH is billed as the largest educational center on funeral heritage in the United States. Designated as a not-for-profit organization, the museum relies totally on contributions from funeral aficionados and ordinary citizens. The NMFH hosts a pair of golf tournaments each year to further the effort, funneling the proceeds into additional exhibits and upkeep, which breathes new life into a museum firmly committed to death.

A Grave Situation

To think of the NMFH simply as a repository for old caskets and a few old hearses, however, is to sell the operation short. This facility traces the death journey in myriad ways and features world-class exhibits that any mainstream museum would, please pardon the pun, kill for.

While moving amongst the museum's exhibits, visitors will find a full-size mockup of an old casket factory. They will also learn how woods were chosen, the various tools and glues used in the process, and how the craft was passed down from generation to generation. The museum also displays its share of burial oddities: Coffins shaped like fish, automobiles, a chicken, an outboard motor, and even a KLM airliner prove that people can be just as bizarre in death as they are in life.

Life—for the Living *and* the Dead

The museum's motto reads: "Any day above ground is a good one." Though this sounds like a reasonable statement, it does run counter to the museum's mission. After all, the NMFH demonstrates that "six feet under" isn't necessarily the gloomy affair it's been made out to be. Whether or not such glorious departures will signal a safe arrival on the "other side," no one can say. But if a glimpse into life's big ending is what a person's after, he or she need look no further than the National Museum of Funeral History. When it comes to the final end, their coverage is dead-on.

Blue Light Cemeteries

Under the full moon, some cemeteries in Texas are known for eerie, flashing blue lights and ghostly figures hovering over certain graves.

Texas's many intriguing mysteries include "blue light" cemeteries. Many people believe that these blue lights and figures are ghosts, angels, or even demons. Others blame the phenomena on swamp gas or foxfire, a luminescent fungus that glows in the dark. The more likely explanation is more simple . . . and perhaps more mystical.

Geologists explain that normal flashes occur when the mineral labradorite is exposed to bright, natural light. Although they can happen at any time, these flashes become especially obvious at night. The effect is so unique, it's called *labradorescence.*

No Need to Be Alarmed

Labradorite is a blue-green stone that's found in Finland, Nova Scotia, Newfoundland, and Labrador. The mineral has been used for gravestones, especially in Louisiana and Texas. Unfortunately, natural cracks and refractions within the mineral cause it to crumble, especially after years in the hot sun.

Thus, in cemeteries throughout Texas, pieces of crumbled labradorite glisten beneath the moon. Hidden in the grass, those shards reflect moonlight and spark ghost stories.

Or Is There?

According to folklore, labradorite can connect the living to the spirit world. Some psychics use labradorite to communicate with "the other side." Perhaps labradorite gravestones connect the worlds, too.

One of Texas's most famous blue light cemeteries is just west of Houston near Patterson Road. For more than 20 years, curiosity seekers have ignored poison ivy, spiders, snakes, and barbed wire to explore Hillendahl-Eggling Cemetery. It's been called "Blue Light Cemetery" since the 1940s when the surrounding German community moved to make room for a Houston reservoir. Other Texas "blue light" cemetery locations include Andice, Cason, and Spring.

Texas Timeline

(Continued from p. 165)

February 8, 1924
The electric chair at Huntsville Prison, "Old Sparky," is used for the first time. Five convicted murderers are executed this day.

November 4, 1924
Miriam "Ma" Ferguson is elected the first female governor of Texas.

September 1, 1927
Passenger air service begins at Dallas's Love Field. This is the city's primary airport until the massive Dallas/Fort Worth International Airport opens in 1974.

February 11, 1933
The Texas Bankers Association issues a recommendation that all bankers carry guns in an attempt to reduce the alarming number of bank robberies statewide.

June 20, 1935
The formation of Big Bend National Park is authorized by an act of Congress. The mountains and canyons of Big Bend comprise one of the largest parks in the United States.

October 6, 1935
The famed Texas Prison Rodeo, featuring prisoners as clowns and competitors, is held for the first time at Huntsville Prison.

January 26, 1945
Audie Murphy, a native of Kingston, receives the Medal of Honor for valor in action in France. He goes on to become the most decorated soldier in the history of the U.S. armed forces.

April 9, 1947
A massive tornado strikes the Texas Panhandle. The mile-wide twister is part of a tornado outbreak that travels for 200 miles, killing 181 people in three states. The total Texas death toll is 68.

April 16, 1947
More than 500 die and the town of Texas City is leveled when a chemical-laden French ship explodes, igniting a second ship carrying 1,000 tons of ammonium nitrate.

November 22, 1963
President John F. Kennedy is killed when a gunman fires on his motorcade as he travels through Dallas with Governor John Connally and their wives. Kennedy is pronounced dead at Parkland Hospital, while Connally recovers from his wounds.

November 24, 1963
Suspected Kennedy assassin Lee Harvey Oswald is shot and killed on live television while being led from the Dallas police station's basement. Local businessman Jack Ruby pulls the trigger.

April 23, 1964
The Houston Colt .45s' Ken Johnson becomes the only pitcher in the history of Major League Baseball to take a loss on a complete game no-hitter. The unlikely happens when Reds star Pete Rose comes home to score on an error that was preceded by a ground out and another error.

(Continued on p. 255)

 Taste of Texas

- On the first Saturday of November, more than 10,000 "chiliheads" convene in Terlingua for two annual chili cookoffs: the Chili Appreciation Society International and the Frank X. Tolbert/Wick Fowler World Chili Championships. The four-day celebration, just outside Big Bend National Park, includes a proclamation from the governor declaring "Chili Appreciation Day" and four nights of live music by some of the best bands in Texas.

- On President's Day weekend, Laredo hosts its annual Jalapeño Festival and Parade, capping a month of festivities. Along with all the festival food menus, visitors can walk across the international bridge to Neuvo Laredo for some truly authentic Mexican cuisine.

- Since 1971, the East Texas town of Athens has thrown a Black-Eyed Pea Jamboree each year. Past jamboree recipes have included black-eyed peas in green Jell-O, pea pizzas, enchiladas, quiche, and even black-eyed pea wine. Bill Perryman, an Athens oil man, invented a jamboree favorite, the peatini—a martini with marinated black-eyed peas instead of olives.

- Sulphur Springs hosts the annual World Champion Hopkins County Stew Cook-off in September. The local tradition dates to the late 1800s, when schools celebrated the end of the year with stew suppers cooked over open fires. Squirrel was once a mainstay ingredient, giving way in recent years to beef and chicken. More than 100 teams prepare at least 10 gallons of stew each, feeding dozens of judges and more than 5,000 cook-off attendees.

- The South Texas town of Linn hosts the annual Linn–San Manuel Country Cook-off, featuring grilled meats and food cooked over burning hardwoods for a real smoke-scented Tex-Mex experience. Favorites include beef ribs cooked over mesquite coals, spit cooked cabrito (baby goat), and chili cooked with chile piquín—a South Texas wild pepper.

- If Texas is the center of the salsa world, Austin is the hot sauce capital of Texas. In August the city hosts the annual Austin Hot Sauce Festival, when 15,000 people descend on Waterloo Park to taste hundreds of hot sauces. The categories include "special variety" condiments—dried pepper sauces, mango-habanero salsas, and other entries that don't fit neatly into the standard "red" and "green" categories.

That's Just Like...

Here are a few more examples of how to talk like a Texan.

- If he were any faster, he'd catch up to yesterday.
- That girl's faster'n a Texas blue norther tearin' through the Panhandle.
- He's so fat that he has to put his underwear on with a winch.
- She's as mean as a bobcat in a burlap sack.
- His mouth was a-goin' like a cotton gin in pickin' time.
- I'm as happy as a pig in a peach orchard.
- It's hotter than a black Cadillac in July.
- I'm hungry enough to eat a bear with the hair still on it.
- Anytime you pass by my house, I would appreciate it.
- They call her "blister" because she shows up when the work is done.
- He don't know big wood from kindlin'.
- You're as mad as a rooster in an empty hen house.
- She's as nervous as a long-tailed cat in a room full of rocking chairs.
- He's heavy in the middle and poor at the ends.
- She's got lines in her face from trying to straighten out the wrinkles in her life.
- He's mean enough to steal his mama's Christmas money.
- She was so poor she had a tumbleweed for a pet.
- He's old enough to have been a waiter at the Last Supper.
- I'm mad enough to eat rattlesnakes.
- She's so poor she had to fertilize the sill before she could raise the window.
- He's not afraid of hard work, 'cause I've seen him lay down and go to sleep right next to it.
- She's as pretty as a speckled pup in a red wagon.

Town for Sale

The Grove, in Coryell County, is one of dozens of ghost towns that dot the Texas landscape—and perhaps the only one that is for sale.

Located north of Fort Hood and Killeen, between the cities of Temple and Gatesville, The Grove is actually a "Historical Museum Town," with about 60 residents. Founded around 1860, The Grove was named for its large stand of live oak trees and sits on the fertile edge of the Leon River Valley. The town's first well was dug by hand through solid rock in 1872 and has supposedly never run dry, even during the most severe droughts. By 1900, The Grove was one of the most prosperous towns in the county, with nearly 500 residents, a school with two teachers and 60 students, and a number of businesses.

The Beginning of the End

In 1936, however, the Texas Highway Department told residents they would have to place a cover on their town well if they wanted Highway 36 to run through The Grove. Residents refused, and the highway bypassed the area, cutting businesses off from considerable traffic that would have flowed through town. Expansion of the nearby Fort Hood army base in the 1940s and the completion of Belton Dam a few years later took hundreds of thousands of acres of land away from many of the area's farmers, accelerating the town's steady decline into obscurity. Today the hamlet continues as home

to a few dozen families while filling its new role as a historic museum town, thanks to Austin antiques dealer and collector Moody Anderson.

Anderson, who has been collecting antiques for nearly 50 years, discovered The Grove in 1972 and tried to buy several antique items in the W. J. Dube general store. Proprietor John Graham refused the sale. When Anderson offered to buy the whole store, lock, stock, and barrel, Graham agreed.

Anderson had already amassed a huge collection of artifacts from the state's frontier past, stored at a warehouse outside Austin. For more than 20 years he's rented many of his treasures to nearly 100 film and television productions, including the *Lonesome Dove* miniseries and movies such as *The Best Little Whorehouse in Texas, The Newton Boys, Spy Kids*, and *The Alamo*.

A New Niche

With The Grove, Moody Anderson saw another opportunity and began buying more buildings near the general store. The hamlet's other historic museum buildings include a blacksmith shop and the sheriff's office next door to the store. The Cocklebur Saloon is a short block away and opens every weekend with local bands playing dance music for crowds that often number in the hundreds. A doctor's office is in another nearby building.

Dube's, which Anderson has turned into the Country Life Museum, remains the center of town. The old store is jam-packed with all things old fashioned, including household goods and groceries, patent medicines, hardware, hand-crank washing machines, and even a coffin or two, all dating to the 19th and early 20th centuries. The Planters State Bank, established in the early 1900s, occupies one corner of the store, its original fixtures—including a walk-in safe—just as they were when the bank was robbed in 1927. The Grove U.S. Post Office, established in 1874, is on the opposite side of the general store. Anderson has rented a number of the store's antiques to movie companies, including a bathtub used by Farrah Fawcett in the movie *The Substitute Wife.*

On the third Saturday of every month, musicians from around the state gather to play and sing at The Grove. A two-day homecoming is held each fall, with a parade, music, and dances. The Grove is open for tours on Saturdays and Sundays.

Anderson, who is now more than 80 years old, has listed The Grove for sale with an Austin real estate company, hoping to find a buyer who will preserve the historical museum town and keep it open to the public for years to come.

Going Batty!

Bats love Texas—and Texans love their bats.

Bats have never been nature's most popular animals. In fact, they give most people the willies. But their reputation as creepy is undeserved: Bats benefit humans and the environment by helping to control pesky insects (especially mosquitos) and pollinating fruit trees.

In Texas, bats also provide entertainment. Several regions throughout the state have become popular tourist attractions where people congregate in the evenings to watch the mammals, which often number in the millions, fly en masse from their dark, dank homes to grab a quick bite of dinner.

A whopping 32 species of bats currently call Texas home, among them the Mexican long-tongued bat and the hairy-legged vampire bat. Fossil skeletal remains also suggest that four other species used to flit about the Texan night sky. Bats congregate in a variety of places, including caves, under bridges, and in abandoned buildings.

Where to Go

In Mason, the Nature Conservancy of Texas opened the Eckert James River Bat Cave Preserve so families could experience the wonder of evening bat emergences. Each summer and early fall, an estimated 4 million female Mexican free-tailed bats visit the cave to give birth and raise their young.

A similar spectacle can be witnessed outside the tiny town of Fredericksburg at the Old Tunnel Wildlife Management Area. The abandoned railroad tunnel there is home to an estimated two or three million bats, which exit the tunnel as a group every evening about an hour before sunset. (A word of advice to visitors: Wear a hat.)

Meanwhile, in Austin, crowds gather nightly to watch nearly 1.5 million Mexican free-tailed bats emerge from under the Congress Avenue Bridge. Across the street, you'll find a sculpture titled *Nightwing*, which honors the bug-munching beasties. A smaller colony of bats can be found about 15 miles north of Austin, beneath the I-35 underpass at McNeil Road, Round Rock.

Bragging Rights

- **The Air Power Museum:** Located in Midland on the grounds of the Commemorative Air Force Headquarters, the museum is home to a fleet of 160 airplanes, making it the largest flying museum in the world. These historic aircraft, known as the Ghost Squadron, represent 60 different types of American and foreign aircraft from World War II. Museum members keep the planes in flying condition to participate in air shows and demonstrations. More than 10 million spectators visit the museum annually to view the planes and learn the role they played in aerial combat missions.

- **Texas State Capitol Building:** The capitol building in Austin is known as the largest capitol building in the United States. Although it is also popularly believed to be the tallest capitol building, Louisiana has it beat by 142 feet. Texas, however, holds the record for largest square footage: 360,000 square feet on 2.25 acres. It was constructed between 1882 and 1888 with limestone from present day Oak Hill. Unfortunately, the limestone discolored because of its iron content. The owners of Granite Mountain in Marble Falls offered pink granite to cover the limestone, which gives the building its unique facade. Over the years, renovations and additions have given the building 400 rooms and more than 900 windows along with the rotunda, foyers, and chambers.

- **Tyler Municipal Rose Garden:** Since it opened in 1952, the 14-acre rose garden in Tyler has drawn visitors from far and wide and is the site of the annual Rose Festival. But it is more than just a popular Texas tourist attraction; it is the largest rose garden in the United States. The garden is divided into display gardens where visitors can stroll and view the vivid displays of roses, including more than 30 varieties of 19th-century roses and hundreds of modern rose varieties. The trial gardens grow roses that have not previously been introduced in the United States; during the two-year trial period, they are tested for vigor, flower characteristics, and disease resistance. A demonstration garden offers new ideas for rose gardeners and features not only roses but more than 90 varieties of flowers, trees, shrubs, and plants. It is a destination for horticulturists, rose enthusiasts, and armchair gardeners.

Texas Has Heart

Heart transplant pioneers Drs. Michael DeBakey and Denton Cooley have opened up new ways of extending life in Houston. But personal relations between them were anything but cordial.

Partners turned bitter rivals, Dr. Michael DeBakey and Dr. Denton Cooley revolutionized heart surgery and made Texas the leader in cardiac research. Over the years, heads of state, celebrities, princes, and regular folk have all come to Houston for treatment and surgery by one of these renowned physicians. Their competition, however, made a few headlines of its own.

A True Pioneer

Born in Lake Charles, Louisiana, in 1908, DeBakey made a name for himself as a heart physician early. While still a student at Tulane University, he invented the roller pump, a component of the heart-lung machine used during open-heart surgery. During World War II, he served the U.S. surgeon general and was instrumental in developing the mobile army surgical hospital (MASH) and the Veteran's Affairs hospital system.

Joining the faculty of Houston's Baylor College of Medicine in 1948, DeBakey later launched the first National Heart and Blood Vessel Research and Demonstration Center there. With a team of researchers and surgeons, he devised more than 50 surgical instruments, performed the first coronary artery bypass, led a team in a multiple transplant procedure, and developed an artificial heart.

A Rival of Like Mind

Dr. Denton Cooley, son of a prominent Houston family, was a bit more than a decade younger than DeBakey. After training at the University of Texas and Johns Hopkins University in Baltimore, he joined the faculty and staff of Baylor in 1951. While there, Cooley worked with DeBakey on many projects and research in developing the artificial heart. However, his personal caseload and research grew until it was in direct competition with DeBakey. It became difficult

for two doctors of such talent and
ambition to work together.

By 1962, Cooley founded the
Texas Heart Institute at St. Luke's
Hospital in Houston. In 1969,
he became the first surgeon to
implant an artificial heart into a
patient. DeBakey felt betrayed
and publicly denounced Cooley's
actions, accusing Cooley of stealing the artificial heart being devel-

Dr. Denton Cooley

Dr. Michael DeBakey

oped in DeBakey's lab. The much-publicized feud between the two
hung over the heart-surgery community for decades. It even landed
on the cover of *Life* magazine in 1970.

Although they did not speak again until years later, both continued
to seek new breakthroughs in heart medicine. In conjunction with
NASA, DeBakey invented the DeBakey Ventricular Assist Device,
a miniature apparatus implanted in the heart to increase blood flow
for those suffering from congestive heart failure. He also consulted
worldwide to develop cardiac medicine and surgery programs and was
extremely influential in establishing the National Library of Medicine.

Cooley pioneered many techniques used in cardiac surgery. He
was instrumental in designing techniques now used for coronary
bypass and repair of aneurysms, and he contributed to the development of methods to repair and replace diseased heart valves and
operations to correct congenital heart conditions. He was also one of
the first in the United States to perform a human heart transplant.

Putting the Feud to Rest

Although various parties tried to bring the two rivals together
through the years, such attempts would always fall through one
way or another. Finally, however, Cooley's Cardiovascular Surgical
Society offered DeBakey a lifetime achievement award in 2007. No
one was certain whether the surgeon would appear to accept it until
the ceremony itself, but when he did, it made the *New York Times*
and papers across the nation. A few months later, in May 2008,
DeBakey returned the honor, inducting Cooley into his own surgical
society. DeBakey died in June 2008 at age 99.

Fast Facts

- In 1960, the inaugural year of the Dallas Cowboys, the team's best effort was a tie against the New York Giants; its season record was 0–11–1. For the first few weeks of its existence—before the season actually got started—the team was called the Dallas Steers.

- Judge Roy Bean, who lived through most of the 19th century, was known as "The Law West of the Pecos." He was a tough judge, but perhaps less well-known was his great generosity. Behind his gruff exterior was a steady flow of his own money (augmented with fines he collected) that he shared with the poorer locals.

- A Rice University gathering could include former All-NFL end Buddy Dial, tycoon Howard Hughes, NFL/AFL quarterback Tobin Rote, Advanced Micro Devices CEO Hector Ruiz, science-fiction author Elizabeth Moon, former U.S. Attorney General Alberto Gonzales, NFL quarterback and Ph.D. Frank Ryan, and astronauts Peggy Whitson and Shannon Walker.

- Karen Michelle Johnston, known for her folk music, grew up in a rigorous Mormon household in Gilmer. That upbringing didn't exactly take. And that name may not ring a bell, either. The singer's stage name was introduced when she was arrested at a political convention; asked to identify herself by arresting officers, she felt shell-shocked enough to answer "Michelle Shocked."

- Would it be so wrong for someone to replace the HOLLYWOOD sign with IRVING? Many famous films have been shot at the Movie Studios of Las Colinas in Irving: Robocop, Silkwood, JFK, and Forrest Gump, for example.

- A death mask is a plaster cast of a corpse's face. Anyone who wants to see a nice collection of them from the Old West should travel to Midland, where the historical museum has masks purportedly for Jesse James, Robert Ford, Wild Bill Hickok, Clay Allison, Butch Cassidy, and more.

The Biggest Texas Political Scandals

Next to football, politics may be the most popular sport in Texas. But with politics often comes scandal, and Texas has had more than its fill of that.

- **Johnson wins by a nose:** Controversy dogged Lyndon Johnson in his first two runs for the U.S. Senate. In 1941, the member of Congress and future president ran for a vacant Senate seat in a special election against Texas governor W. Lee "Pappy" O'Daniel. Johnson initially appeared to be the winner but lost when some questionable returns were counted. He ran again in 1948, finishing second in a three-way Democratic primary to Coke Stevenson, but a runoff was forced when Stevenson failed to win a majority. Johnson won the runoff by 87 votes amidst accusations of fraud, including one that involved votes brought in by campaign manager (and future governor) John B. Connally that appeared to have been cast in alphabetical order. After a friendly judge struck down Stevenson's appeal, Johnson went on to win the general election.

- **Estes donates soiled money:** Billy Sol Estes was both a friend and an enemy of Lyndon Johnson. As a wealthy fertilizer salesman, Estes contributed to Johnson's campaigns for the Senate and the vice presidency. Unbeknownst to Johnson, much of Estes's wealth came from sources as odorous as his fertilizer. In the late 1950s, Estes lied about buying cotton from local farmers to obtain bank loans for nonexistent cotton and fertilizer he claimed was in storage. After his accountant and a government investigator died under suspicious circumstances, Estes and three associates were indicted on 57 counts of fraud. Two of these indicted associates also died suspiciously. Estes was found guilty of fraud and sentenced to eight years in prison, with an additional 15 years tacked on for other charges. His association with Johnson nearly caused President Kennedy to dump his vice president. Estes's conviction was ultimately overturned by the U.S. Supreme Court in 1965, however, on the grounds that having TV cameras and reporters in the courtroom (uncommon at that time) deprived him of a fair trial. After Johnson's death, Estes accused his one-time friend of involvement in a conspiracy behind the Kennedy assassination.

- **Bribery makes real estate deals easier:** The Texas Sharpstown Scandal is named for the Sharpstown master-planned community near Houston and its backer, banker and insurance company manager Frank Sharp. Sharp made loans of $600,000 from his bank to state officials, who then bought stock in his insurance company. They next passed legislation to inflate the value of the insurance company, which allowed the officials to sell their stock profitably. The huge profits aroused the suspicions of the Securities and Exchange Commission in 1971, and charges were filed against Sharp and others. The governor, lieutenant governor, and House speaker, among other state officials, were accused of bribery. Sharp received three years' probation and a $5,000 fine. One victim of the fraud, Strake Jesuit College Preparatory, lost $6 million.

- **Questionable congressional ethics:** Democrat Jim Wright represented Texas in Congress for 34 years, serving as Speaker of the House from 1987 to '89. In 1988, Republican Newt Gingrich led an investigation by the House Ethics Committee into charges that Wright used bulk purchases of his book to get around congressional limits on speaking fees and that his wife had been given a job to get around a limit on political gifts. Wright was forced to resign from Congress in 1989, and Gingrich eventually became Speaker of the House with his own subsequent ethics violations.

- **Corruption as a lifestyle:** George Parr was a political force in Duval County from the 1920s to the '60s. Replacing his brother in 1926 as county judge, Parr used legal and illegal tactics to convince the county's majority Mexican American population to support the Democratic Party. Parr was convicted of income-tax evasion in 1934 and served nine months with little effect on his influence as the "Duke of Duval County." He found questionable votes to help Lyndon Johnson win the 1948 Democratic senatorial primary and was linked to but never accused of at least three murders of political opponents. While appealing a conviction and five-year sentence for federal income tax evasion in 1975, Parr committed suicide.

Talkin' About Texas

"The greatness of Texas lies not so much in its vast extent of territory and its abundance of natural resources as in the character of its people which is a composite—with the good predominant—of qualities peculiar to many lands, whence the citizenship of the state has been recruited."

—Professor George. P. Garrison

"Wildflowers are the stuff of my heart."

—Lady Bird Johnson

"Growing up in the Big Thicket of southeast Texas endowed one with a sense of awe about life and living that marked one's character. The Thicket gave distinctive meanings to words like *work, love, family, home, hope, truth, joy, pain,* and *education.*"

—Jesse Truvillion, preacher

"What . . . makes Texas Texas is that it's ignorant, cantankerous and ridiculously friendly. . . . It's authentically awful, comic and weirdly charming, all at the same time."

—Molly Ivins, journalist

"It is intrinsic to Texan hospitality that you tell visitors all about yourself. That's why Lyndon Johnson used to display his post-operative scars to visitors. Hell, it's only neighbourly to make strangers feel at home."

—Stephen Brook, author

"I wasn't born in Texas, but I got here as soon as I could."

—Popular bumper sticker

"The fertile lands, delightful climate, and wonderful resources of Texas, all combine to attract within her borders the intelligent and enterprising of every State, and indeed of almost every land."

—*The Vicksburg Times,* 1870

"The bluebonnet . . . arrives overnight in spring, thickly coating fields and highway shoulders in a spectacle of deep blue that would have given Renoir a lump in his throat."

—June Naylor, author

Texas as a Republic

For a short time between its independence from Mexico in 1836 and its annexation by the United States in 1845, Texas (or Tejas, as it had previously been known) was an independent, sovereign nation.

Today, Texas is a vital part of the United States of America. It's the largest state of the lower 48, and it's hard to imagine what the country would be like without it. Likewise, it's hard to imagine how life in Texas would be if it weren't part of the United States. But, as every schoolchild knows—especially every Texas schoolchild—for nine years, that's exactly what Texas was.

In the 1830s, many Texians, particularly those who had moved in from the United States to the east, desired independence from Mexico. A representative group of them gathered in Washington-on-the-Brazos, about 70 miles northwest of Houston, and signed the Texas Declaration of Independence on March 2, 1836. Two weeks later, they also approved the Constitution of the Republic of Texas. A military victory by General Sam Houston over Mexican president Santa Anna at the Battle of San Jacinto on April 21 sealed the deal. Three weeks later, Santa Anna signed a peace treaty and ordered Mexican troops out of the newly formed Republic of Texas.

Self-Government

So now that it had broken off from the Mexican government, what was a new nation to do? The republic's first full-term president was war hero Sam Houston, who defeated Stephen F. Austin for the job. Houston served from October 1836 to December 1838. One of his main desires as president, however, was not to lead a newly independent republic but to become part of the United States. If nothing else, this would strengthen Texas's defensive position against Mexico. He oversaw a popular vote held in 1836 that supported annexation by a wide margin. But when Texas's diplomatic representative in

Washington proposed the matter to President Martin Van Buren's government, the U.S. response was lukewarm, at best. By the end of Houston's presidential term, the idea had been withdrawn.

In these early years, much of Texas's territory had not been yet fully settled, and the nation's capital moved several times. After Washington-on-the-Brazos was evacuated to escape Santa Anna's advancing army, the revolutionary government moved to Harrisburg and then on to Galveston, Velasco, and Columbia. With Sam Houston's inauguration, the ad interim government was replaced by the constitutional government of Texas, and in 1837, the capital settled in Houston, where—with the city's namesake as the country's president—it seemed it would stay. Just two years later, however, when Mirabeau B. Lamar became Texas's president, it was moved again, this time to Waterloo. Today, that city is better known by its new name: Austin.

In Defense of Texas

Though Texas had claimed territory down to the Rio Grande, the republic didn't have the troops necessary to defend its borders. And Mexico, still smarting after its defeat at San Jacinto, had never officially acknowledged Texas's independence.

Nonetheless, Mexico had problems of its own and was in no position to offer an immediate threat. In 1841, President Lamar sent an expedition west to the Mexican town of Santa Fe in modern-day New Mexico in an effort to extend Texas's borders. He believed that Texas should reach the Pacific Ocean. Unfortunately, the effort was poorly conceived and carried out, and Mexican forces easily bested the Texans without firing a shot. Sam Houston soon returned as president.

On September 11, 1842, nearly 1,000 Mexican troops seized control of San Antonio. Texas tried to retaliate, but the result was Dawson's Massacre, in which Nicholas Dawson and his company of 53 Texans crept up behind 850 Mexican soldiers. The Mexicans turned and fought, and the battle was over within an hour. If the republic didn't join the United States, it might be forced into rejoining Mexico.

Fortunately, the United States under President John Tyler was now more open to the idea of annexation. Negotiations began, and on December 29, 1845, Texas became the 28th state.

Fast Facts

- *Edgar Byram Davis was rich even before he hit Texas sweet crude near Stairtown in 1922. He became a major (if odd) philanthropist; for example, a friend wrote a mediocre Broadway play called* The Ladder. *Davis liked it and kept it running for two years by purchasing all the tickets.*

- *Sometimes the Spanish legal heritage of Texas can be noticed in today's law. For instance, in a direct legacy from Castilian law, if someone is going to sue another person over a particular event, they must sue that person where they live, not where the event took place.*

- *In 1978, Baylor football coach Grant Teaff told his Bears a loopy motivational story about Eskimos, fishing, and worms. To cap it off, Coach Teaff then ate a worm himself. Somehow or other, the motivation worked. Waco's Baptist sons gave the University of Texas a total immersion, 38–14.*

- *In 1806, Spain and the United States tried to establish a neutral zone between the Sabine and Calcasieu rivers, just east of modern Texas, but it became such a lawless haven for every thug, cardsharp, smuggler, and bandit in the South that Spanish and American authorities united against them.*

- *The Ellis County Courthouse in Waxahachie is decorated with a variety of odd-looking faces. One story suggests that the stone carver had been in love with a local girl whom he immortalized in stone but who had refused his interest. As the carving continued, the girl's face was distorted more and more. Waxahachie authorities insist that the story isn't true, but it does offer an explanation for the strange expressions.*

- *During George W. Bush's 1994 Texas gubernatorial campaign, he used the Spanish slogan "Juntos Podemos," which means, "Together, we can." The Houston Chronicle misreported a campaign sign as saying, "Juntos Pedemos," which, delicately translated, means, "Let's have gas together."*

The Deadliest Texas Tornadoes

Texas sits at the southern end of a geographic area called Tornado Alley. Each year, during spring and summer months, deadly tornadoes wreak havoc through the countryside. Here are the deadliest tornadoes in modern Texas history.

1. The Waco Tornado, May 11, 1953: The day after Mother's Day wasn't a good one as this F5 tornado, about a third of a mile wide, raged through town, killing 114 people and hurting 597 more. About 600 buildings and homes were destroyed, and another 1,000 were damaged.

2. The Goliad Tornado, May 18, 1902: This F4 tornado also had a death toll of 114. It demolished hundreds of buildings including a Methodist church where many citizens had taken shelter. A total of 250 people were injured.

3. The Rocksprings Tornado, April 12, 1927: This F5 tornado demolished 235 of the town's 247 buildings. Almost one-third of the population was affected by the twister, which resulted in 74 fatalities and 205 injuries.

4. The Sherman Tornado, May 15, 1896: This F5 tornado took a path straight through the most populated section of the town of Sherman, killing 73 citizens and injuring 200.

5. The Glazier-Higgins-Woodward tornadoes, April 9, 1947: A massive two-mile-wide tornado was part of a family of storms that started in Texas and moved on to Oklahoma and Kansas. In Texas, the monster twister destroyed the town of Glazier, resulting in 17 deaths and 40 injuries, and severely damaged the town of Higgins, which recorded 51 fatalities and 232 injuries.

6. The Wichita Falls Tornado, April 10, 1979: This mile-wide F4 tornado took a direct path into Wichita Falls. When the winds subsided, citizens found 3,000 homes destroyed and significant damage done to public buildings and schools, as well as 42 fatalities, 1,700 injuries, and as many as 20,000 homeless.

Lone Star Lexicon

- **Coke:** Although a distinct trade name in its own right, it is commonly used to refer in generic terms to any flavor or brand of carbonated soft drink. "Hey, y'all want a *Coke*? The Dr Pepper is on me, I'm buying!"

- **fixin' ta:** The preparatory action preceding the main action, getting ready to do something; usually issued within a warning, e.g., "I'm *fixin' ta* have a hissy fit!"

- **eat up:** Corroded, oxidized, or destroyed; describes someone consumed by emotion, e.g., "She's all swole up about what happened and *eat up* with hatred for Billy Joe."

- **frog-strangler:** A rainy downpour of biblical proportions that not only activates the hibernating frogs burrowed in the earth but threatens to drown them at the same time.

- **gully-washer:** The same as a *frog-strangler*, the only difference being that in this case it is the ground that is affected by the rain, creating deep rivulets and streams where once there were none.

- **blinky:** An adjective used to describe milk that has gone sour or a plan that has gone south, e.g., "Hell's bells, Cletus, the whole shootin' match went *blinky* on us, and we lost our shirts."

- **nu-uh:** Sometimes used in place of the more common "nossir," this is the typical response heard when the person is speaking formal Texan and insisting that the answer is "no."

- **tarred:** Used to describe one's state in regard to sleep, noting a deficit of the same, e.g., "Forget the rodeo, ahm *tarred* and got to git me some shut eye."

- **ridin' high:** A throwback to the days when the animal one rode determined socioeconomic status. Poor people rode a burro or a plug (and were low to the ground), while rich people trotted around on a Tennessee Walker and hence, were *ridin' high* in the saddle.

From Aggies to Owls

How did the top Texas university sports teams nab their nicknames? Find out here.

- **University of Texas Longhorns:** The editorial staff of the *Daily Texan* newspaper decided to call the university football team the Longhorns during the 1903 season. They reasoned the name, which referred to the tenacious breed of cattle, would be accepted by the school's students. Eventually they were proven right, and in 1906, the school officially adopted *Longhorns* as the sport sobriquet.

- **Texas Agricultural and Mechanical College (Texas A&M) Aggies:** Many agricultural institutions have adopted the nickname *Aggies,* a slang term for farmers. The most famous of these schools is Texas A&M, whose football team has appeared in 30 bowl games and captured 18 Southwest Conference championships. Utah and New Mexico State also call themselves Aggies.

- **University of Texas at El Paso (UTEP) Miners:** Although it's generally presumed that sports teams competing at UTEP called themselves the *Miners* because the school was originally founded as the Texas State School of Mines and Metallurgy, there is no evidence the nickname was officially put forward. It is possible that a faculty member named John Kidd, an avid football fan who financially supported the team, dubbed the club the Miners and, over time, the name simply stuck.

- **Texas Christian University (TCU) Horned Frogs:** Legend has it that when the TCU football team first gripped the gridiron in 1896, someone observed that the team resembled a horde of horned toads, the state reptile known for its sharpened quills and unpleasant disposition. Another school of thought purports that a committee of students, looking for a name for both the university yearbook and the school mascot, chose the name *Horned Frogs.*

- **University of North Texas Mean Green:** There are various versions of the tale of how the school adopted its malicious moniker. One concerns verbosity and an overabundance of alcohol. The other involves a turbulent tackle by All-America linebacker Charles "Mean Joe" Greene, who played at the school from 1966 through 1968. After bruising an opponent with a brutal blow, a fan in the crowd yelled, "That's the way, Mean Greene!" The battle cry caught on, and before long, the team itself was dubbed *Mean Green.*

- **Texas Tech Red Raiders:** Originally known as the *Matadors,* the Texas Tech football team was first referred to as the *Red Raiders* by journalist Collier Parris. In 1932, he wrote in a sports column, "The Red Raiders from Texas Tech . . . swooped in the New Mexico University camp today." In 1936, the new nickname became official.

- **University of Houston Cougars:** Coach John Bender, who joined the Houston faculty from Washington State University, suggested the cognomen *Cougars.* Although Houston wouldn't field a football team until 1946, the school needed a name for its student newspaper. Bender proposed the name *Cougar,* and the graceful and powerful beast became the school mascot.

- **Baylor University Bears:** In 1914, Baylor University president Samuel Palmer Brooks initiated a contest to decide on a nickname for the school's athletic teams, which had been competing since the 1890s without a manageable moniker. More than two dozen entries were considered, including buffalo, antelope, frog, and ferret. The students themselves tagged the team the *Bears.*

- **Rice University Owls:** The appellation *Owls* was inherited from the design of the school's official academic seal, which features three Athenian owls, the symbol of wisdom.

- **Southern Methodist University (SMU) Mustangs:** Originally, teams at SMU were generally referred as the *Parsons* because of the large number of theology students on the team. After the SMU women's basketball team captured the state championship in 1917, however, it was decided that a more appropriate appellation was required. On October 17, 1917, *Mustangs* was selected over *Bisons* and *Greyhounds* by the student body.

Billy Bob's Texas: The World's Largest Honky Tonk

Billy Bob's takes the idea of beer drinkin' and boot scootin' to a new level. Thirty-two bars, a barbecue restaurant, and an indoor rodeo arena are only the tip of the steer's horn.

When good ol' boys brag about how "everything is bigger and better in Texas," some might greet the comments with skepticism. That is, unless the good ol' boys are flappin' their jaws about Billy Bob's Texas, a dancehall billed as "The World's Largest Honky Tonk." Named the country music club of the year by the Country Music Association and the Academy of Country Music ten times between them, it's an icon within the Fort Worth Stockyards.

The building that houses Billy Bob's began its life as an open-air barn in 1910, and livestock events were held here until 1943, when the stock show moved to the Will Rogers Memorial Complex in downtown Fort Worth, or "Cowtown" as it is sometimes called. During World War II, the building was a factory for Globe Aircraft, and during the 1950s, it became a department store so large that the stock boys wore roller skates so they could serve customers faster.

The Birth of a Legend

In 1981, the building's true destiny was realized when it was reopened as Billy Bob's Texas. Since then, it has been working its way into the popular culture of Texas one country music act at a time. Opening night featured Larry Gatlin and the Gatlin Brothers, who were followed that first week by Waylon Jennings, Janie Fricke, and Willie Nelson. The word was out: Billy Bob's was *the* place to be if you wanted to experience a contemporary honky tonk.

And what are honky tonks? After World War II, they were typically small joints located on the outskirts of town, hubs of musical creativity. Many were rowdy clubs, where fights were frequent and chicken wire protected the bandstand from the audience. A variation of country and western, honky tonk music peaked between 1948 and 1955. It's known for its distinct fiddle-'n'-steel sound and its two-step shuffle beat. When artists such as Hank Williams sang and played, lyin', cheatin', and broken hearts never sounded so good.

Today, Billy Bob's has taken the essence of the early honky tonk and gentrified it for the masses. Unlike its predecessors, this club is a cavernous space, with 127,000 square feet—that's three acres—able to host more than 6,000 visitors at a time. Thirty-two individual bar stations serve up Shiner Bock, ZiegenBock, and Lone Star beer (as well as a host of other libations) to the thirsty urban cowboys and cowgirls who venture out nightly to do a little Texas two-steppin'.

By the Numbers

With that many bars at its disposal, Billy Bob's holds some impressive records: The most bottled beer sold in one night—16,000 bottles—was registered during a Hank Williams Jr. concert. Not to be outdone, singer Merle Haggard once bought a round of drinks for the entire club and set a new world record.

Since 1981, more than 15 million visitors have ambled through the front door. Many come to see the live pro bull riding, held every Friday and Saturday night at the indoor rodeo arena. There's no mechanical bull on the premises, but tenderfoots can have their picture taken with the "photo bull," which provides the illusion of a real bucking bronc ride.

But mostly, visitors favor this venue of the Fort Worth Stock-yards to eat the barbecue, hoof it on the Texas-size dance floor, and listen to some great live country music. When they leave, they come away with two facts that are far from bragging: First, that Billy Bob's is a Pure-D slice of Texas, and second, that it really is the World's Largest Honky Tonk.

* *What do you do if your wife absconds with your child, your dog, and all your stuff? If you're rockabilly musician Reverend Horton Heat from Dallas, you write a country song entitled "Where in the Hell Did You Go with My Toothbrush?"*

Let Me Finish!

*Software magnate Ross Perot had a relatively low
national profile until he decided that he might like
to be president of the United States in 1992.*

Dismissed by many as merely an eccentric, self-made Texas billionaire Ross Perot created a political storm in the 1992 presidential election by mounting the most serious challenge to the two-party political establishment in modern history. In June '92, Perot led the polls with 39 percent compared with 31 percent for incumbent Republican George H. W. Bush and 25 percent for Democrat Bill Clinton. Come November, Perot secured 18.9 percent of the popular vote, making him the most successful third-party candidate since Theodore Roosevelt in 1912. Considering his colorful background and unpredictable temperament, Perot would indeed have made an unusual choice for president.

The Myth of Perot

The future candidate was born in Texarkana in 1930 to a Texas horse trader and cotton dealer. Many of the details about his early life have been embellished over the years, not least by the man himself, so it can be tricky deciphering fact from fiction. One popular story has it that as a boy Perot delivered newspapers on horseback through a dangerous neighborhood of Texarkana so he could escape any potential muggers. When an unauthorized biography of the Texan was published in 1990, the author claimed that Perot in fact rode a bicycle rather than a horse. For six months, Perot barraged the author and his editor with witness accounts supporting the horse story, demanding a retraction. (He never received one.)

Perot graduated from the U.S. Naval Academy at Annapolis. He was unhappy with what he saw as the Navy's stifling bureaucracy and the immoral behavior of his comrades, but he served his four-year obligation. Working in sales at IBM proved more to the young Perot's liking, and he quickly became one of the company's top salespeople. In 1962, he fulfilled his annual sales quota as early as January. This accomplishment, he claims, caused IBM to force him to sit idly for the next six months because the company didn't want its sales representatives earning more than their managers. This may be another myth, however, as his former colleagues refute these claims, saying that sales reps were actively encouraged to sell more than 100 percent of their quotas and thus earn more commission.

The Birth of EDS

Perot began the road to fortune in 1962 by founding Electronic Data Systems, or EDS, a company that provided computer systems to other companies without their own machines by outsourcing idle time on still other companies' computers. When he sold the company to General Motors in 1984, the deal made Perot a billionaire and GM's largest stockholder until the company bought him out two years later.

Popular myth has it that Perot launched EDS with a mere $1,000 in the form of a check from his wife, Margot. Even Perot himself acknowledges that this claim isn't entirely accurate. The $1,000 check merely covered the registration fee for the new corporation, not the entire start-up costs. Still, Perot propelled the Texarkana-based company to incredible growth, despite some highly unusual business practices.

Under Perot, EDS employees were required to sign an agreement whereby, if they were fired or quit within two years, they had to repay the company $9,000 to cover their training expenses. Men had to wear dark suits with white shirts and a tie and always keep their hair cut short. Facial hair was banned, and recruiters were allegedly directed not to hire any man with a weak handshake in case he turned out to be a homosexual. Perot also decried marital infidelity, which he was known to punish by firing. While women made up 44 percent of the EDS workforce, only 5 percent of senior personnel were female. This was in part because Perot preferred hiring former military men for key positions.

Conspiracy Theories

Perot's affinity for the military extended to supporting covert operations. In 1978, when two EDS executives working in Iran were arrested by revolutionary forces there, Perot recruited a retired U.S. Army officer to lead a group of volunteers in a secret mission to break them out. That story formed the basis of Ken Follett's thriller *On Wings of Eagles.* Perot also helped fund Oliver North's arms-for-hostages deal that came to light in the Iran-Contra scandal of 1986.

A renowned conspiracy theorist, Perot believed that U.S. government officials were actively involved in covering up the existence of American POWs still being held in Vietnam after that war ended. In 1985, he offered the Vietnamese $10 million for every American released, and in 1987, he traveled to Hanoi in order to directly negotiate with the Vietnamese authorities. At no time, however, did Perot reveal any evidence to support his claims. It was Perot's allegations of another conspiracy (this time aimed at him personally) that many political commentators believe were very costly to him in the 1992 election.

Politics as Usual

Despite leading the polls in June, Perot dropped out of the race in July. Just as suddenly, he resumed his bid on October 1. In an appearance on *60 Minutes* the week before the election, Perot made unsubstantiated claims that he dropped out of the race because the Republican Party had threatened to release compromising photos of his daughter prior to her wedding.

Perot's strong showing in the '92 vote meant that he qualified for federal funding for the 1996 election. But this time, running on the Reform Party ticket, Perot didn't fare quite as well at the polls. Many attribute this to his debate with Vice President Al Gore on CNN's *Larry King Live.* Perot's repeated requests to "let me finish" turned him into a figure of fun and ultimately signaled his political demise.

Since that time, Ross Perot has mostly kept a low political profile. In terms of business, after he was bought out by GM, Perot and his associates founded Perot Systems, an information technology company that rose to join the Fortune 1000. In 2009, the computer company Dell agreed to buy it for $3.9 billion in cash. That wouldn't be considered a bad way to finish in anyone's book.

You Can Thank Texas

Anyone who has ever made a mistake while typing and used Liquid Paper to fix it has Bette Nesmith Graham to thank.

Shortly after World War II, Graham, a Dallas divorcée with a young son to raise, went to secretarial school and found employment as an executive secretary. A perfectionist, Graham loathed the fact that her typed pages often contained errors and thought long and hard on how to fix them.

Graham was an aspiring artist who knew that painters often covered over their mistakes on canvas with more paint, so she mixed some specially tinted tempura in her kitchen and brought it to work. The stuff worked like a charm, covering over her errors as if they'd never been there, and her boss was none the wiser. Graham's colleagues in the secretarial pool soon took notice and asked if they could get some of her special correcting fluid. Graham obliged, placing it in a bottle labeled "Mistake Out."

Graham knew she was on to something and turned Mistake Out, which was later renamed Liquid Paper, into a home business. She worked hard to improve her formula, mixing batch after batch in her electric mixer and using her family and friends to fill orders for customers.

Graham was ultimately fired from her secretarial job, but she took the opportunity to focus exclusively on Liquid Paper, which became a huge success. By 1968, she had moved into her own plant and had 19 employees; six years later, a massive new corporate headquarters and manufacturing facility opened in Dallas. In 1979, she sold the Liquid Paper Company to the Gillette Corporation for $47.5 million. She had little time to enjoy her windfall, however, dying only six months later at the age of 56.

Graham's son, Michael Nesmith, who helped her during the early days of her business, is also quite famous in his own right. He was a founding member of the '60s rock band The Monkees and later had a part in the creation of MTV.

The World's First Rodeo

Although different towns in several states make the claim, most historians believe the world's first rodeo was held in the West Texas town of Pecos.

In the days of the Old West, Pecos was little more than a dusty cowboy town, an outpost on the cattle-driving trails linking Abilene to Montana, then a stop on the Texas and Pacific Railway. In the 1880s, it became known as a violent frontier town where arguments frequently ended in a hail of bullets and a body being dumped quietly into the Pecos River. However, when a group of cowboys at Red Newell's saloon began arguing about whether Trav Windham or Morg Livingston was the best at riding and roping, they kept their guns holstered and decided instead to hold a roping and bronco-busting competition.

Windham was a well-known figure in the area, first as a cattle driver then as a ranch foreman. Livingston, on the other hand, had a reputation as an accomplished roper. The two men chose to compete on the flat land on the west side of the river, roughly where the city's courthouse stands today. The year was 1883, and they chose the date of July 4, as it was a public holiday, which enabled more ranchers, cowboys, and townsfolk to attend.

The Stakes Are Raised

Once word of the contest spread, other cowboys clamored to take part. Cowpunchers such as Jim Mannin, John Chalk, and Brawley Oates traveled from ranches with names such as the Hashknife, the Lazy Y, and NA and descended upon Pecos to compete. They were joined by spectators who arrived from every direction in wagons and buggies, on horseback, or simply on foot. Local ranchers put up a

$40 purse while a young girl donated blue ribbons from the hem of her dress as prizes.

The first contest in the competition was won by Trav Windham when he roped and tied a steer in a time of 22 seconds. Morg Livingston then beat his rival in the matched roping contest. Other winners included Pete Beard of the Hashknife and Jeff Chism. According to reports, the youngest entrant, Henry Slack, didn't fare quite as well. When he attempted to rope a steer, his lasso broke, which sent him crashing from his saddle. The young man was knocked unconscious, thus missing out on the prize money, the bragging rights, and a possible blue ribbon.

The First or Not the First?

Much of the controversy surrounding Pecos's claims to holding the world's first rodeo stems from the fact that the contest didn't become an annual event in the town until 1929. But Pecos has not maintained that it holds the *longest-running* rodeo on record. Concerning its actual claim of the world's oldest, the *Encyclopedia Britannica* examined signed affidavits from many who either took part in or attended the 1883 event and concluded that Pecos had indeed held the "world's first public cowboy contest wherein prizes were awarded to the winners of bronc riding and steer roping."

In 1936, the West of the Pecos Rodeo Committee built the Buck Jackson Memorial Arena as the permanent home for the annual West of the Pecos Rodeo. Today, the event is the largest outdoor rodeo in Texas. Spectators no longer arrive by wagons or in horse-drawn buggies, but the spirit of the rodeo remains much as it was in 1883. Instead of settling their arguments in a hail of bullets, cowboys compete to decide who is the best at roping and riding. And while the defeated may miss out on the prize money and bragging rights, they never end up facedown in the Pecos River.

* *Circus strongman "Stout" Jackson (Perrin; 1890–1976) was best known for feats such as playing tug-of-war with horses. South Texas Tejanos, however, remember Stout and his wife Beatrice as* amigos *of the community, always there to lend a hand, let them use the phone, or help midwife a baby.*

The Weird Animals of Texas

Texas is full of unusual critters. Here are some of its strangest.

- The Texas state small mammal is the nine-banded armadillo, an insect-eating relative of sloths and anteaters. Originating in South America, the armadillo migrated to Texas via Mexico in the 19th century. Its fear response is to jump in the air, which is why so many are found dead on Texas highways. Selling armadillos is illegal in Texas because they're the only animal besides humans to carry leprosy.

- The horned toad, horny toad, or horned frog is really a horned lizard and the Texas state reptile. The mistaken identities come from the lizard's round body and blunt snout, and the name comes from the scaly spikes on its back, sides, and head. Unrelated to the name, the male also has two sexual organs.

- The Houston Toad is an endangered toad species discovered in and around Houston in the late 1940s. Only between a few hundred to a few thousand remain, and they're gone from the city that gave them their name. The largest group of these loud amphibians is in Bastrop State Park.

- When people think of Texas, they often think of the longhorn. Longhorn cattle are a hybrid descended primarily from the first cattle brought to the United States by the Spanish and mixed with English cattle. The horns can measure 120 inches tip to tip for steers (which are castrated males) and up to 80 inches for cows and bulls. Longhorns might have been bred out of existence if not for members of the U.S. Forest Service who saved a herd of breeding stock in 1927.

- At five feet in height, the whooping crane is North America's tallest bird and an endangered species. An estimated 340 exist in the wild. The largest group spends the summers in Wood Buffalo National Park in Alberta, Canada, and migrates south in the winter to the Texas Gulf Coast, settling primarily near Corpus Christi on the Aransas National Wildlife Refuge and Matagorda Island.

- Found only in the Guadalupe and a few other Texas rivers, the Guadalupe bass is the Texas state fish. A black bass and member of the sunfish family, the Guadalupe bass is called the "Texas trout" by fishers because of its fighting ability.

- Mexican free-tailed bats live in caves across the western and southern United States, but the largest colony—nearly 20 million bats—hangs out in Bracken Cave, north of San Antonio. Another huge colony of 1.5 million free-tails spends its summers under the Congress Avenue Bridge in Austin, just ten blocks from the state capitol building, making it the largest urban bat colony in North America. Those numbers helped make the Mexican free-tailed bat the official "flying mammal" of Texas.

- The greater roadrunner, a member of the cuckoo family, believe it or not, is a year-round resident of Texas, although it can be found in other southwestern deserts, as well. It can fly if necessary, but it prefers to stay on the ground, where it can reach speeds of more than 15 miles per hour. Although roadrunners try to stay clear of coyotes, they are willing to attack a snake for a nice meal.

- At the small end of the Texas critters scale, the Texas leafcutter ant is a fungus-farming ant species that likes to dine on more than 200 types of plants. Considered a major pest by Texas farmers, leaf-cutter colonies can contain as many as 2 million ants, and one colony with high hopes can strip a citrus tree of its leaves in less than a day.

- It sounds strange, but many Texans, particularly goat farmers, fear a creature known as the Chupacabra—Spanish for "goat sucker"—because of its reputation for attacking goats and other livestock and then drinking their blood. Unexplained livestock disappearances are often blamed on this creature, which is said to be the size of a small bear with fangs and huge claws, have spines down its hairless leathery back, and be bluish-greenish-gray in color. In 2004, a San Antonio rancher killed a creature many believed to be a Chupacabra, but DNA analysis identified it as a coyote with a mange problem. Even though no credible evidence of such a creature exists, it has built up quite a reputation.

Fast Facts

- *Bonnie Parker wasn't the first famous Parker from Texas. Chief Quanah Parker of the Comanche, born around 1850 to white captive Cynthia Ann Parker, never lost a battle to the white settlers. He spent his later life trying to get justice for the Comanche, with more success than many.*

- *Lots of Texans believe the biblical story of Ezekiel and the wheel. Pittsburg's Reverend Burrell Cannon decided to build a modern flyable version of it; some claim it actually flew. In 1902, sadly, high winds blew Cannon's wheel off a train near Texarkana, wrecking all his work.*

- *Roy Rogers and Dale Evans had a rough experience during their halftime performance at the very first Dallas Cowboys' home game at the Cotton Bowl in 1960. As they circled the field after singing, young fans began pelting them with ice cubes and other projectiles. Rogers went to midfield and lambasted the crowd for its rudeness.*

- *From 1896 until 1946, when it was closed by the Texas Rangers, Miss Hattie's Gentlemen's Social Center (a very fancy name for a brothel) operated in San Angelo. Miss Hattie herself lived to be 104, dying in 1982. The property is now Miss Hattie's Bordello Museum, complete with guides in old-style "soiled dove" attire.*

- *While the Texas Brigade of Lee's Army of Northern Virginia is often identified with General John Bell Hood, it was commanded for much of the war by General J. B. Robertson. Why? Hood's command was impressive, and he was promoted to division and then army command—where he wasn't nearly as effective.*

- *Folks with ties to the University of Houston include singer Kenny Rogers, NBA athlete Clyde Drexler, astronauts Bonnie Dunbar and Bernard Harris, actor Dennis Quaid, track star Carl Lewis, rapper Chamillionaire, actor Brent Spiner, ESPN broadcaster Robert Flores, TV journalist Dan Rather, and Cy Young Award–winner Doug Drabek.*

That's Just Like...

Here are a few more examples of how to talk like a Texan.

- I feel as restless as a chicken on a hot stove.
- She walks so slow that you had to set stakes just to see if she was movin'.
- He can show 'em where the bear sat in the buckwheat.
- She's so tight, she'd crawl under the gate to save the hinges.
- You're so strong you can crack walnuts with your toes.
- He's so stupid he uses a shotgun to hunt corn.
- That girl's about 12 cookies shy of a dozen.
- He's so skinny he could take a bath in a shotgun barrel.
- I'm thirsty enough to spit cotton.
- That's wrapped up tighter than the bark on a tree.
- My get-up-and-go has done got up and went.
- She's as tough as the calluses on a bartender's elbows.
- He's ugly enough to stop an eight-day watch.
- She looks like she was pulled through a knothole backwards.
- He couldn't get a date at a chicken ranch with a truckload of fryers.
- She looks like something the cat drug in and the dog won't eat.
- His breath's strong enough to cripple an ox.
- She's so ugly she has to sneak up on the kitchen sink.
- Them folks are as welcome as an outhouse breeze.
- No use cryin' after the jug's busted.
- He's as worthless as a milk bucket under a bull.
- She's got so much money some of it has gone to bed.
- That's as worthless as two buggies in a one-horse town.
- He wouldn't loan you a dollar unless Jesus cosigned the note.

Marfa: An Unlikely Art Capital

Is it really so surprising that a small town known for ghostly lights and a literary name should sprout an artistic community?

Perched in the high desert a ways north of the Mexican border and four hours from the nearest airport, at first glance Marfa looks like many small Texas towns—dusty, hot, underpopulated. But Marfa is anything but ordinary. For starters, it's home to the mysterious Marfa Lights, which bring thousands of visitors to town annually to witness unexplained lights in the night sky. Then there's the iconic "Reata," the set for the movie *Giant,* filmed there in the '50s. Film buffs also know Marfa as the place where *No Country for Old Men* and *There Will Be Blood* were filmed more recently.

But chief among its attractions is Marfa's thriving art scene, a cultural phenomenon that has put this sleepy town on the world map. With a year-round population of more than 2,000, it boasts more than 15 art galleries and artists' studios, several arts-oriented foundations, a growing community of working artists, and some of the most mind-boggling modern art pieces to be found anywhere.

Perhaps the town's literarily inspired name foreshadowed its future as an arts destination. Founded as a railroad watering stop in the mid-19th century and named for a character in a Dostoevsky novel, by the mid-1970s Marfa was down-at-the-heels and headed nowhere—and then artist Donald Judd arrived.

The Desert Blooms

Judd, a minimalist artist from New York, was in search of an expansive setting for the oversize art he and his colleagues were creating. He hit upon a former army post, Fort D. A. Russell, and over a few years bought up most of its 340 acres and, indeed, much of the town itself. Barracks, warehouses, gymnasiums, artillery sheds, hangars, and houses all were renovated and became home to dramatic art installations.

Judd was assisted in his vision by the Dia Foundation, and when it ran out of money, he formed his own Chinati Foundation. While

Judd believed passionately that art needed to be displayed in suitable settings, he was not particularly concerned about whether the public actually came to see it. So, Marfa's growing importance to the art world was very much on the q.t. for years, until the Chinati Foundation started to promote Judd's legacy after his death in 1994.

Artists Begin to Colonize

By the early 1990s, as Judd's extraordinary complex became known to the rest of the world, more artists and art lovers flocked to Marfa. They were drawn by the quiet, the extraordinary desert light, the serene landscape, and Judd's inspiration. Soon bookstores, coffee houses, and fine restaurants came, galleries opened, and artist studios bloomed. Newspapers, art magazines, and, of course, realtors took note.

Today, in addition to its full-time community of artists, more than 10,000 people visit Marfa annually to see Judd's work and other Chinati Foundation projects. Another organization, the Judd Foundation, manages still more facilities, including the house where Judd lived. The Lannan Foundation provides in-residence writers space and time to write. And at the Ballroom, an eclectic mix of art, performance art, and music is on the bill.

The work of artists such as Dan Flavin, John Chamberlain, John Wesley, Ilya Kabakov, Richard Long, Claes Oldenberg, and Coosje van Bruggen—huge works in aluminum, concrete, and neon—is seen to its most dramatic advantage set in repurposed buildings or outdoors in the wide-open spaces of the Big Bend. Judd's own installation of hundreds of large aluminum cubes set inside two enormous buildings is perhaps the most eye-catching. Also appealing is a Prada store, or what looks like one, anyway. Artists Michael Elmgreen and Ingar Dragset built a mock-up of the high-end chain store but sealed it tight, so it would always appear to be abandoned.

On a visit to Marfa in 2006 for the wedding anniversary of friends, singer David Byrne found the town's vibe appealing. As he blogged, "Marfa is in a dry flat area in between these outcroppings that you reach after winding through various hills and canyons. In some ways it is a typical small Texan town with a beautiful old central courthouse, a train track running through the middle, grain and cattle loading facilities . . . but that's where the ordinariness ends."

Top Ten Texas Movies

Hardly a year passes without the Lone Star State showing up in a movie. Filmmakers first fell in love with Texas in the early 1900s. From Wings, *a 1927 Best Picture Oscar winner, to chainsaw massacres to love stories, a complete list of Texas-oriented movies would fill an entire book. Here are some highlights.*

- **Red River** (1948). Directed by Howard Hawks this movie stars John Wayne as one of the first Texas cattlemen. Montgomery Clift, Walter Brennan, and Joanne Dru join the Duke for a tale that includes murderous Apaches, the Chisholm Trail, gun battles, and true love.

- **The Best Little Whorehouse in Texas** (1982). Dolly Parton stars as the madame of a famous brothel (based on the real-life Chicken Ranch in La Grange and filmed in Austin and Halletsville), and Burt Reynolds is her friend—and the local sheriff—who tries to fend off trouble. Charles Durning snagged an Oscar nomination for his portrayal of a mealy-mouthed governor.

- **The Alamo** (1960). The quintessential Texas legend has been put on film before and since, but this is the good one. John Wayne again, this time as Davy Crockett. Shot in Brackettville, this is an epic film that still evokes tears. Laurence Harvey plays William Travis, and Richard Widmark is Jim Bowie. Wayne directed.

- **The Last Picture Show** (1971). Some say this film, directed by Peter Bogdanovich from a screenplay by Larry (*Lonesome Dove*) McMurtry, is the single best picture ever made about Texas. Filmed in Archer City, it is a poignant coming-of-age tale set in fictional Anarene, a fading small town, in 1951. Timothy Bottoms and Jeff Bridges star as Sonny and Duane, with Cybill Shepherd shining as Jacey, everyone's fantasy. Cloris Leachman and Ben Johnson won Oscars for their performances. And then how about Ellen Burstyn, Eileen Brennan, Clu Gulager, and Randy Quaid?

- **Giant** (1956). Cattleman Bick Benedict (Rock Hudson) butts heads with oilman upstart Jett Rink (James Dean) over the course of two generations in this classic, filmed around Marfa. Trivia: The part of Benedict's wife, Leslie, an iconic role for Elizabeth Taylor, was originally offered to Grace Kelly.

- **Blood Simple** (1984). The first Coen Brothers movie, set in an unnamed Texas town, where bar owner Julian Marty (Dan Hedaya) hires a detective to spy on his wife Abby (Frances McDormand) and his bartender Ray (John Getz), whom he suspects are having an affair. If only things were that simple. A complex, gripping thriller.

- **Hud** (1963). The movie's ads crowed, "After lovin' Hud liked fightin' best ... after fightin' Hud liked lovin' best!" 'Nuff said. Who can ever forget Paul Newman as Hud Bannon, cheating, lying, amoral cad, with the greatest blue eyes in the world? Newman was nominated for an Oscar; Melvyn Douglas as his father and Patricia Neal as his girl both won Academy Awards for their performances. Filmed in Claude.

- **Urban Cowboy** (1980). Hardly anybody outside of Texas had heard of mechanical bull riding before this film made cowboy ultra cool. Today, there are men who still get weak-kneed thinking of Sissy (Debra Winger) bucking and whirling on the thing. Bud (John Travolta), country bumpkin turned refinery worker, felt the same way. Much of the film is set in Mickey Gilley's club; an outstanding soundtrack record netted a Grammy nomination.

- **Dazed and Confused** (1993). Another great coming-of-age film, set in another small Texas town, this time in 1976. A rowdy group of high schoolers hazes next year's freshmen on the last day of school. Jason London and Wiley Wiggins have lead roles, but Matthew McConaughey, Ben Affleck, Parker Posey, and Milla Jovovich are all part of the fun.

- **Friday Night Lights** (2004). No top-ten Texas movie list is complete without this definitive Texas high school football flick. Billy Bob Thornton plays coach Gary Gaines in this real-life story of the 1988 Permean High School Panthers, the pride of Odessa. More than just an inspiring football tale, it deals with racism, poverty, and community.

Stand Tall, the Texas Rangers

Among the most revered of Texas's iconic institutions must be the Texas Rangers, whose rich history and daring frontier exploits have thrilled generations. These were those who could not be stampeded.

The oldest law enforcement agency in North America, the Texas Rangers has been compared with the FBI, Scotland Yard, and the Royal Canadian Mounted Police. The group's heritage began with the earliest settlements in Texas, and it became a significant part of the story of the Old West and its mythology.

Getting Off the Ground

In Mexican Tejas, the Comanche and Tonkawa raided Texian settlements on a regular basis. Stephen F. Austin, responsible for founding and developing many of these settlements from America, realized he needed a militia of some kind to ward off Native American raids, capture criminals, and patrol against intruders. He set up two such companies, which today are considered the ancestors of the modern Texas Rangers.

In 1835, in what is often considered the official founding of the Rangers, the Texas council of representatives created a Corps of Rangers and set pay at $1.25 per day. These enforcers of the law had to provide their own mounts, weapons, and equipment. As they were often outnumbered during battles, many carried multiple pistols, knives, and rifles. The most popular weapons were Spanish pistols, Tennessee and Kentucky rifles, and Bowie knives. Later, Sam Colt built his reputation on the fact that the Texas Rangers were the first to use the Colt revolver.

Like the state of Texas itself, the Texas Rangers had multi-cultural roots. Company rosters show that Anglos, Hispanics, and American Indians served in the ranks. In addition, a number of immigrants were also present; Ireland, Germany, Scotland, and England each contributed native sons to the Rangers.

As the cause for independence from Mexico heated up, the Rangers played a key role in protecting civilians fleeing Santa Anna's army, harassing Mexican troops, and providing intelligence to the Texas army. And it was the Rangers who responded to Colonel William Travis's last minute plea to defend the Alamo. Even so, the Rangers did not participate in actual combat as often as they may have preferred.

Texas president Sam Houston sought good relations with Native Americans, so a fighting force to be used against them was not high on his list of priorities. Texas's second president, Mirabeau B. Lamar, however, felt differently and strengthened the Rangers and their responsibilities when he got into office. He wanted them to clear the frontier of Native Americans who were in the way of Texas settlement and expansion, and the Texas Rangers rose to that call very effectively. The Cherokee War of 1839 expelled most Cherokee from Northeast Texas, and the Battle of Plum Creek moved the Comanchee farther west out of central Texas. When Houston regained the presidency in 1841, he recognized the Rangers as an effective frontier protection agency and threw his support to them.

Making Their Name

In the Mexican-American War that followed closely after Texas annexation, the Texas Rangers distinguished themselves as ferocious fighters. They supported the U.S. Army under Generals Zachary Taylor and Winfield Scott, working as scouts and extremely effective warriors. This brought them a worldwide reputation as *Los Diablos Tejanos,* the Texas Devils.

For a time after the war, however, it looked as though the Rangers might have had their best days behind them. Once Texas became a U.S. state, the protection of its frontier was a federal issue, and there was no obvious place for the Rangers. Although it wasn't dissolved, the agency saw its purpose wither away and its best officers leave for greener pastures. There was a slight revival under Captain John S. "Rip" Ford in which the Rangers attacked and killed Comanche leader Iron Jacket, but the coming Civil War gave those interested in fighting another focus. Many Rangers and former Rangers served with the Confederacy, but there was no official connection. Reconstruction, likewise, offered little opportunity for the

Texas Rangers, as their former frontier duties were handled by the Union Army.

Back in the Battle

That all changed, however, when the Democrats took back the governor's mansion in 1874. The state legislature passed a bill that year formally creating the Texas Rangers (thus making that name official). The Reconstruction government hadn't been entirely successful in maintaining order, so the Rangers had their work cut out for them. Two branches were created by the legislation: the Special Force, focusing on law enforcement, and the Frontier Battalion, protecting the western frontier and borders. The Special Force did what was necessary to get the job done. In one particular infamous incident, Rangers took the bodies of dead cattle rustlers and stacked them in the Brownsville town square as a show of force.

The Frontier Battalion, focusing on gunfighters in addition to Native Americans, had its share of high-profile captures, as well. Not bound by the borders of the state, Ranger John Armstrong captured one of Texas's deadliest outlaws, John Wesley Hardin—reputed to have killed more than 30 people—on a train in Pensacola, Florida. In the course of the capture, Hardin was knocked out, and one of his three companions was killed; the remaining two surrendered. Another famous train and bank robber, Sam Bass, was killed by four Rangers in an 1878 shoot-out at Round Rock.

By the 1890s, Texas Rangers were upholding the law in mining towns and tracking down train robbers. They were once even called upon to prevent an illegal prizefight. Records show that in one year, the Rangers scouted nearly 174,000 miles, made 676 arrests, returned 2,856 head of livestock, assisted civil authorities 162 times, and guarded jails on 13 occasions.

Into Tomorrow

The role of the Texas Rangers has continued to evolve. Today, they are part of the Texas Department of Safety, and a Ranger is far more likely to have a laptop computer than a horse. Even so, they continue to investigate cattle thefts as well as other major felony crimes. And the stories of their heyday during the early days of Texas live on to support the mythos of the officers who stand tall.

🍽️ Taste of Texas

Roadside diners may not have originated in Texas, but the state has more than its fair share of such definitively local eateries.

- The Cottonwood Café in La Grange, the Feed Mill Restaurant in Bonham, Goodson's Café in Tomball, and the Bluebonnet Café in Temple have all been cited as having "the best" of a Lone Star favorite, chicken fried steak. And the battle goes on. In the West Texas town of Strawn, the two primary businesses in town—Mary's and Flossie's—go head-to-head every day for the title of best chicken fried steak in Texas.

- The best place to eat a burger in Texas is often called a toss-up between Kincaid's Grocery in Fort Worth—where patrons stand at a wall counter and eat—and Wise County's Greenwood Grocery in Decatur, which always has old westerns playing on a vintage TV set.

- Although beef is the national entrée of Texas, chicken often figures prominently in daily dining. The Cowboy Chicken diner in Dallas features chicken roasted over a hickory fire. Some claim that Babe's Chicken Dinner House in Roanoke has the best fried poultry in the state.

- The Shady Grove Restaurant in Austin harks back to a sadly passing era when the Texas capital still felt like a groovy little college town. Although the Tex-Mex menu is good, the main attraction is ambience, with patio seating under a pecan grove and live music on Thursday nights. It's located on Barton Springs Road, just down the street from the famous public swimming hole; patrons often bike in wearing their swimsuits.

- While technically not a diner, no list of Texas in-and-outs is complete without the H&H Car Wash and Coffee Shop. This El Paso landmark could be a time capsule from the 1960s, where diners can get an old-fashioned hand wash for their car while enjoying some amazing huevos rancheros or carne picada with freshly roasted chiles. The H&H is always packed with locals and has been visited by no less than Julia Child—it's also won a coveted James Beard culinary award for its masterful Tex-Mex menu. The car wash operates from 9 A.M. to 5 P.M. during the week and from 9 A.M. to 3 P.M. on Saturdays.

Stationed in the Heart of Texas

Fifty miles southwest of Waco, 60 miles northeast of Austin, and right next to Killeen lies Fort Hood, a bustling place that is home to more than 100,000 men, women, and children.

Like any successful small city, this community boasts a hospital, schools, shops, a wide variety of housing, mass media, cultural and community activities, and an eager, well-trained workforce. Sound like a nice place to live? Well, anyone who's ready to commit a few years to defending the nation could make a home here, too. Welcome to Fort Hood, the largest U.S. active-duty military installation in the world.

Sprawling across 340 square miles, Fort Hood is the only U.S. post that is able to serve as home to two U.S. Army armored divisions, the 1st Cavalry Division and the 4th Infantry Division. In addition, the Headquarters Command III corps, the 3rd Air Support Operations Group, and numerous other Army outfits whose duties range from finance to dentistry to battlefield surveillance are also stationed here.

Built to Last

Known as "The Great Place"—though some grunts have called it other things over the years—Fort Hood began life as Camp Hood in 1942. It is named for Confederate General John Bell Hood, commander of the Texas Brigade named for him during the Civil War.

With 44,000 military personnel and 9,600 civilian employees, the fort is the largest single-site employer in the state of Texas. In 2005, the state comptroller estimated the direct and indirect impact of the fort on the Central Texas economy at $6.09 billion annually.

What's life like on a base that's bigger than most of its residents' hometowns? Well, mobile, for one thing. More than 85 percent of the units stationed at Fort Hood served at least one one-year tour of duty in Iraq, with many returning for second and third tours. That's a tough life for soldiers and families alike, and the Army is more sensitive to families and the base community these days than ever before, offering educational activities, community outreach, counseling, and a wide variety of activities and programs to help families cope with the stresses of military life. Base housing has been improved, and schools have stepped up in importance.

The Carl R. Darnall Army Medical Center at Fort Hood is a teaching hospital partnered with several civilian hospitals and medical education institutions. The center serves 163,000 care recipients within a 40-mile radius of the base, including active military, retirees, and families. Among its training programs are those in obstetrics and gynecology (the center averages seven births daily!) and the top emergency medicine residency program in the country—whether military or civilian.

Staying at the Ready

The area's dry, flat, Central Texas terrain makes Fort Hood an ideal place for all kinds of military training (one old joke maintains that if you go AWOL from Fort Hood, the MPs won't come after you for days, because they can still see you). Indeed, all kinds of training take place here, making the sound of distant weapons fire just a normal part of everyday life. Of the base's 215,000 acres, 136,000 are used for maneuvers. Fort Hood is home to the Army's only Battle Command Training Center, which provides command and control training in the field while replicating battlefield conditions using actual tactical units, virtual-reality battlefield situations, or computer-supported war games. The area is so large and diverse that battalion task-force operations can go on for weeks. Nearby Lake Belton provides additional opportunities to train in water, while the world's largest combat aviation training area—15,900 square miles, beginning at Fort Hood and traveling through four counties—trains troops in highly realistic situations.

As fiercely impressive as this all seems, consider the softer side of life at Fort Hood, which anyone can easily follow on Twitter (twitter.com/forthood) to catch up on the day's events and issues, from back-to-school pool parties and cheerleading tryouts to free tax assistance and activities in honor of Gold Star families. Though the work is serious, the life often arduous, the sacrifice never-ending, for more than 100,000 people, Fort Hood is still just home.

Texas's Largest Ranches

A popular image of Texas is longhorn cattle, ranches, and oil. Texas is home to many of the largest ranches in the country. Most of them have interesting heritages and are operated by descendants of the original owners to produce cattle, crops, oil, and gas.

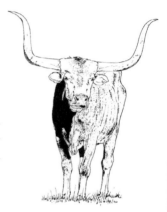

- The King Ranch covers 825,000 acres over six South Texas counties, making it the largest ranch in both Texas and the United States and one of the largest in the world. The ranch consists of four divisions, and only two of those four actually border each other. Captain Richard King and Gideon K. Lewis purchased a Spanish land grant in 1853 and founded the ranch. In the 1990s, the ranch had around 60,000 head of cattle; it also raises crops (grain sorghum, cotton, sugarcane, and wildflowers), manages oil and gas drilling and refining through King Ranch Oil and Gas, has a timber company, raises horses, and is a prime hunting and tourist spot. The ranch is still partly owned and operated by descendants of Captain King.

- Briscoe Ranches is actually a number of ranches in nine Texas counties. The 640,000 total acres are owned by former Texas governor Dolph Briscoe Jr., making him the largest individual landowner in the state. Founded in 1939, the ranch is used for raising cattle and Angora goats, farming, and producing oil and gas.

- The Waggoner Ranch got its start in 1849 when Daniel Waggoner settled near what is now Decatur with his wife and son William Thomas (Tom) Waggoner. When Tom Waggoner died in 1934, he stipulated that the ranch couldn't be divided into parcels, so today the tract of approximately 520,000 acres is the largest ranch in Texas surrounded by one fence. Waggoner Ranch is used for cattle, oil, horse breeding, and farming.

- O'Connor Family Ranches began when Thomas O'Connor and his uncle James Power sailed from Ireland to Texas in 1834. Later that year, the Mexican government granted the 17-year-old O'Connor 4,428 acres as a settler in what is now Refugio County. The O'Connor Family Ranches today total approximately 500,000 acres, which are used for cattle ranching by about a dozen descendants of the founder.

- The Jones Family Ranches were founded in 1897 when William Whitby Jones bought 6,000 acres in Jim Hogg County. Today the 380,000 acres of ranches are owned and operated by his descendants, who use it for cattle, oil and gas, and wild game hunting.

- According to Texas legend, the Four Sixes (6666) Ranch and cattle brand owe their origin to a poker hand of four sixes that gave the ranch to Samuel Burk Burnett. A more likely story is that Burnett worked as a trail boss on a cattle drive for his father and used the money to buy the ranch in Denton County with the 6666 brand in 1871. Burnett's brother Bruce flipped the brand over and used 9999 on his ranch. The 350,000-acre ranch is now located in King County, managed by Burk Burnett's great-granddaughter and used for raising cattle and horses.

- What little is known about the East Family Ranches is that rancher Tom T. East married Alice Kleberg, the granddaughter of King Ranch founder Richard King, in 1915 and lived on East's San Antonio Viejo Ranch near the King Ranch. Tough times forced the Easts to sell the ranch to Kings, but when Alice Kleberg died in 1935, the title was transferred back to the East family. Her descendants own 340,000 acres in eight counties used for raising cattle and producing oil and gas.

- The 272,000-acre La Escalera Ranch south of Fort Stockton is one of the largest cattle-only ranches in the state. The land had originally been given to the GC&SF Railway in exchange for money and materials used to the build the Texas capitol, then it was sold to Edwin Giddings in 1884, when it was called Elsinore. In 1992, Gerald Lyda Sr. bought the land from Giddings's grandson, Douglas, and renamed it La Escalera, the Spanish word for "ladder." Now owned by Lyda's sons and daughter, La Escalera is known for its Black Angus cattle.

Texas Timeline

(Continued from p. 211)

April 9, 1965
The Houston Astrodome is inaugurated with an exhibition Astros-Yankees matchup. This first-ever indoor baseball game ends with a 2–1 Astros victory.

August 1, 1966
In one of the worst mass murders in U.S. history, Charles Whitman embarks on a shooting spree from the tower at the University of Texas at Austin. He takes 17 lives.

July 18, 1970
In the last reported train robbery in Texas, two AWOL soldiers attempt to hold up the miniature train in San Antonio's Brackenridge Park.

January 1971
"Me and Bobby McGee," the biggest hit of Port Arthur singer Janis Joplin's career, reaches number one on the *Billboard* charts three months after Joplin's tragic death.

July 9, 1972
Texas superstar pitcher Nolan Ryan strikes out three Boston Red Sox players on nine pitches, becoming the only player to accomplish such a feat in both leagues. He did the same thing in 1968 while pitching for the New York Mets.

August 17, 1973
The Manned Space Center in Houston is renamed in honor of late President Lyndon B. Johnson.

October 14, 1987
Eighteen-month-old Jessica McClure falls down an eight-inch-wide well in Midland. The international media is riveted by the successful 58-hour rescue operation.

July 18, 1988
Texas state treasurer Ann Richards delivers the keynote address at the Democratic National Convention, famously claiming Republican candidate and fellow Texan George H. W. Bush was "born with a silver foot in his mouth."

July 30, 1990
Nolan Ryan, the 100-mph flame-thrower with the Texas Ranger baseball club, records his 300th career win.

April 19, 1993
A two-month standoff between federal agents and members of a Waco cult ends in tragedy when the Branch Davidian compound goes up in a flurry of flames and gunfire. Eighty-one cult members, mostly women and children, are killed along with leader David Koresh.

May 2002
The Cadillac Ranch, a roadside attraction that features ten half-buried Cadillacs in a field west of Amarillo, is repainted, restoring the site to its former glory.

February 1, 2003
The Space Shuttle *Columbia* disintegrates on reentry, breaking up over Texas and spreading debris from one end of the state to the other. It is determined that a missing heat shield tile is the cause of the disaster.

Weird Museums

*Does Texas have more than its share of eclectic
and interesting museums? Maybe so.*

- **Robert E. Howard Museum, Cross Plains:** Robert E. Howard, the creator of Conan the Barbarian, was born in Peaster and spent most of his short life in Cross Plains. Howard committed suicide at 30 years old after hearing that his mother was terminally ill. Loyal fans and a community organization, Project Pride, purchased the Howard home and have turned it into a museum devoted to the beloved writer. The town celebrates Robert E. Howard Remembrance Day yearly with tours of the home and a display of his original manuscripts at the public library.

- **House Moving Museum, Fort Worth:** Since 1985, this family-owned collection of dollies, jacks, rollers, boomers, and tools has been a destination for professional movers and those curious about the process of moving a house.

- **Texas Prison Museum, Trinity:** Established in 1989, this museum gives visitors a glimpse into the history of the Texas prison system from the perspective of inmates and employees. In fact, most of the employees and volunteers at the museum are prison-system retirees. The museum's most cherished display honors General Manager Lee Simmons, who was responsible for starting the now famous Texas Prison Rodeo and hiring Frank Hamer to kill Bonnie and Clyde. The gun found in their death car is part of the exhibit.

- **Toilet Seat Museum, Alamo Heights:** Barney Smith, a retired plumber, can't get away from his work. Thirty years ago, when he needed to mount a set of deer antlers, he turned to a familiar item, a toilet seat. That started a creative endeavor that continues to this day. Smith currently has almost 700 decorated toilet seats on display at his home. A local company donates the wood-finished seats, and Smith adds the imagination and materials to create each unique work of art.

- **Wooden Nickel Museum, San Antonio:**
The adage, "Don't take any wooden nickels," certainly doesn't apply at this unique museum and nickel-processing plant operated by Herb Hornung. Hornung acquired a wooden nickel–processing machine from the Old Time Wooden Nickel Company and began making and selling wooden nickels.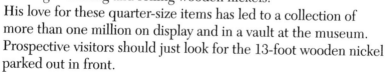
His love for these quarter-size items has led to a collection of more than one million on display and in a vault at the museum. Prospective visitors should just look for the 13-foot wooden nickel parked out in front.

- **Devil's Rope Museum, McLean:** Any self-respecting cowboy knows that devil's rope is barbed wire, and in McLean the curious can visit a museum dedicated to the multiple types and uses of this wire. Collectors from the United States, Canada, and Australia 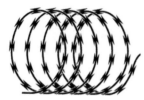 donated specimens of common and rare forms of barbed wire, as well as the tools used to construct and maintain fences. And if that's not enough, visitors can learn how to make their own barbed wire via daily demonstrations.

- **Texas Route 66 Museum, McLean:** Located in the same building as the Devil's Rope Museum, this archive contains close to 700 artifacts from the section of Route 66 that crosses Texas. In addition to road signs and advertising memorabilia, visitors won't want to miss the giant snake that once graced the entrance to Regal Reptile Ranch.

- **Cockroach Hall of Fame, Plano:** Michael Bohdan is a pest control specialist who takes his love for his job to a new and interesting level. On the premises of his retail store, Bohdan has created a loving homage to cockroaches. Dead cockroaches are dressed in costumes and placed in shadow box displays representing historical and cultural figures. Those who might be more interested in live cockroaches, however, can hold a Madagascar hissing cockroach while touring the museum.

The Biggest Bulldog: The Story of Bill Miller

Texas has proudly produced more than 700 major league baseball players and 19 big-league managers, three of whom have guided teams to the biggest prize in the game—a World Series title. While baseball fans around the world recognize the names of Texas-born bench bosses such as Tris Speaker, Frank Robinson, Rogers Hornsby, and Eddie Mathews, the name Bill Miller is not so well known. Miller was never in the majors as a player or a manager, but his accomplishments on and off the diamond are anything but minor league.

Bill Miller learned the lessons of the game of baseball at La Grange High School, a community best known for the house of ill repute located on its doorstep and immortalized in the Broadway musical and movie *The Best Little Whorehouse in Texas*. An all-star hurler renowned for his poise on the mound, Miller helped lead the La Grange Leopards to the 1973 Class 3A Baseball State Championship. After graduation, Miller attended Texas Lutheran University, located in Seguin near San Antonio. With the Bulldogs, Miller was named Big State All-Conference as a pitcher in 1975 and also captured the Big State Conference MVP award. During his tenure at State, Miller compiled a 20–13 record.

A Little Help

It's impossible to tell Miller's story without paying tribute to Ray Katt, the man who taught Miller that success as an adult and an athlete can only be gauged by strong moral character and a commitment to academic excellence and achievement. A former major league catcher with St. Louis and a member of the World

Series–winning New York Giants in 1954, Katt was best known for his compassion and competitive spirit, a resounding endorsement considering his on-field accomplishments. Under Katt as Texas Lutheran coach, Miller refined his skills as an athlete and defined himself as a benevolent humanitarian.

After graduation, Miller continued to mix scholastics with athletics, doubling as a teacher and assistant baseball coach at Spring Woods High School in Houston, where a young Roger Clemens was one of his students and protégés. Miller moved from Houston to the outskirts of San Antonio, settling in Converse, where he was named head baseball coach at Judson High School.

Stepping Up

After seven sensational seasons with the Rockets—where he compiled a 125–50 record—Miller was asked to return to his alma mater in 1992 to assume Ray Katt's position. Although he was apprehensive in replacing his mentor in the dugout, Miller realized it was an opportunity to bring both his academic and athletic career full circle. He accepted the post with the promise he would coach only if he could do it for all the right reasons—for his players. He continued to preach and teach Katt's philosophy that excellence on the playing field must be matched by distinction in the classroom.

Miller served as the Bulldogs' bench boss for 15 seasons, from 1993 until 2007, compiling a coaching record of 530–191–3. His winning percentage of .734 is the third-best all-time mark among Texas-based managers in NCAA history. During his decade and a half as dugout disciplinarian, Miller was named ASC West Coach of the Year four times, and he was the 1999 Heart of Texas Conference Coach of the Year. His Bulldogs appeared in the NCAA Division III Baseball Championships on three different occasions and made six appearances in the NAIA district and regional playoffs. Most importantly, the Bulldogs appeared in postseason play in 11 of Miller's 15 seasons, a gauge of success few coaches can claim.

Katt had also been TLU's director of athletics, and Miller took on that role, as well. One of his accomplishments in that position has been to move TLU from NCAA Division II to Division III, in which schools do not offer athletic scholarships, strengthening again Miller's focus on achievement in the classroom.

Fast Facts

- From the Prohibition days to the Kennedy years, anyone who wanted to hustle or be hustled at golf went to Tenison Glen in East Dallas. The situation eventually got so bad there that the course had to ban "spectators" (a more polite name for bettors) from following players around the links by car.

- Travelers full of jukebox nostalgia should pull into Pharr, home to Smitty's Jukebox Museum, containing more than 70 functional, classic boxes. Some date back to the 1920s; others are very rare. Even the mix of colors has a surreal beauty.

- General Claire Chennault, the contentious, granite-faced leader of the American Volunteer Group (also known as the "Flying Tigers") over China in World War II, may have grown up in Louisiana, but he was born in Commerce on September 6, 1893.

- On November 23, 1968, the Houston Cougars were beating the University of Tulsa 51–6 after three quarters. With about a dozen Golden Hurricane starters down with the flu and injuries, Houston ran it up to 100–6 by the end of the game.

- Jim Bowie is likely known by anyone who's even heard of Texas. What's less well known is that, as a commander, he was extremely careful with the lives of those under his command. His specialty was winning battles without taking unnecessary casualties, so it's no wonder his troops would follow him to Hell and back.

- North Texas alums and affiliated people include NFL Hall of Famer "Mean" Joe Greene, pro wrestler Steve Austin, actress Joan Blondell, Miss America and broadcaster Phyllis George, singer Don Henley, TV shrink Dr. Phil McGraw, commentator Bill Moyers, activist Jim Hightower, and former U.S. House Majority Leader Dick Armey.

- Why did Texas billionaire environmentalist Ed Bass sink $200 million and more into a sustainability enclosure called Biosphere 2? He thought it would lead to discoveries. It did: Among other things, participants discovered how to feud over the basic purpose of Biosphere 2! The experiment soon fell apart.

Feuds as Big as Texas

Forget the Hatfields and the McCoys. Texas's feuds are larger and more colorful than anything that can be found outside the Lone Star State. Here are 10 candidates for the title of "Top Texas Feud."

• The Regulator-Moderator War of East Texas broke out in 1839 when the Regulators—a group of vigilantes—used lethal force to stop bands of outlaws. When a new group formed to "moderate" the Regulators, violence became rampant. The fighting ended five years later, when Sam Houston and 500 militia members took charge of the local area for two weeks until both sides signed an agreement disbanding both factions.

• The Lee-Peacock Feud is a classic tale. The Lees and their cousins defended the Confederacy, and the Peacocks and their kin supported the Union. One night in 1868, after the war was over, Lewis Peacock and his friends robbed Bob Lee at Choctaw Creek Bottoms. Gunfire followed, and the feud had begun.

   Bob Lee was killed the next year, but the feud continued, killing as many as 50, until 1871 when one of Bob Lee's followers shot Lewis Peacock. Everyone seemed to agree that the matter was settled.

• The 1875 Blood Feud is often called the Mason County War or the "Hoodoo War." The problems began when German settlers staked land claims later disputed by returning Confederate soldiers.

   After the Germans elected a mystery man, John Clark, as sheriff of Mason County, a group called the "Hoodoos" took the law into their own hands. Hired guns such as John Ringo became part of the fight, which exploded across the area.

   Peace was restored when a battalion of Texas Rangers arrived late in 1875. Sheriff Clark resigned, and John Ringo headed west to Tombstone, Arizona, to meet the Earp brothers in another feud.

• The 1877 Salt War was a conflict concerning the rights to a salt mine near San Elizario. Various disputes among Mexicans, Anglos, and African Americans led to a free-for-all. When the fighting stopped, at least a dozen people had been killed—some of them mutilated—and at least 50 were wounded. Community leaders left town, and El Paso replaced San Elizario as the county seat. The site of the salt war never recovered its prefeud importance.

- The Bastrop County Lynching Feud broke out after a June 1877 dance when four men were lynched. As in many other feuds, the combatants were organized outlaws opposed by vigilantes. Additional hangings continued for nearly ten years, when the anger seemed finally to abate.

- From 1888 to 1890, Fort Bend County was the site of the Jaybird-Woodpecker War. The Woodpeckers had favored Reconstruction and were elected by African American voters, while the Jaybirds were white citizens who opposed them. A series of grisly killings led to the "Battle of Richmond." The feuding ceased in 1890 when a Jim Crow whites-only primary voted the Jaybirds into power. In 1953, the U.S. Supreme Court reversed the law in favor of equality, but by that time, the feud had become just a vague memory.

- The Colorado County Feud may be Texas's longest-lasting feud. It began in 1890 in the lovely town of Columbus. After the July 4 barbecue, Marshal Larkin Hope shot and killed Bob Stafford and his brother John. Soon after that, Hope ran for sheriff and was shot dead in a downtown Columbus alley. The departing sheriff was also killed in a downtown gunfight, and central Columbus became known as "Hell's Half Acre." It took 20 years for state law enforcement to restore peace to the community. Today, Columbus is known for its art and antiques...and its ghosts.

- The Broocks-Border-Wall Feud was one of the last big Texas feuds to erupt. Lycurgus "Curg" Border had hated the Roberts and Wall families since childhood. One April afternoon in 1900, Curg and his buddies were drinking in Ephraim Talley's saloon across the street from the courthouse. One of Curg's group shot Sheriff Wall, who'd been taking a nap just inside a courthouse window. The sheriff's family retaliated by killing Curg's cousin, Ben Broocks. The shootings continued through early June and included a gunfight around the the courthouse in which Sid and Felix Roberts were killed. A new sheriff ended the feud by killing Curg Border.

Pigskin Propulsions of Prodigious Proportions

The football field goal is rarely given the respect it deserves, despite the fact that more games are decided by the accuracy of a carefully calibrated kick than a perfectly pitched pass. In Texas, however, the field goal has been able to transcend the touchdown.

The three longest field goals in the history of top-tier football all have a distinct Texas connection. The longest three-point play in gridiron history was generated by a Swedish-born, soccer-style kicker named Ove Johansson. A junior at Abilene Christian University, Johansson was playing in only his sixth football game when he con-

nected for a 69-yard gem in a game against East Texas State on October 16, 1976. A serious knee injury ended Johansson's college career and hampered his attempts to translate his record-setting kick into a successful professional career. Johansson returned to Texas after a brief NFL fling and settled in Amarillo, where he became a well-respected investment broker, certified estate counselor, and motivational speaker.

Close, but Not Quite Enough

The second most prodigious three-pointer in football folklore—and the longest in NCAA Division I competition—was punched by another Texas placekicker less than a year later. On October 1, 1977, Russell Erxleben of the University of Texas Longhorns lined up a 67-yard field goal attempt against Rice University and successfully punched the pigskin through the posts, helping the Longhorns lasso the Owls by a score of 72–15. Erxleben, who became the first placekicker to be picked in the top 12 of the NFL draft when he was selected 11th overall by the New Orleans Saints in 1979, played six seasons in the NFL, mostly as a punter. After he retired, he became a successful financial investor before being jailed for money laundering and securities fraud, a charge that cost him $28 million in restitution, $1 million in fines, and seven years in a federal penitentiary.

A Tie for Second

Ironically, Erxleben was also present and in uniform when his two-week old record was equaled by an opposing kicker. On October 15, 1977, Steve Little of the University of Arkansas Razorbacks matched Erxleben yard-for-yard and inch-for-inch when he also connected for a 67-yard three-pointer in a game against Erxleben's Longhorns. Despite Little's Herculean heft, the Horns sliced through the Razorbacks to record a 13–9 victory. Unfortunately, Little's life off the gridiron also paralleled his Longhorn counterpart. Although he was a promising professional prospect, Little couldn't find the consistency needed to forge a successful NFL career. In the fall of 1980, the St. Louis Cardinals released him. Within hours of getting the pink slip, Little was severely injured in an automobile accident, a mishap that left him paralyzed from the neck down. He died in 1999 at the age of 43.

A Record Set and Taken Away

The third-longest Texas field goal was made on the same day that Ove Johansson was etching his name in the lexicon of legends. Tony Franklin of the Texas A&M Aggies established his own legacy in an Aggies 24–0 win over Baylor. For a few brief moments, Franklin held the record for the longest three-pointer at 64 yards. Later that afternoon, Johansson made his kick, and even Franklin's kick of 65 yards, still later in the day, wasn't enough to wrest the record back. Although his mark was quickly surpassed, however, Franklin's name remains in the record books. He is the only kicker to boot two 60-yard field goals in the same game.

* On December 28, 1969, with Dallas losing the divisional playoff game to Cleveland, Cowboy kicker Mike Clark set up for an onside kick. His leg swung, the players clashed . . . then everyone realized Clark had whiffed. The ball was still on the tee.

The Glory of Goliad: Where the Texas Revolution Began

The stirring and symbolic slogan "Remember the Alamo!" may have unified the masses and inspired the military campaign that eventually defeated the armies of Santa Anna and delivered independence to Texas, but the spark that lit the fire of freedom was first fueled in a small town along the San Antonio River that has become synonymous with sacrifice and solidarity.

The first shots in the Texas Revolution were fired during the Battle of Gonzalez, but it would be in the tiny town of Goliad where they would begin to reverberate. The Gonzalez altercation took place on October 2, 1835, when a group of rebellious Texians seized a cannon from Mexican troops guarding

COME AND TAKE IT

the town. The settlers, upset with the dictatorial polices of Mexican president Antonio López de Santa Anna, refused to return it as a display of protest. When Mexican troops threatened to use force to retrieve the artillery piece, a small posse of 140 militia and citizens attacked them and forced them to retreat from the vicinity. The "battle" was a minor skirmish—only one Mexican soldier was killed and one colonist injured—but it galvanized the festering unrest among the colonists toward Mexico and its soldiers. Hundreds of freedom fighters poured into the territory and formed small bands of counterforces intent on crusading down the coastline and disrupting trade routes.

On to Goliad

Seven days after the Gonzales incident, a marauding mass of Texian militia captured the town of Goliad and assumed control of the settlement and of the fort that protected it. The first declaration of Texas independence was formulated, written, and eventually signed by 92 of the town's citizens on December 20, 1835. An ensign featuring a bloody knife and arm on a white background was raised above the captured garrison. It became known, unsurprisingly, as the "Bloody Arm" flag and is considered to be the first banner of Texas independence.

In early 1836, a large army of several thousand troops under the command of Santa Anna descended upon San Antonio, where a squad of 260 Texians had taken command of the Alamo. While Santa Anna prepared to make his assault on the small mission, he directed General José de Urrea to take a large contingent of soldiers, reopen the supply lines along the San Antonio River, and recapture the fort in Goliad.

The Goliad Massacre

Meanwhile, the Goliad contingent of Texians, a collection of soldiers, freedom fighters, and colonists under the command of Colonel James Fannin, were ordered by General Sam Houston to abandon their fortress and retreat to the Guadalupe River near Victoria. A series of mishaps and mistakes followed, mostly due to the inexperience of Fannin and the sheer fear instilled by the dominant number of Mexican troops closing in. On March 19, the Goliad garrison began its march toward Victoria only to be quickly surrounded by Urrea's troops. After a feisty one-day battle, Fannin and his troops accepted Urrea's terms of surrender under the false impression they would be freed within a matter of weeks. The Mexicans, however, had other plans. One week after their capture, the 342 Texian prisoners of the Goliad Campaign were marched into the open prairie and executed.

The massacre of Fannin and his troops, although serving as further notice of the brutality of the Mexican dictator, has been largely lost in the sands of time. Only days after the Goliad garrison was gutted, Santa Anna's army destroyed the Alamo, killing prominent historical figures such as Davy Crockett and Jim Bowie. Although the Alamo may be the battle the world was called upon to remember, the glory of Goliad was equally significant in molding the legend of the Lone Star State.

Snake Farm—Exit Soon

Since 1967, billboards for the Snake Farm in New Braunfels has been enticing tourists and local residents off Interstate 35 and into its environs.

People seem to be hot or cold on snakes. Some come to the Snake Farm and rave about the variety of snakes and the petting zoo. Others describe the attraction as "creepy" and recommend it only for people who love reptiles and crawly things.

The Snake Farm—officially known as Animal World & Snake Farm—is a modern-day legend and roadside attraction between Austin and San Antonio. But the farm is more than just a tourist site; it's dedicated to raising some of the biggest and most dangerous snakes in the world.

Making a Name

The origins of the Snake Farm are murky. Several stories point to a man named Mack—with no last name—who'd previously lived in LaPlace, Louisiana. There, his Snake Farm was widely known as a tourist attraction . . . with a brothel rumored to be in the back.

Moving to Texas, Mack started a new business with a chimpanzee. He put a sign by the side of the road that invited travelers to stop and buy a ticket to see his "gorilla." In the years that followed, Mack's carnival-style attraction evolved with several snakes in display pits. (A few old-timers, however, insist that the snakes were just a front for a "bawdy house," the same as Mack had built in Louisiana.)

The attraction was made famous by billboards along the highways of Texas, each showing a huge snake and directing people to the New Braunfels site. In fact, far more people likely know the notorious Snake Farm from the ubiquitous billboards than by ever actually darkening its door.

The Snake Farm changed hands several times after Mack moved on to other projects. Gradually, the attraction became what the signs said: a genuine snake farm.

A Variety of Reptilian Delights

Texas is home to more species of snakes than any other state. It was only natural, then, to build a farm to display them and educate the public about snakes. Today, all 15 varieties of Texas's venomous snakes are featured at the Snake Farm, along with a wide range of other reptiles, amphibians, and exotic animals.

John Mellyn and his wife, Susan, owned and ran the Snake Farm for about 13 years, starting in 1994. They transformed it into a more upscale attraction while still retaining its 1950s-style charm. Mellyn had a habit of freezing his deceased snakes, rather than disposing of the bodies. This once inspired Dorothy Cross, an artist from Dublin, Ireland, to create a cathedrallike exhibit of frozen snakes in a San Antonio art museum.

In December 2007, the Snake Farm was purchased by Eric and Dara Trager. Today, this husband-and-wife team is dedicated to the more than 500 animals in their care.

Moving into the Future

Despite a tragic fire that damaged part of the farm in late 2008, the Tragers and their staff have rebuilt and steadily expanded the facilities and the range of animals kept there. They're proud of what they've accomplished, and their hard work has produced great results. Parents and travel experts list the Snake Farm as a "must-see" on any road trip across Texas.

Most visitors to Animal World & Snake Farm give it a thumbs up. From time to time, however, someone comes in expecting a full-scale, traditional zoo and is disappointed. Herpetologists—people who study reptiles and amphibians—and children who love the "ick" factor may be the most enthusiastic Snake Farm guests.

The site has been especially popular since it was featured on the TV show *Dirty Jobs* in 2007. In the episode "Snake Wrangler," star Mike Rowe carried huge pythons, moved western diamondback snakes from their pit, and then, shirtless, helped clean the alligator and crocodile tank with the Snake Farm crew.

Lone Star Lexicon

- **ole cuss:** Age is not a prerequisite for use; this term can either refer to an old rascal or a *galoot* who exhibits a tough, irascible nature and/or is bad-tempered.

- **plug-ugly:** Based on the word *plug*, the slang used to describe a worn-out horse, this term is a derogatory description utilized to describe either males or females with hideous looks.

- **dinner:** Depending on the preference of the Texan using it, this term functions as a double-duty descriptor, referring to either the meal consumed at noon or in the evening.

- **supper:** Depending on the Texan who is using this word, it can either mean the noon meal or the evening meal, leading to great confusion when heard by non-Texans.

- **ball:** Refers to the Texas pastime (a religion to some) known as football, the "Friday night lights" ritual that dominates sports culture in both small and big towns alike.

- **come hell or high water:** Showcases the Texan's boundless (obstinate) endurance and determination, regardless of the problems or obstacles, e.g., "*Come hell or high water,* you will graduate high school!"

- **yankee/damnyankee:** Since the influx of people from all regions into the state, the use of this derogatory term and its amplified variant has diminished somewhat in recent years; refers to any individual from north of the Mason-Dixon line.

- **hissy fit:** Not to be confused with the *conniption fit*, the *hissy fit* is characterized by a state of extreme agitation, marked by shrieking, violent movements, and other histrionics.

- **waller:** A vague verb that is used as a past participle along the lines of wear down or tire out: "The Lone Star Lexicon lessons he read in this book wallered down and gave him a good base on which to communicate with other locals"; also used to describe a hole that is hollowed out or made larger.

The King of Ragtime

Scott Joplin, the most famous ragtime composer of all time, was a Texan. He became known as the King for compositions including "The Entertainer" written in 1902, although he may have gained his greatest fame and renown more than 50 years after his death as composer of the music in The Sting.

Despite his enduring musical legacy, the details of much of Scott Joplin's early life remain imprecise. His birth date is often recorded as November 24, 1868, although it seems likely that it may have been as much as a year before that. He was born near Linden, where Jiles Joplin, his father and a former slave, worked as a laborer. It appears as though Mr. Joplin boasted at least a rudimentary knowledge of music that he delighted in passing on to his son.

By the time that he was seven years old, Scott Joplin was already an experienced banjo player, and when his family moved to the Texas/Arkansas border town of Texarkana, he was introduced to the instrument that would make him famous. His mother, Florence, did domestic work for a neighboring attorney, who allowed young Scott to experiment on his piano.

The Father of Ragtime

The elder Joplin saved enough money to buy his son a used piano, and Scott's talent quickly blossomed. At age 11, Joplin began taking free lessons from Julius Weiss, a German-born piano teacher who helped shape Joplin's musical influences, including European opera. As a teen, Joplin formed a vocal quartet and performed in the dance halls of Texarkana before venturing out as a pianist on the saloon and honky-tonk circuit that stretched from Texas to Louisiana, Missouri, Illinois, and Kentucky.

In St. Louis, Joplin encountered a style of music that featured abbreviated melody lines called "ragged time," or "ragtime" for short. Joplin adopted the principles of ragtime into longer musical forms including a ballet—*The Ragtime Dance,* written in 1899—and two operas—*The Guest of Honor* in 1903 and *Treemonisha* in 1910. While the orchestration scores for both operas were sadly lost during the copyright process, a piano-vocal score for *Treemonisha* was later published. It was, however, Joplin's shorter compositions that earned him the title "The King of Ragtime."

From the Maple Leaf to New York

One of his first compositions to be published, "Maple Leaf Rag" in 1899, went on to sell more than one million copies of sheet music. The piece was named after one of the music clubs Joplin enjoyed playing in Sedalia, Missouri, the Maple Leaf Club. Joplin occasionally returned to Texarkana to perform, but by 1907 he was living in New York City. It was here that he wrote his instructional manual, *The School of Ragtime.* In 1916, Joplin's health deteriorated in part due to syphilis, which he'd contracted a few years before. His playing became inconsistent, and he was eventually forced to enter the Manhattan State Hospital, where he died on April 1, 1917. Joplin was married and divorced twice, and his only child, a daughter, died in infancy.

Legacy

It wasn't until years after his death that Scott Joplin achieved the full recognition his work deserved. In 1971, the New York Public Library published his collected works, but his music found a whole new audience with the release of the popular 1973 Paul Newman and Robert Redford movie, *The Sting.* Joplin's work, adapted by Marvin Hamlisch, was featured heavily in the film's score, which won an Academy Award. "The Entertainer," released as a single from the movie, became a bona fide top ten hit.

Joplin himself was posthumously awarded a Pulitzer Prize in 1976 for *Treemonisha,* which has been recognized as the first grand opera by an African American composer. Today, a large mural on Texarkana's Main Street depicts the life and accomplishments of one of the town's most famous sons.

Fast Facts

- *Spain built replicas of Christopher Columbus's Niña, Pinta, and Santa María for the 1992 500th anniversary of the explorer's discovery of some Caribbean islands. Like the originals, these replicas were seaworthy enough to sail the Atlantic. Corpus Christi was their destination, and they're on display there to this day.*

- *Billionaire Dallas Mavericks owner Mark Cuban has been fined more than $1 million by the National Basketball Association over the years, usually for complaining about officiating. He's probably the only professional sports owner who should have "Fines" as a budget line item.*

- *Before women's suffrage, a law in Texas denied the vote to "idiots, imbeciles, aliens, the insane, and women."*

- *Almost half of Texas's strawberries come from Poteet. In standard Texan fashion, the town has not one but three giant strawberry monuments around town. Need it be added that there's an annual festival? Visit in April.*

- *Waco is the land of secret society museums: the Improved Order of Red Men, the Scottish Rite, and regular Freemasons each maintain one. The Red Men might have the most interesting collection, which includes Aaron Burr's desk and a painting by Adolf Hitler.*

- *Molly Ivins, the famous progressive journalist who grew up in Houston, may have bequeathed to us the most succinct summary yet written about Texas politics: "We gave the world Lyndon Johnson and you cowards gave him right back."*

- *According to early explorer Álvar Núñez Cabeza de Vaca, homosexuality was accepted among some Native American cultures in South Texas.*

- *The world's first photograph, an 1826 Niépce image predating daguerreotypes, is among the vast, eclectic collection at the Harry Ransom Center maintained by the University of Texas in Austin. If the collection can be said to have a specialty, it would be literary and movie memorabilia.*

Real or Hollywood?

The Texas cowboy in Hollywood and TV westerns is one of the most enduring characters in popular culture. The fact that many of the fine actors who played these roles were born far from Texas is a credit to their skills. See if you can pick out and put a check mark beside the names of the real Texans by birth from this list of famous Hollywood Western actors.

1. _____ Chill Wills

2. _____ James Arness

3. _____ Gene Autry

4. _____ William Boyd (Hopalong Cassidy)

5. _____ Roy Rogers

6. _____ Dale Evans

7. _____ Gabby Hayes

8. _____ John Wayne

9. _____ Clint Eastwood

10. _____ Richard Boone

11. _____ Glenn Ford

12. _____ Gary Cooper

13. _____ Dennis Weaver

14. _____ Audie Murphy

15. _____ Alan Ladd

16. _____ Tom Mix

17. _____ Tex Ritter

18. _____ Slim Pickens

19. _____ Randolph Scott

20. _____ Will Rogers

21. _____ Richard Widmark

1. ✔ Yes—Seagoville, Texas; 2. No—Minneapolis, Minnesota; 3. ✔ Yes—Tioga, Texas; 4. No—Hendrysburg, Ohio; 5. No—Cincinnati, Ohio; 6. ✔ Yes—Uvalde, Texas; 7. No—Wellsville, New York; 8. No—Winterset, Iowa; 9. No—San Francisco, California; 10. No—Los Angeles, California; 11. No—Ste.-Christine, Quebec; 12. No—Helena, Montana; 13. No—Joplin, Missouri; 14. ✔ Yes—near Kingston, Texas; 15. No—Hot Springs, Arkansas; 16. No—Mix Run, Pennsylvania; 17. ✔ Yes—Murvaul, Texas; 18. No—Kingsburg, California; 19. No—Orange County, Virginia; 20. No—Oologah, Oklahoma; 21. No—Sunrise Township, Minnesota

---

273

Index

Contributing Writers

Jeff Bahr is author of *Amazing and Unusual USA* and *Weird Virginia*. His work has also appeared in *The Last Survivors, The Gigantic Reader, The Book of Myths & Misconceptions*, and other Armchair Readers™. He considers himself much like the city of Austin, Texas—an off-kilter town that cozies-up to the slogan "Keep Austin Weird!"

Fiona Broome is a prolific writer and researcher who has contributed to *Weird, Scary & Unusual Armchair Reader™*. She moved to Texas—and found true love—in 2003, but that hasn't stopped her from chasing ghosts around the United States, the U.K., and Ireland. Her website is FionaBroome.com.

James Duplacey, when not writing for *The Origins of Everything, The Colossal Reader, The Book of Incredible Information*, and other Armchair Reader™ projects, can be found researching and writing absorbing anecdotes about culture, sports, and history. He is a resident of Calgary, Alberta.

Laura Hill is a freelance writer and former reporter for the Nashville *Tennessean* who lives in Franklin, Tennessee. She has loved Texas deeply ever since meeting Molly Ivins while covering Elvis's death, and she became even more smitten when she attended and wrote about a Willie Nelson picnic in Austin.

J. K. Kelley has a B.A. in history from the University of Washington in Seattle and has contributed to *The Amazing Book of History, The Last Survivors, The Origins of Everything*, and numerous other Armchair Readers™. He resides in the desiccated sagebrush of eastern Wash-ington with his wife, Deb; his parrot, Alex; and two dogs, Fabius and Leonidas.

Bill Martin is a freelance writer whose diverse portfolio of creative, corporate, and media writing includes *The Book of Myths & Misconceptions, Armchair Reader™: World War II*, and numerous other Armchair Readers™. He currently plies his trade in his hometown of Toronto, Ontario, but looks forward to one day actually kickin' back in the Lone Star State with his wife, Marianna.

Winter D. Prosapio, a syndicated writer, award-winning humor columnist and travel writer, fifth-generation Texan, and second-generation smart aleck, is coauthor of *Bathroom Book of Texas Trivia.* Her work has appeared in essay collections, newspapers, and national magazines. Find more of her work online at winterdprosapio.com.

Lawrence Robinson is a Los Angeles–based novelist and screenwriter who has written for *The Gigantic Reader* and *The Book of Myths & Misconceptions.* From time to time, he also updates his website www.britwriter.com.

Bill Sasser is a freelance writer and journalist who lives in New Orleans. He writes for the *Christian Science Monitor* and Salon.com, among other publications. His work has also appeared in *The Book of Myths & Misconceptions, Amazing Book of History,* and *Armchair Reader™: World War II.*

Paul Seaburn has spent more than half his life in Spring, Texas. He has written for *The Tonight Show, The New York Times, The Extraordinary Book of Lists, The Colossal Reader,* and numerous magazines, web sites, humor books, and comedians. He's also head writer for the family comedy "Taylor's Attic," and he occasionally updates his Web site, www.humorhandyman.com.

Donald Vaughan is a freelance writer whose work has appeared in an eclectic array of publications, including *Military Officer Magazine, Nursing Spectrum, MAD* magazine, and the *Weekly World News.* He has also authored, coauthored, ghosted, or contributed to more than 30 books, including *The Book of Myths & Misconceptions* and *The Origins of Everything.*

Nanette Lavoie-Vaughan is a regular contributor to *Military Officer Magazine* and a columnist on eldercare for *Today's Officer.* Visit her website, www.nanettelavoie-vaughan.com, to find out about her next adventure.

Michael Witzel is an award-winning author who resides in the Texas Hill Country near Austin. His work has appeared in *American Heritage of Invention & Technology, Texas Highways,* and *Rider* magazines. When possible, he haunts the local 'cue joints, signing copies of his most recent book, *Barbecue Road Trip: Recipes, Restaurants, & Pitmasters from America's Great Barbecue Regions.*